T0243614

Dreaming in Яussian

a memoir

Anya Gillinson

Skyhorse Publishing

To my husband, Clive

Skyhorse Publishing books may be purchased in bulk at special discounts for sales promotion, corporate gifts, fund-raising, or educational purposes. Special editions can also be created to specifications. For details, contact the Special Sales Department, Skyhorse Publishing, 307 West 36th Street, 11th Floor, New York, NY 10018 or info@skyhorsepublishing.com.

Skyhorse® and Skyhorse Publishing® are registered trademarks of Skyhorse Publishing, Inc.®, a Delaware corporation.

Visit our website at www.skyhorsepublishing.com.
Please follow our publisher Tony Lyons on Instagram @tonylyonsisuncertain.

10 9 8 7 6 5 4 3 2 1

Library of Congress Cataloging-in-Publication Data is available on file.

Cover design by David Ter-Avanesyan
Cover photograph courtesy of the author
Interior design by Chris Schultz

Print ISBN: 978-1-5107-8212-9
Ebook ISBN: 978-1-5107-8213-6

Printed in the United States of America

Acknowledgments

I WANT TO THANK MY HUSBAND FOR HIS TIRELESS PATIENCE WITH me during the past three years while I was writing this book. He has not only been my sole source of encouragement, but my one and only source of courage which enabled me to travel this journey.

I want to thank my mother, the chronicler of my life, the sole living witness to everything that took place in this memoir. Reading through the manuscript was hardest for her, but true to her fearless self, she never faltered in her belief in my vision for this book.

From the very beginning my dearest friend Rabbi Shmuley Boteach has been my unofficial agent and his contribution to this project has been instrumental. Most importantly, he has also been one of my greatest champions in my decision to write this book. I thank him for his confidence in me, for every word of wise advice he has given me, for his kindness and for always staying loyal.

Introduction

I REMEMBER SITTING NEXT TO A NICE LADY AT SOME FANCY DINNER party telling her about my life in Russia, about my parents, grandparents, then the major tragedy that had transformed my life, about my tumultuous immigration and ending with my scandalous divorce, leaving with two small children my husband of thirteen years for another man; she was fascinated. Wanting to pay me the biggest compliment she could think of, she exclaimed: "You are a strong woman, which is no surprise, seeing how you come from such a long line of strong, powerful women!"

I knew she meant well, and it's not a good idea to pick fights with nice ladies at dinner parties, so I must have mumbled something reminiscent of gratitude at this. Inside, though, I cringed at her words, because there are few things that I scorn more than the labels "strong woman" or "powerful woman." I do not consider myself such a woman. Strong women frighten me, because this strength of which they are so proud deprives them of their femininity.

Strong women hide their insecurities underneath their shield of strength, and it is these insecurities that make them vulnerable and therefore human and feminine. Too often, women are forced to become strong, because of either hardship, or great sadness; too often these misfortunes fall upon a woman when she either has no man to love her and protect her, or when she has a man, but he is a useless kind who provides neither love nor protection for her. Men fear strong, formidable women and shy away from them. Yet there are other types of strong women, who despite having quite satisfactory husbands and good lives, are so obsessed with notions of being equal to men in everything, that in the process they end up utterly emasculating their male partners. This is a Western trend, particularly an American one. This new woman announces to her man that she has no need for his strength, the source of his pride for thousands of years, since the dawn of time. She lets him know that he is not needed, for she can do everything on her own. As a result, men become weak, spoiled, and lazy. This goes against their nature, and it is bad for them. Men want to be needed for their power, for their ability to provide security to women. When they are told they are not wanted for that, they acquire other qualities—complacency, softness, appeasement—which these strong, manly women may find attractive. Rigid, confident, lonely, and angry with herself and the world around her, the strong woman marches on through life, fending off foes and always suspicious of friends. A strong woman without a man in her life is not in her natural state, when she must be strong for herself and for the man whose strength she had appropriated. On the other hand, women who have strong and kind men by their side have no need to be strong and therefore rigid, because they do not spend their days fighting for self-protection and security. This is not some outdated wisdom, but an eternal truth, a stubborn fact, which our society is forced to deal with every day. The natural order of things is for men to be strong and for women to be soft; everything else is a compromise that helps women to adjust to life's viciousness, nastiness, and loneliness. I am not a strong woman, and even though in my life there were many times when I had to act with strength, confidence, and defiance, I did so with resentment because I always felt these qualities devoured my softness, shaving off my femininity.

My life since the day I was born has been defined by one man only. My Father. My creator, the architect of my life, the inventor of my character, my judge, and my true protector. His way of life and the way he understood it made me into the person I am, forcing me to reveal to myself the unfashionable truths about the nature of things.

I grew up in Moscow during the mid-80s. Russia is a profoundly patriarchal society that has held a deeply traditional set of values for more than a thousand years. The Revolution of 1917 upended Russian society, but everything that concerned family values and relations between sexes remained as it had always been, old, traditional, patriarchal. Very briefly, the revolution toyed with the idea of female emancipation and open marriage, but this Western frivolity was soon abolished. The country was devastated by two wars and a revolution in between, the population was destitute, and there were a million orphans. The dictator Josef Stalin decided what Russia needed was stability and a return to old values, where a father was the king, and a wise and capable mother took care of the home, while the young always respected the old, and the legends about the courageous knights fighting for the honor of their graceful maidens were still told. Soviet life was not kind to its women, demanding from them to be laborers, mothers, and wives. The exigencies of social struggle left a woman little time for her children and almost no time for herself. In theory, she was an equal of a man, but in reality she had to work twice as hard, because most Soviet men ended up either killed in wars, jailed, or drunk. So, against this morbid backdrop, Soviet women found solace in tears that darkened their faces and dulled their hearts. They had children more out of duty than out of pleasure; and few families had more than one child. Abortions were widespread because life was hard, because women were not happy, and children were frequently not a source of happiness, but a source of added hardship to many Soviet families.

In silent grief, women continued to labor and stand by their doomed men because this was the Russian way, the way it had always been. Soviet life turned women back into the serfs they had always been, only now they were educated serfs.

And it was partly because of this harsh reality that it was femininity, not feminism, that determined relations between the sexes in Soviet Russia. When it came to things like female wants, needs, and desires, Soviet women were no different from Russian women who lived under the tsar. Both types craved the protection and attention of men, whom they hoped would be smart, brave, strong, and kind, who would smile at them, and caress them from time to time, and occasionally would spoil them with gifts. In return, these women, these creatures made of flesh and desire, were ready to give them their loyalty and even love. A woman wanted to be a lady, a seductress, a temptress, a vixen, not a fighter on barricades. She wanted to give in to her weaknesses and be praised for them, not shamed or scolded, as she was under the Soviet rule, and likewise in the atmosphere of the modern progressive feminist, #MeToo type movements in America and Western Europe.

But even more than the country, it was the family I was born into that determined my place in the society, as well as in my future family, as a persona and as a woman.

When I was thirteen, my secure, well-paced, traditional life in Moscow, where I wanted for nothing, ended when a personal tragedy changed the trajectory of my life forever. And yet, despite all the unplanned experiences I was to live through, no matter what sort of lifestyles I had to adapt to in the future in order to survive, I never became a different person. Stubborn customs of my old country became part of my bone marrow, along with my deeply seated sense of the feminine, not feminist, identity which was defined and given to me by my father.

At the age of fifteen I became an immigrant in America, the country of my father's dreams and his greatest aspiration for me. I wanted everything my father wanted, and I was ready to accept everything America was to lay at my feet: its vast opportunities, the recklessness of its freedom of speech, the promise of the pursuit of happiness (a concept unknown to a Russian mind), and the acceptance of a society profoundly different from the one that had given birth to me. One of the most difficult things about immigration is compromise. If you want to fit in in America as an immigrant, you must compromise, unless you are a billionaire or a genius. Very few immigrants are. Almost immediately I sensed I was living in a society which zealously believed, or at least wanted to believe, in a myth of sexual egalitarianism. At first, I played along trying to observe and absorb the rules and codes of its conduct. So, I had to fit in by playing the part of a woman who believed in America's sexual revolution, where women are equal to men in virtually everything, and if they are not yet equal to men, they should strive to become such, and even better. For about thirty years I diligently yet unsuccessfully tried to play the part, until I finally understood how much I resented the role imposed on me by this society. In America I always dated lighthearted, well meaning, egalitarian minded, emasculated American males. I eventually made the mistake of marrying such a man, a good man, but a wrong man. It took me a very long time to admit to myself, that after almost thirty years, I was more of an immigrant than I was when I first came here in 1992, and that my core was forever cemented in this particular Russian state of being, which is more than just culture, tradition, or custom. My old unfriendly land finally spoke to me after years of silence.

Women are different from men physically, and because of that emotionally. Their roles in life and their relationships with one another have been defined by this difference for thousands of years. It is this difference that has contributed to the evolution of civilization as we know it. Men are made stronger so that they can be hunters to provide food for their families, while women are given sexual powers permitting their bodies and their minds to be both feminine and wise. In this way, they tame the brashness of their men, cultivating in them a stronger desire to be better breadwinners and protectors.

My parents had a union of unequals, who completed and complemented one another precisely because they were unequal.

America loves fairness, justice, and equality. It worships principles of egalitarianism in every sphere of its multicultural, yet sensitive and fragile society, frightened by uncomfortable words and unpopular thoughts. A long time ago I too was charmed by these words, but in time I saw they bore no relevance to my irreversibly Russian state of being. I came from the culture of unfairness and inequality, where male/female relationships and their daily lives are not driven by obsessive egalitarianism, but honest laws of nature, which if not interfered with, can sometimes create harmony.

I.

The Man Who Defined My Everything

MY GRANDPARENTS HEARD THE NEWS OF MY FATHER'S MURDER in New York on the Voice of America in the middle of the night, a couple of hours after they put my younger sister and me to bed. The Voice of America news anchor announced that at four a.m. on June 24, 1990 in New York City, Dr. Arkady Novikov, a physician from Moscow, was fatally wounded by 23-year-old Eric Wilson during an attempted robbery as he shielded his wife, Galina Novikova, from the attacker.

The murder made the news in New York and in Moscow. "Soviet Widow Mourns Doctor Slain in Queens" said the headline in the *New York Times*.

For the next three weeks, every Soviet newspaper, every radio station, and every TV news program would talk of nothing else, offering updates on the case as soon as they were available. My sister and I, however, were the only two people who knew nothing. I found out much later that when my grandparents first heard from my mother after the murder, she had told them not to tell us anything until she got back.

My parents had been excited to go to America, but my sister and I couldn't wait for them to come back. It would be like when they came

1

back from Europe a year before, only bigger because, surely, a trip to America was worth five trips to Europe. This summer Papa arranged for my sister and me to stay at the peaceful resort *Otradnoye*, which means either Joy or Happiness in Russian. The place was located about two hours from Moscow, amidst tall Russian trees and not so tall Russian hills. It was a beautiful place, almost poetic, were it not for other guests of the busy resort. A few long weeks had passed since our parents' departure for America when we were suddenly told by my grandmother that they were due back a week early. We were ecstatic! It was July 7, a bit rainy, and my wait for their arrival began the moment my sister and I woke up that foggy morning. We waited all day as I kept staring at the clock's stubborn hands, and I was sure that time had decided to stop for me that day. There were no cell phones, and we were in the country with poor phone connection to the city, so there was no way for us to find out about the status of their flight in case it was delayed. So, I waited nervously and impatiently, when suddenly I was told that they were here, and I ran toward my father's embrace. My wait was over. I looked for Papa. I was planning to jump into his arms, but I couldn't see him anywhere. I was gaping at the crowd of strangely familiar people, whose presence was beginning to seem both meaningless and alarming. My mother was wearing one of the flowery dresses I loved so much. She stood there, right in front of me, with her arms wide open in the most unnatural way: they wanted to embrace me, but they were also nervous about something. Her entire body was hesitating. I saw it right away.

"Mama, where is Papa?" I asked. She replied: "He is in America" and then muttered something, or I thought she did. Then she added: "He is in a hospital." Something dropped within me, and I think I looked at my mother to see the sign of a lie on her face. All mothers lie to hide from their children the ugly realities of life, but my mother had an extra thick blanket of illusions that I was able by now to recognize. I took another look at the people gathered around and they were not strangers, they were my parents' friends. Their familiar faces looked frozen, helpless, like a decoration or a set of some tasteless play. Almost hoping to hear a lie, I asked my mother: "Is he alive?"

"No," she answered.

I had asked, and she had told me. I thought she had no right to give me that answer. Never in my whole life had I ever received an answer like that.

I never knew what really stood behind a "no," or being denied or refused anything. My parents were my endless childhood, they were my fearlessness, and the prism through which life could seem very charming at times. They assured me that the world was magnificent. Of course, I knew that life ended in death, but that would come only at the very, very remote end. My mother's "no" was perhaps the first completely honest answer she had ever given me, and I saw from the look on her face she wasn't going to change it for me.

I walked inside the house. In the horror of that moment I saw my glamorous grandmother, star of Soviet showbiz, sitting on a messy coach like a common woman, with her legs spread rather far apart and a cigarette in her thick fingers. She hadn't touched a cigarette since the war, when they all smoked to appease their hunger and because they might die before the cigarette was through. I knew that there was no one I desired to be consoled by more than her. Strange sounds were coming from her throat. I couldn't understand whether that was her crying or if it was some other peculiar way of expressing grief. She moved her body back and forth when she was embracing me with her thick, strong arms and commanded me to cry. "Cry,

Anuta, cry..." she said, and, in that voice, I heard notes of truth and strength.

My love for my father was absolute. He was my king. And as true kings go, he was neither a good king, nor a bad king, but a great one. He did great things because as a physician he healed people, he saw through their bodies and their minds. I wasn't just his daughter, but also his collaborator, his confidante. His hopes for me made him demanding toward me, sometimes even unkind, but that did not diminish his greatness. He was a dreamer. As I was growing up in his presence, I was keenly aware of my obsession with him. His own singular living self was the only source of my love for him. I knew who I loved and why I loved. I have always looked at my narcissistic femininity through the prism of his magnificence. He was taken from me so suddenly, so irrationally, and it has marked me for the rest of my life.

Arkady Mikhailovich Novikov was of medium height, with a wiry athletic body. He moved lightly and gracefully. He got his large courageous nose, unruly black hair, and large flappy earlobes from my grandfather. Nearsighted since he was a teenager, he wore large glasses that magnified the effect of his eyes, which were large and brown, inherited from his mother.

He was born in 1942, in Ishim, a remote place in the western part of Siberia, where he had been evacuated with his mother, Anya, and his older brother, Yuri, after Russia was invaded by Nazi Germany. My grandfather, Mikhail Novikov, was serving as a surgeon in the Red Army, operating in makeshift army hospitals under German bombs, until they reached Berlin in 1945. He lost an eye when a bomb went off over the operating tent. The doctors never could get all the fragments out.

My father's older brother, Yuri, was weak and sickly, perhaps also feeble minded, and died young. No one in the family wanted to talk about that, or about his older sister, Kira, who had died in a terrible accident in the bathtub for which my grandmother Anya blamed herself until the day she died. From time to time, my aunt's name came up, softly, fluttering like a butterfly. Kira, K-i-r-o-ch-k-a. My grandfather's one good blue eye would sparkle when he said it. He was a hard man, five years of constant surgery under enemy fire had amputated his sense of sympathy and numbed his tenderness, as it had for many men who fought in that war of wars. Those men returned home to their wives, parents, and children as victors, yet broken by war and humiliated by death. Their families missed them, loved them, and forgave them. They forgave their cruel, prodigal men-soldiers because they were broken and humiliated by war. My Dedushka, what you call your grandfather in Russia, was the patri-arch of the entire family. He was well into his seventies, for those times and for that country a very advanced age, but still in excellent health and as feisty as ever. He was an indispensable part of our lives as we were growing up in Moscow.

My father, his youngest and now only child, was his shining star. My father did not choose medicine, it was chosen for him by my forceful Dedushka. In Soviet Russia, there was no career more pres-tigious or respectable. Although he had not become the surgeon Dedushka had hoped, as he tended to faint at the sight of blood, it turned out his sensitivity made him an inspired diagnostician. My father was a softer, more diplomatic, more sophisticated version of Dedushka, but he did inherit his independent spirit, stubbornness, and uncompromising willpower. These qualities are what it takes for a man to survive in Russia, whose soil is made up of dirty dandelions and trampled bluebells.

On the one hand, doctors were seen as part of the despised intelligentsia elite, but on the other hand they were forgiven that sin, since their skill made them irreplaceable. Because of that, doctors were also seen as part of the proletariat class. "*Prestizhno*," they called it, prestige, and this was worth a lot in a country where nobody made any money from their profession. Even if they had to share a toilet with their neighbors, they were still called "Doctor."

It was the best future available in that time and place, and so my father entered the First Medical School of Moscow. Dedushka badly wanted him to follow in his footsteps and was embarrassed at his fainting spells. The surgery professor, a Red Army colleague of his, made some ugly remarks about his scrawny bespectacled weakling of a son. My father didn't take it nearly so hard. One of his great skills that eventually brought him fame was listening quietly to his patients' stories. He had to win their trust and then get accurate answers to his questions. It all began with the way he took out his stethoscope and pressed it to the patient's body, gently, quietly, patiently; he never forced the answers, but instead simply rephrased the questions, making sure the patient did not know the difference.

When father was younger and Dedushka was stronger, they would bicker often, but as an adult my father was a great comfort to his old father. He took charge of his affairs and made sure he lacked for nothing money could buy. He also hired a housekeeper for him. Even when Dedushka began to slip, becoming increasingly impatient and obstreperous, if still very charming, father was infinitely patient with him, dressed him like a king in Italian suits ordered from tailors abroad, took him everywhere, and paid him the greatest respect.

Dedushka had a terrible bleeding stomach ulcer which frequently flared up painfully, accompanied by severe bleeding. Certain

Western medications helped. My father got them through his contacts in the foreign embassies, or through his European friends. He also put him on a very strict diet with very special foods which could only be purchased in those *Beryozka* stores with the pig-faced guards, where only foreigners or very influential people could go and everything cost a fortune in foreign currency that had to be obtained "on the black market." I never went to the black market, but my parents knew where it was.

My grandfather was a poor patient, never kept to the strict diet my father prescribed and his ulcer always started bleeding in the middle of the night, whereupon he would summon not the ambulance but his son. I could never allow my father to go out in the middle of the night without me. And so, no matter how late it was, whatever the weather, we got dressed, got into his Volga, and drove across Moscow. When we got there, Dedushka would be in agony, spitting up blood and uttering terrible soldier's curses. He needed an injection, with an old-style syringe that required sterilization in a metal box carefully placed in a pot of boiling water. The aroma of alcohol, of the boiling water, the medicine, the syringe, gauze pads and cotton wool, all made my head spin with pleasure. I had a proud sense of purpose: I was assisting my doctor father in saving the world, starting with my Dedushka. It was the world at its worst and at its best, with blood, pain, and Red Army style cursing from the patient and a wonderful, cool, wise doctor on the other side.

My grandfather was vehemently opposed to my intimate participation in this type of procedure, unaware, since his back was turned to receive the shot, that I was the one who was giving it to him. My father had taught me how. Whatever we gave him, it worked, and Dedushka would turn sweet again, with his sparky blue eyes and soft white hair, always glad to see his granddaughter. He would shout for

Glafira, his maid: "*Gla, Gla, our baby girl is hungry! Our boy is looking famished! Where is that pie of yours? What the hell?*"

In theory, the Bolshevik revolution was supposed to erase the line between fathers and sons, but somehow with so many fathers dying in the Revolution and the wars, and the replacement of one authoritarian government with another claiming to be its opposite, the gravity of a father's word still mattered. Socialism also proved strangely unable to eliminate the patronymic; children still carried their father's name right next to their first name. Arkady Mikhailovich, the son of Mikhail. Both were deeply traditional men, products of the patriarchal society that formed them.

My Dedushka was one of those Russians who simply could not accept anything that was contrary to his will, no matter how obviously logical it might be. So, for the first time, Arkady contradicted his father by deciding not to go into surgery but into a different branch of medicine. He was interested in the branch of medicine known as cardiovascular therapy, and he needed a PhD if he wanted to have a successful career, and not be sent to some remote locale of our vast motherland. But he was a Jew, and all graduate institutions had a quota on Jews, and in the political environment in Russia at the time, even my Dedushka's status didn't do him much good.

Russia and Jews. Jews and Revolution. Volumes have been written on it. At the beginning, it appeared as if the Revolution was going to bring hope to the plight of the Russian Jews, whose conditions were intolerable under the tsar. This had reached a fever pitch in the late nineteenth century, when waves of pogroms—violence against the lives and property of Jews sanctioned by church and state—overtook towns, villages, and neighborhoods with mostly Jewish residents and resulted in waves of Russian Jewish immigration to the United States. Jews like Trotsky, Sverdlov, and Zinoviev were at the forefront of the revolution; Lenin himself had Jewish blood on his mother's side. For the first time in Russian Jewish history, the Jews had come out of their shtetls into the world, and side by side with their seemingly friendly non-Jewish comrades overthrew the cruel hateful tsar.

It was a hopeful moment. The creed of the Revolution was equality for all. Under the Soviet slogan of solidarity, all ethnicities and all races were to be equal, brothers and sisters: Jews, Ukrainians, Russians, Georgians, Kazakhs, Turkmens, Mongols, Kalmyks, and all the rest. Marx had written that religion was the "opium of the masses," and the new Soviet government undertook to stamp it out. Since there was no God and no religion of any kind (except for communism), then there was no Judaism and no Jews as a religious minority. On the other hand, Jews as an ethnic minority were promised to become equal members of the new Soviet society. From 1917 until about 1948, there was no open persecution and my Dedushka got to go to medical school. Stalin tolerated Jews and even promoted some of them into his inner circle. At the same time, during Stalin's purges of the 1930s, millions of Jewish and non-Jewish intellectuals and regular people disappeared without a trace.

Stalin turned against the Jews over the state of Israel, even though the Soviet Union voted for the UN partition plan in 1947, and when Israel was founded in 1948, The Soviet Union officially recognized it as an independent state. Initially Stalin was sympathetic, hoping Israel would be a socialist state, but when Israel aligned itself with the United States, he turned against it. When 50,000 Soviet Jews greeted the newly appointed Israeli ambassador Golda Meir shouting: "Am Yisroel Chai!" ("The People of Israel Live!") and she replied, "Thank you for remaining Jewish!" Stalin turned against his own Jews. He closed the Yiddish theatre and all Jewish cultural institutions. The director of the famous Moscow State Jewish Theatre, a friend of my grandfather's, died in one of those hit-and-run car accidents that kept befalling enemies of the state.

Official antisemitism was suddenly back. The Soviet passport, which needed to be carried everywhere, identified the bearer by ethnicity: Russian, Ukrainian, Mongol, Georgian, Armenian, or Jewish, on line five of the document. Every teacher had an official list of students' names and their corresponding ethnicities. People with obviously Semitic last names all had the experience of being told by some clerk in some office that with a name like that there wasn't a chance.

This is the world that my father was facing in early 1962, as he graduated from medical school and sought to get his PhD. The alternative was to go straight into a residency and start a hands-on medical career, but there was no prestige, no future in doing that. Most PhD candidates had mentors, members of the faculty who advised them on their dissertation: assisted them with research, helped them write. Members of disfavored groups, however, had either to find and pay for their own mentor, or go without.

My father went without. He took a night shift job as a hospital orderly and began to prepare for the dissertation on his own. He was one of the first people in his entire year to defend the dissertation on congenital heart disease and earn his PhD. He was twenty-five years old.

For the next decade, he practiced medicine in one of Moscow's main hospitals affiliated with the First Medical School, specializing in cardiovascular illnesses. At twenty-six, he was already married to my mother, a young concert pianist. He was very interested in bronchial asthma, and his treatment approach made him famous all over the Soviet Union; people traveled from far and wide to seek his advice.

At that hospital, one of the best in Russia, my father came to loathe the Soviet healthcare system. He saw bureaucracy, inertia, stupidity, lack of resources, and negligence toward patients that was not personal so much as it was systemic. As a doctor, he could make his own decision about how to treat his patients, but again, only to a limited degree. There was always a "suit" reprimanding him for being too autonomous, too entrepreneurial, too independent. My father's professional manner was serious, yet serene; he spoke to his patients as if they belonged to him personally, he thought of medicine as something that belonged to him.

Officially, of course, like every doctor in the USSR, he worked for the state and drew a modest salary. Fee-for-service medicine was illegal, and even established doctors were afraid to practice it for fear of being prosecuted for the crime of parasitism. The punishment was prison, psychiatric treatments, or most often, a forced-labor camp. My Dedushka, from time to time, took a few private patients, in a very unofficial capacity, as a favor for friends or relatives.

Social parasitism or unemployment (in Russian, *tuneyadstvo*) was a crime in the new worker's heaven, where everybody had to be employed by some sort of department or organization. Those who fell out of favor at work and got fired were subject to arrest if they couldn't get another job right away. This law was often used to intimidate dissidents, who were forced to work menial jobs to stay out of trouble. Forget being in business for yourself, that was a sin against socialism.

Despite the danger, he began to see patients at home, after work, on Saturdays and Sundays. It started with just a few patients a week, then slowly grew to fifteen patients a day. I remember our modest apartment swarming with people almost every day of the week, coughing, sneezing, breathing heavily and nervously, emitting odors acquired on the long train trip. Some talked in loud voices, while others were too timid to ask where the toilet was.

Most of them came to try his asthma treatment; but he was also an excellent specialist in other cardiovascular illnesses. Asthma is characterized by a shortness of breath and is brought on by environmental factors and stress, which was why it was one of the biggest killers in the Soviet Union. My father saw miners, factory workers, people living in polluted areas and in proximity to industrial plants and highways. Many of his patients had been misdiagnosed or mistreated for many years. It fell to him to unravel their cases. He knew what to look for, how to touch a patient's body, how to ask the right question. My father took only the most severe cases. A typical patient would be a severe asthmatic, with various accompanying illnesses such as diabetes, high blood pressure, and obesity, or a lifetime of smoking. Each consultation lasted around forty-five minutes, sometimes longer. On busy days, he didn't go to bed until two in the morning.

His method involved a complex combination of various drugs, which needed to be taken in various dosages many different times a day throughout weeks, which then needed to be replaced by other, less strong drugs to lessen side effects, but still substituted by other drugs to keep the effect going. He wrote out the instructions, he read them to the patient, he made the patient read them back to him making sure his directions were understood. The drug therapy was complemented by a specially designed diet, tailored to each patient's needs. Under my father's method, his patients usually began to feel better within a week, but they remained under his watch for months and sometimes years. They had to maintain the regimen, which he altered with time, depending on the state of their health. No other doctor in the Soviet Union treated patients like that. A large percentage of my father's patients who had given up on poor Soviet health care at the same time stayed loyal to Russian folk medicinal cures. They believed in miracles. Their story was always the same: up to ten emergency calls a night, due to repeated asthma attacks in remote areas with no communication, extremely high mortality rate among children and adults, which could have been avoided had paramedics reached those families in time. If people didn't die, they suffered from deteriorating health, missed school, missed work, broken marriages, infertility. Still, so many of them feared medical progress and science in general. Betrayed by their country's healthcare system, they desired and trusted the unproven wonders of the occult sciences. When these patients met my father, he initially detected fear and distrust in their eyes when he explained his rational medical treatments. In Russia, thousands of people would rather drink urine in hopes for a cure than adhere to a medical treatment coming from an educated doctor. So, my father despised the system because he knew it was at least partially responsible for people's agony, for how distrusting they were toward modern science. And yet, through word of mouth, my father, not some shaman in the mountains, so often ended up being those people's last hope. He made them not afraid of him, and he won their trust. People from some of the most remote regions of the Soviet Union used to learn the name of this wonder doctor who lived in Moscow and saw patients privately, at home, that he was rather young, and that even though he was Jewish and used regular scientific methods, he knew how to heal, and he did no harm.

From an early age, I glued myself to my father's chair in his study. He never sent me away. Together we saw his patients. I would greet my father when he came home, bring him his slippers. I guess at that time he still worked a few hours at the state hospital, just to satisfy the authorities. Then I would follow him into his study, climb into his chair behind him, and get myself ready to receive his patients.

He liked having me there with him and his patients didn't seem to mind. I would go into the long narrow hallway and announce: "Next, please." I felt so empowered, so pleased, hoping my voice was pleasant enough for the adoring looks those tired, sick patients gave me; I also hoped I was helpful to my father. I wanted so much to be useful to him. I would perch almost on top of him, my fingers constantly playing with his big flat earlobes as he talked. As soon as school was over, I was back home assisting him. Some of his patients were mathematicians and physicists with Nobel Prizes, who were kind enough to help me with my homework.

At the beginning, we could contain the patients inside the apartment, but with time the line began to stretch onto the staircase and then outside the building and the neighbors began to complain. They threatened to go to the authorities about this shameless flouting of the law. We were living in the Soviet Union, after all, but all he said was: "I would like to see how successful these authorities will be in turning these sick people away. Most of them traveled three days by train to see me, spent most of what they had on the ticket; they sleep at the train station waiting to see me. I am their last hope. These people are not going back." These same neighbors became my father's patients, and the authorities came to see the doctor as well, because everyone in Russia had trouble breathing.

Eventually, the list of my father's patients came to include the most powerful people in Moscow: members of the ruling Politburo, diplomats and ambassadors, heads of neighboring Soviet Socialist republics, bosses of big factories. Americans ask with naïve suspiciousness how he got away with it. The answer, I am afraid, is too simple to believe: they needed him more than he needed them. He was the best in his trade, and those who suffered from those terrible illnesses wanted to be treated by the best. He possessed a certain non-Soviet charm which was curiously irresistible to the rulers of the empire.

The tricky part of Soviet capitalism was asking for money. My father could spend hours with each patient and be the most charming, enticing, lighthearted doctor imaginable, but the minute some timid patient whispered: "Doctor, how much do we owe you?" his response was curt and coarse: "It's your own decision. I don't get involved in such matters." Then he would leave the room, and the discomfited patient would be left looking at me.

Back in those days Soviet people were modest about money. Salaries were limited so as not to allow people to feel free and independent. It was just enough to survive. Most people lived from paycheck to paycheck. The government said money was bad for you, a sin in a country where essential services were provided free of charge: free medicine, free education, free housing. Everything else was simply cheap: transport, food and drink, museums. Yet, somewhere deep in their hearts, together with the shame and discomfort that they felt toward money, they were also in awe of it. Still, on a regular-day basis, even talking about money was considered undignified, and certain dealings in it were illegal. In this way, a visit to the doctor's was something like a drug deal, something the police might ask you about later. So, when my father left his patients to ponder over the fee, their faces would flush with embarrassment and confusion. My father understood his audience: he knew people needed to pay something for their doctor, otherwise they would not trust him. In the end, each one left what they could, what it was worth to them. In most cases they could not afford much, but others among his patients were mighty rich, and they displayed a fine sense of responsibility in the way they paid. Some left 120 rubles, the entire monthly salary for a lesser doctor; and then there were those who paid him no less than 500 rubles.

At the end of the day, my father would ask me to count the money he had made. My math was not all that good, but he didn't care. He wanted me to count and not be afraid of money. He was training me in the forbidden science of capitalist economics, to the horror of my mother and our relatives who thought that speaking of money was dirty and unbecoming. I wanted to please him and make him think I was smart. So, I counted his money, and if I got muddled somewhere in the middle, he pretended not to notice. He thanked me, and I was happy. I asked if he thought I was smart, and he told me I was still a very silly girl.

I wanted to be an actress and to be famous like my grandmother Marina. My father thought it silly and superficial of me. Being a doctor, who could help people and make a living anywhere, was the thing to do, especially if we wanted to go to America one day. His vision for me, for us, was very practical. He almost enjoyed telling me how in America all actors waited tables, while waiting a lifetime for a phone call from an agent for that one-in-a-million shot. I kept insisting that I was the exception. He laughed at me.

My father came of age in the period known as the Khrushchev Thaw. After Stalin's death in 1953, Krushchev acknowledged Stalin's crimes and released millions of political prisoners from the Gulag. Censorship was relaxed, allowing the publication of Aleksander Solzhenitsyn's *One Day in the Life of Ivan Denisovich*. What was not allowed had become permitted, what had lain hidden, canceled, and anathemized, was reborn. There was a renaissance of the arts, as people read again the literature and poetry that had been censored for thirty years, and enjoyed new currents in prose and in poetry, music and film. Voices of such artists as Tarkovsky, Evtushenko,

Shostakovich, Akhmatova, were not afraid to expose the country's false ethics; they spoke of their pain, of human vulnerability, of sanctity of life, and Russia's obsessive glorification of death.

My father loved poetry and loaded my mind with verses I had no way of understanding. Yes, perhaps, I had a glib understanding of Pushkin or Lermontov, but I was desperately lost when I heard Mayakovski's uncomfortable rhymes, when he recited to me Akhmatova's strange, proud verses, or Tzvetaeva's poems soaking with shamelessness and passion. He read from Pasternak, from Mandelstam and Gumilev, and a host of others whose names are not well known in the West. As soon as I thought I had captured one idea, it escaped from me like some frisky butterfly. My father always told me understanding poetry was not necessary, but feeling it was. Poetry gave him a sense of freedom, which meant everything to him.

Many of my father's school friends, those freedom- and poetry-loving Thaw youngsters, all sobered up when the time came. They got proper jobs with proper wives, and with the exception of those who emigrated to Israel or America, they all turned into proper Homo Sovieticus. They wanted freedom in theory, but they could live without it.

My father couldn't do that; he challenged the absence of freedom in every way he could. By introducing me to poetry, by reciting it to me, almost insisting that I let it run through the fibers of my body, by making me understand and accept what its duplicity meant, he showed me it was a mechanism through which one could exercise independence of spirit.

My father enveloped me with his thoughts, his ideas, and defended me against the outdated provincial attitudes of some of my loving relatives. He took personal responsibility for my education, deciding when I was six that I was to go to the best school in

Moscow, the In-Depth English Language Program School #23. If we were going to America, I had better learn how to speak English. He interviewed the teachers in that school, to see which would best suit my personality and my educational needs. No parent in the Soviet Union dared to handpick teachers for his or her child, that was the height of bourgeois arrogance, a confusion of traditional roles. In the Soviet Union a teacher was an important figure, vested with his authority by the state, commanding the respect of the child and parents whether freely given or not, and above all not to be questioned or argued with. A student could consider himself lucky if he was taught by a wise and sympathetic teacher, but nobody got to go shopping the way my father did. I wasn't even supposed to be in that school, reserved as it was for the children of the party elite. We didn't even live in the neighborhood. But my father, with his contacts and his charm, somehow got me in. He wanted the best for me, not only the quality of education, but the sort of people I was surrounded by, who my friends were. It was about my education, my life, my future.

Today I can see that he was right, and I was silly to quarrel with him about the theatre. I would have ended as a used up eastern European bimbo, always at someone's beck and call, with larger-than-life table-waiting experience, still waiting for that phone to ring.

In today's America, my father might be criticized for not giving enough respect to his daughter's dreams, but in Russia, my opinion counted for exactly nothing. My father might have been more sensitive than Dedushka, but he was no less serious about his plan for family success. This plan required his daughter to play a role. He never praised me to my face, but he told my mother about my good memory, about my writing, about my willingness to discuss things. He was raising me to be his successor. We were going to America, and I was going to be a doctor and that was that, but unless I wanted it, unless I chose it freely, this plan would never work. By surrounding me with his gravely ill patients whose helplessness and cluelessness left one feeling both humble and sad, taking me on night expeditions to save our Dedushka or his other patients, he was showing me the joy of his profession.

Years passed, and as my father became even more famous, our family moved to a new apartment in the center of the city at Kutuzovsky Prospect #18. Our new neighborhood was the most fashionable and prestigious in Moscow, where Leonid Brezhnev lived. It was an imperial apartment, five rooms with high ceilings and huge windows off a long, arched hallway. He wanted it very much, for his vision was to build an oasis and live the kind of life that was inconceivable by Soviet standards, in a grand Moscow apartment where he could see his patients and raise his family.

Such was the nature of the Soviet Union that the apartment my father found was a *kommunalka* with five families sharing a toilet. It was also the nature of the Soviet Union that anything was possible if you had enough money and influence, and he did. Huge bribes had to be paid to any number of officials and nice apartments were secured for all five families, who happily moved out to make way for a nine-month renovation project.

Soviet people typically did not renovate their own apartments or hire tradesmen. There were no stores where you could buy things like plumbing fixtures or floorboards. Every door, windowpane, every light bulb, every switch, tile, can of paint, every basic piece of furniture, and curtains, had to be specially ordered from factories. My father had patients in every sphere of the manufacturing and consumer goods industry. He charmed, bribed, overpaid, and the work went forward.

Our father's study, where he saw patients, was my favorite, a large hexagonal room with three oversized windows overlooking the magnificent avenue. A wall-to-wall built-in bookshelf was filled with Russian literature, Western literature, medical books in English and in Russian, art books with wonderful pictures. Across, right next to those bright windows, stood a friendly beige sofa complemented by two friendly chairs. Finally, to the left was my father's desk, and a leather chair for the patient to sit.

The desk was a late nineteenth-century mahogany partners desk with a green leather writing surface, a relic of an older world, painstakingly restored. He bought it in some antique shop in Moscow at a time when no one wanted to buy antique furniture, only to sell their old relatives' stuff for a few miserable rubles. Its most miraculous feature was the drawers: their quantity, their size, their secret chambers. This was where my father kept his money. One day after he died, I sat at the desk thinking of him, opening and shutting those drawers, inhaling the sweet wooden aroma. I reached deeper inside and felt a couple of thick sturdy envelopes. It was money! We were in such need of it at that moment.

When the apartment was finished, it was the only one of its kind in the city of Moscow, a bourgeois fantasia like you'd see in Paris, or New York. In the USSR, everyone had to be equal, but since everyone else's standard of living was equally mediocre, everyone had to live in an equally mediocre way. Soviet people's apartments differed only when it came to their bookshelves; they were the only thing where you could collect as many of as you wanted as long as they were the right kind of books. Even those who had money were not allowed to desire things that had traces of luxury, because wanting things other people didn't have so as to excite their envy belonged to the realm of capitalist inequity and selfish individualism.

Individualism was a bad word in the USSR, to be an individual went against the Soviet paradigm and was strongly discouraged by the authorities, starting in school. You had to be just like everyone else, because if you were different, you stood out and if you stood out you attracted attention and you quickly learned that was not good for you.

Only the elite were allowed to retain the trappings of imperial Russia and enjoy the luxuries of the decadent West. These were the people in my new neighborhood: members of the Politburo, top ministers, cultural superstars, important scientists. They had regal apartments, dachas in the country with chauffeured cars to take them there, specialty supermarkets, exclusive vacation spots, fancy clubs and restaurants ordinary people couldn't even enter. This way the system rewarded its most important servants, ensuring their loyalty and devotion.

As a good Soviet, you were not supposed to want to join the elite. You were supposed to wait to be invited. Certainly, a Jewish doctor openly and notoriously engaged in the illegal private practice of medicine down the street from Brezhnev's apartment had no place in it, but somehow my father turned the Russian paradox inside out. He created for us an oasis of autonomy in the heart of an empire whose only creed was obsession with control over all its citizens. Somehow, none of these stony-faced apparatchiks, who ran the fearsome army and the ten thousand jails, ever objected to having a doctor in the neighborhood. From formidable officials they turned into regular patients, desperate parents of sick children.

Into this beautiful bourgeois apartment came a parade of characters representing all of Russia: peasants in traditional clothes waited alongside the Foreign Minister, forsaken aristocrats rubbed elbows with Nobel Prize winners, mediocre apparatchiks, former political prisoners, policemen, firemen, prostitutes, priests, former political prisoners, movie stars, writers, scientists, teachers, everyone coughing and sneezing and wheezing and often not smelling too good. Sometimes, coming home from school, I would find exhausted patients resting in our beds, strange, sickly children playing with our toys. Sometimes they even ate with us. This was not sympathy, it was empathy; my father felt their physical and emotional despair.

Patients waited in the living room, where the furniture was covered in white sheets. As at the old place, the line continued down the corridor and into the hall, then downstairs into the backyard and the playground. My father saw his first patient at about 9:30 in the morning; his last patient left sometime in the middle of the night, sometimes as late as three in the morning. He took his time with each patient, and many quarrels were had, and friendships made in his waiting room.

I remember parents carrying in a son who was so sick, he could not walk, the skin on his face blue with asthma. They had brought him from far away to see my father. "Doctor," the parents said, like all the others, "please help." My father got them into the room, he put his big hand on the boy's shoulder and told him that he was going to get him to run up a hill within two weeks, possibly less, if he followed the doctor's orders. He did get better, that boy.

I once walked into my father's study after lunch and saw a Muslim man kneeling to kiss his hand to express gratitude for saving his son. My father was a bit taken aback at this gratitude, but somehow it was all right. We opened our door to the non-elite stratum of the USSR, the poor and the sick, and they were the ones who fed our family, bringing with them sacks of potatoes that they grew, an unimaginable variety of homemade cheeses, eggs, fresh meat, huge jars of honey, jams, pickled goods, cured meats and smoked fish, middle eastern spices and delicacies, handmade wool clothes, intricately designed scarfs, sheepskin coats, and kilos of caviar.

Our neighbors, the elite who ran the government, famous scientists, police officers, famous authors, entertainers, sat together in the same room with the non-elite crowd waiting for their turn to be seen. They were just as grateful and generous in making sure the good doctor never had a problem. One of my father's patients was the boss of the only auto repair shop in Moscow—one of the wealthiest people in the city and a very important man to know if you were lucky enough to have a car. For the very special patients, close friends or important individuals, my father kept hours on special days, clearing his schedule to take time out for important conversations with people he respected about business, or about the state of world affairs or developments in science. It was very hard to contain the flow of patients. There were suitcases filled with letters from patients, either begging to be seen on behalf of a dying son, mother, wife. Many letters were expressions of gratitude for saving lives. The egalitarianism of the waiting room notwithstanding, my father did not believe in a classless society. Workers behaved, thought, and felt like workers, intelligentsia had different thoughts, no matter how much the government tried to tell them they were the same. My father could talk to anyone; he respected and felt for all people, but he could not overlook the fact that notwithstanding its socialist order, the reality was that he lived in a deeply hierarchical society. As a wealthy man who lived in a socialist country, he understood that it was only due to his exclusive status that he was able to live well and protect his family. Although he was a modest man, he enjoyed his wealth and his status tremendously, proud of what he was able to achieve in a country that anathemized it.

I understood it when all these people, rich or poor, important or unimportant as they were, asked him the same question over and over again: "Doctor, what can I do for you?" I grew up knowing that nothing was impossible, because of the sort of a father I had. His powerful aura had defined the contours of the sort of a man I would want for myself once I was all grown up. My father was a king, and I decided I wanted nothing less for myself one day.

II.

My Mother's World

PHYSICALLY, MY GRANDMOTHER COULD TOLERATE ALMOST ANY-
thing except the feeling of hunger. Whenever she got hungry,
no matter where we were together, on a subway or at some fancy
gathering, she would manage to get herself some bread and swallow
a piece. My grandmother, Marina Karaseva, had survived the siege of
Leningrad. She never complained when she got sick, neglected doctors' advice, made fun of hypochondriacs and people who entrusted
themselves to psychologists, and yet she always had a tear in her eye
whenever she chewed on her piece of bread. She would say "Anya,
how lucky you are that you don't know what it's like..."

My grandparents never volunteered to talk about it, and I could
never make them tell me the whole thing in chronological order,
but at the same time everything they did, ate, loved, or enjoyed in
peaceful times was connected through some invisible thread to what
they called at school the Great Patriotic War. It was the same at
school, where the soldiers who had faced the German tanks were
invited to tell us what they had seen. The Nazis surrounded the city
of Leningrad for nearly three years and laid it to waste, 1.5 million
were bombed and starved to death. Sometimes the soldiers would
forget they were talking to children, and they would describe their
experiences in graphic detail while we listened with our mouths wide
open. We did not know we were the last generation living under

Soviet rule, listening to these half-broken people tell how they fought for the country whose days were now numbered.

I had already heard from my grandparents how their magnificent Leningrad was turned into a city of frozen corpses, silent apartments, razed buildings, and demolished palatial squares. My grandmother Marina was a sapper, running over the rooftops deactivating incendiary bombs while Nazi planes flew overhead. During the day, she entertained the wounded at the hospital with her one-woman show. My grandmother was not afraid of bombs, but she was afraid of hunger. The only way to bring supplies of food and fuel into the city was in trucks over nearby Lake Ladoga when it froze in the winter. My grandparents told me people were dying on the streets in broad daylight, dying in their apartments surrounded by their families or all alone. The winters, there were three of them, were the worst, with the temperature far below zero and nothing to burn to keep warm. Walking in the street, they told me, your footfall produced no more sound than snow falling off a tree. The people appeared like ghosts on the demolished streets of the imperial city, a museum under the sky, seeming to melt into its frozen air. The black bread of which everyone received 125 grams per day was not made of real rye, because there was none, but of offal, grist, wood shavings, cat food. People drank carpenter's glue and boiled leather belts. They melted snow for water. In order to stay warm, they burned their antique furniture and the frames of their paintings. Driven to madness by starvation, some even resorted to cannibalism, eating corpses, or even grabbing people off the street. My grandmother told me about the time she saw a car making its way toward her with its headlights pointing directly at her (or so she thought), so she threw herself into the darkness of the nearest courtyard.

In this theatre of horror, the worst thing was the continuous feeling of hunger. As soon as she satisfied it and got some of her strength back, it returned with even greater force. She wanted the war to end so that she could have as much canned meat as her heart and stomach desired, and even when it was over, she could never get used to the idea that she was in no danger of starvation anymore.

One bitterly cold winter night, walking home in the dark, my grandparents heard an almost forgotten noise, the childishly squeaky sound of a trolley. They hadn't seen a trolley on that line in months, but soon its unmistakable contours came into view. It didn't stop when they waved. The wind began to blow harder, and it seemed to grow even darker when suddenly the sirens wailed over their heads. They fell into the snow as the bombs began to fall. By and by, the air raid stopped, and they got up and continued walking through the deserted streets, when suddenly they came upon the mangled remains of their trolley. The bombs had turned it to a pile of scorched and twisted metal. Anyone who might have been inside it was surely dead. Everything was a matter of chance. The day they had just lived was still a good day.

In 1944 my grandmother gave birth to my uncle, Evgeniy, and then in 1946, to Galina Soulovna, who would later become Galina Novikova, my beautiful mother.

After the war, my grandparents went on with their lives and their careers. I still remember walking down the streets of Leningrad and Moscow seeing billboards and posters with the glamorous image of Marina Karaseva, announcing her recital dates. She was born with perfect pitch, and she could sing any tune, imitate any sound, any voice. A classical pianist by training, she later developed her own genre: a one-woman show on the piano. She did her own improvisations on the spot, sang popular melodies, juxtaposed various styles, made jokes. She worked with the best lyricists and composers of the day, but her act was unique, improvisational. In all the Soviet Union, there was no one like her.

My grandfather, Saul Karasik, was a promoter and organizer of spectacles. He worked for Lenconcert, the Soviet concert and the-atre administration, and was responsible for booking and organizing tours and promoting the Soviet arts throughout the entire country and all over the world. This made him a big man in Soviet show busi-ness, a revered and beloved figure. After the war, when the country lay in ruins and the survivors had little if any interest in the per-forming arts, he took it upon himself to revive them. The structure of show business in the Soviet Union was rather primitive: the state agency owned the hall, printed the posters, sold the tickets, and paid the artists as it saw fit. Performing artists in the Soviet Union did not have agents or managers. In theory, they were represented by the state, which meant no one represented them at all unless someone like my grandfather took an interest in them.

The business was all about the power of personal relationships, and for a generation of artists in the Soviet Union, he was their biggest promoter, their advocate, their supporter. Gentle and soft-spoken, with impeccable manners, he was famous for never offering or taking bribes, for being principled, for not being a gossiper, for adoring the arts, his family, and for worshipping the city in which he lived.

My mother and her brother grew up in the rigid, unsentimental environment of post-war Russia, but they were privileged children of artistic intelligentsia. They attended music school every day in par-allel with regular school until they were about fourteen, then it was on to music college and then, because they were remarkably well pre-pared on top of being talented, not to mention exceptionally lucky in their connections, the N. A. Rimsky-Korsakov Leningrad State Conservatory. My mother became a concert pianist; her brother played the double bass and was studying to be a conductor.

The walls in my grandparents' Leningrad apartment were splashed with autographed pictures of stars with whom she had shared a stage: Marlene Dietrich, Benny Goodman, Paul Robeson. One of them has my grandmother in some white sparkly outfit sitting at the piano looking up at Marlene, they are surrounded by people, all laughing, smiling, talking. They threw wonderful parties after my grandmother's shows; their home was always full of friends, a glittering crowd from the worlds of classical and pop music.

By the standards of postwar Russia, they led a charmed life. It didn't matter that they lived in a *kommunalka*. Everyone lived like that, especially after the war, when housing was scarce. Their three rooms, a luxury as things went then, were in one of the most beautiful buildings of old St. Petersburg; the apartment had belonged to a famous actor who fled to Europe when the Bolsheviks stormed the Winter Palace.

They also had a full-time nanny-housekeeper named Tasya, an illiterate peasant woman from a little village that was destroyed in the war. When my grandparents found her, she was desperately poor and hungry and all alone. Everyone she knew was dead. They took her in to live with them, and to care for my toddler uncle and infant mother. She was nurse, disciplinarian, mediator, confidant, cleaner, cook. Such arrangements were not uncommon then, so many people were dead and homes destroyed, and many came to bigger cities hoping to find work. Tasya worshipped my grandmother, revered my grandfather, and doted on the children.

She barely spoke of her past and no one dared to ask questions. She recognized only some of the letters of the alphabet, but she knew how to count money. She went shopping for the family and saved for her future. She had no life of her own; her life belonged to my mother's family. She became my grandmother's secretary, remembering all her phone messages, knowing my grandmother's concert and touring schedule. Within a few years from a simple, starving village girl she had turned into a respectable young lady who knew her way around Leningrad, responsible for care of Marina Karaseva's (my grandmother's stage name) and Saul Karasik's two children and playing hostess to my grandparents' important friends. She was kind to the children, but strict in a plain, unapologetic sort of way. Tasya's "no" meant "no"; no explanations, no apologies; but the kids were well fed, clothed, watched, and well-mannered because she knew those things were important.

Kommunalka living was squalid: you had to live next to strangers, hear their secrets, smell their food, know of each other's physical conditions, habits, dreams, and tragedies. There were vicious battles over things big and small, with curses, screaming and yelling, crying, sobbing and quarreling into the night. However, with some people, my mother remembers, like my grandfather Saul and the Widow, people were too embarrassed to quarrel. They passed through the corridors of those noisy, degrading, sad dwellings the same way they passed through life, proudly and gracefully.

The Widow was an old lady called Antonina Vasilyevna. Her husband was an officer in the tsar's army who was murdered by the Bolsheviks as soon as they came to power. My mother remembers a beautiful woman, always dressed in an old-fashioned way in long skirts or dresses, with shirts of exquisite lace, and magnificent handmade woven scarves around her shoulders. She adored my grandmother Marina for her glamour and her connection to the world of the arts, so far removed from the rest of the Soviet reality, which was not to her taste. She wasn't a princess or a countess, but she was a Russian aristocrat. Together with her old-fashioned manners, she had managed to preserve some of her prerevolutionary jewels, and she loved loaning them to my grandmother to wear whenever she had some special performance or important occasion. In defiance of the dreariness imposed on her by the socialist regime, the Widow adhered to her prerevolutionary ways, as befitted a member of the nobility. She took baths, she drank tea and coffee from cups of fine china, which had escaped smashing by the Bolsheviks or the war. She addressed everyone, even those much younger than herself, formally by their patronymic name.

A prostitute lived across the hall. Mother doesn't remember her name, and it probably wasn't her name, anyway. Officially, prostitution was not supposed to exist in the USSR, but it did, and everyone knew it. They didn't walk openly on the streets, but the customers knew where to find them. Hotels were out of reach for regular Soviet citizens, so they brought them back to their wretched dwellings to do the deed. In the evening, she would disappear into her mysterious reality and reappear in the morning, smiling coquettishly and helplessly. It took my mother a long time to understand who those men were that she saw tiptoeing through the hallway in the wee hours of the morning.

The prostitute was a very colorful character, but unhappy, tarnished by war and used up by men. She was in her mid- to late thirties, with rather bad skin made worse by continuous use of toxic makeup. My mother tells me that her hair was always dirty but colored bright yellow and her lips were painted in perfect red. Inside the apartment she wore robes with images of Asian princesses, and in her arms she always held a tiny puppy. Of the inner workings of her business, my mother could tell me nothing. Such women could be nothing more than they seemed, or they could be agents of the state used to elicit information from their lustful clients, or even from their unsuspecting neighbors. My mother says people were used to her, but no one trusted her. Not only because she had sex with strangers but because she did it for money, which in the USSR was even more taboo than sex. Her wavy hips, her fearless gaze, the little dog in her arms, her coquettish robe, and the ease with which she came and went every day was a living reproach to the regime which made its population live in filth while pretending it cared nothing about money and social status.

Indeed, the Bolshevik Revolution proclaimed equality for all in work and society and promised to erase the difference between men and women. Russian women got the vote in 1917, before American women did in 1920, but when Stalin came to power all these newly acquired freedoms lost their meaning. Almost immediately he enforced strict control over people's private lives and promoted traditional, patriarchal family values. Prostitution, however, exists outside of time and despite time, defying even Stalin. The more she is repressed, the more alluring, more precious she becomes. All the neighbor women, my mother tells me, seemed to be envious of her and the looks she got from their husbands. These women worked all day and cooked in their miserable communal kitchens at night, while their men came home, drank, and fell asleep without even glancing in the direction of their lawful wives. The prostitute's secret life seemed more desirable than theirs, with a hint of femininity.

No one knew more about femininity, it seemed to me, than my grandmother.

She appeared on stage almost every day, sometimes twice a day, and spent weeks touring the country. She was lavishly paid by Soviet standards, but she spent a lot, too, because she needed to look like a goddess every time she walked out of the house. Dresses couldn't be purchased, but a good seamstress could make them. For things like pretty shoes or redder than red Dior lipstick, it was the black market or nothing.

My grandmother was the one who made the money for the family, and she loved spending it the most. She loved to buy food, delicacies, gifts for everyone. Things she adored were expensive and impossible to find, but she knew where to find everything she needed. She had friends at every major market or department store in Leningrad and in Moscow, Kiev, and Minsk; she made sure they all got tickets to her concerts. On many occasions she simply became their friend, which meant more to those people than tickets to a fancy concert. Unless she came home with an almost empty wallet, she was not satisfied. She was an absolute performer in that the maniac loyalty of her audiences sustained her in her happiness. Everyone loved her, the glamorous bohemians of Soviet show business, the proud proletarians, even the inmates of the Gulag system where she went to perform. Money was an incidental means necessary to support that inspiration, and also her family. She was not unrealistic about it. It was always an issue because there was never enough, you could never get much for your money because there was always a shortage of everything everyone wanted, but still, money was the only means of getting what you wanted. Knowing the "right" kind of people in the "right" kind of places, along with sufficient sums of money, could eliminate many inconveniences of Soviet life. My grandparents lived generously, and my grandmother had expenses. She needed to spend on her wardrobe, and she also gave parties at home. When she ran out, she borrowed from Tasya, who saved every kopek she made.

As the main breadwinner and generalissimo of the household, my grandmother did not fit the mold of the traditional Soviet

Russian wife. In her family, my grandmother was not a philosopher or an educator but a war general, taking time out from her busy schedule to make rulings on family matters great and small. She didn't involve herself with detail. Her edicts were final, and the answer to any request coming from her kids was always a "no." It was easier for her to say, because it saved her from having to worry about things. My mother's and my uncle's daily schedules, their vacations, their general code of behavior, as well as the main trajectory of their lives, were determined by my grandmother. The execution of the entire operation known as upbringing was left to others. Meanwhile, Saul dutifully got home by six o'clock, unless there was a later theatre engagement, and presided over dinner, doting on the children.

My grandfather had two different lives, one at work where he oversaw a major sector of the Soviet performing arts, and another at home, where he was a soft, indulgent, sentimental father to his adoring children. Like some delicate noble from a novel by Turgenev or Chekov, he took the children on long walks to magnificent parks, to museums and galleries, to silly playgrounds, ice cream parlors. He helped them with their tedious homework, backed Tasya's insistence that they finish every meal to the last bite.

Even though Marina rarely appeared at home she made all major decisions having to do with domestic life and children's education. I always thought of my grandmother as the boss, thought she ruled her husband. I thought of their marriage as the exception to the patriarchate embedded in the Russian soil, but later, after I had come to live in America where roles and customs are more fluid, my grandmother told me I was mistaken. She had always done what she wanted, after all she was a star, and this extended to affairs with other men. At the same time, for sixty-seven years of her life, she remained loyal to her Saul. Once there was this one very special person for whom she was almost ready to leave my grandfather, but she decided that the whole thing wasn't worth it because he was not a king like her husband. My grandmother's bossiness required something bigger, and the only worthy object was Saul, in his grand dignity, in his reserved, understated manner, and finally in her powerful position, into which he had done much to put her. As a performer her star power was almost limitless, but as a woman she knew her limitations. Without her quiet husband she was not as powerful and understanding; her husband defined her strength.

Her advice to me was practical rather than theoretical. "Always be feminine," she used to tell me.

When I was young, I had a lot of opinions on everything and I loved to argue with everybody, especially adults, who were more receptive to this kind of behavior than friends my age. They found it amusing, and politely argued back. Marina never bothered to engage with my silly intellectual diatribes, but sometimes she would blurt out: "Anuta, don't be so pigheaded, you will scare all the men away." "You need to be feminine; you need to have a flexible mind. You can have the same opinions, the same passion, but do it differently."

She never ceased to repeat to me: "Always remain a woman, whether you are cleaning kitchen floors, or dancing in a ballroom like a princess, or if you are at work arguing with other important men and women, or when you are laying naked in bed with a husband or a lover." When it came to men, it was: "Anya, always make sure that your husband is well fed. Even if you are in a quarrel. You don't need to talk to him. You don't need to forgive him. But food he must eat. Serve him his soup with meat, and then leave. This is your duty to him."

I remember my mother in the small and simple kitchen of our first apartment. It was late spring, almost summer; the air, warm and slightly dry the way it always used to get in Moscow in May or early June. It was late morning, the streets silent with everyone at work or school except for me; maybe I was not feeling well. My mother had invented a game to distract me so that I would eat. She had made my favorite breakfast, cottage cheese with strawberry jam, and she was standing on the other side of the table extending her beautiful white arms with the spoon and we were both watching to see if she was going spill it before it was going to make its way inside my chattering mouth. Behind her, the pink and white synthetic window curtains were fluffing in the gentle breeze. The strawberry jam had turned the curds pink; they now tasted less sweet but softer altogether; strawberry seeds teased my gums and the warm seductive scent of strawberries filled our kitchen with joy. There was the sound of my mother's tender whispers, my bumpy laughter, and the street's stillness. No one knows, understands, or loves me better than my mother, but that was the only time I felt completely happy and at peace with her. From time to time this memory reappears to tantalize and sadden me.

My mother is a beautiful musician, her music makes her feel alive and human because she is able to possess it at a deep level. But when she was a little girl, she didn't have this feeling. Her mother had told her she was going to become a concert pianist, and in order to achieve this, she must practice five or six hours a day, like her older brother Yevgeny. Parents in Russia were not to be disobeyed and Saul and Marina least of all, so she went on practicing, five or six hours a day, until she became a concert pianist.

During summers, they went to the beautiful Gulf of Finland, about thirty minutes away from Leningrad, or to some Belarussian village, surrounded by impenetrable forest, with their loyal, stoic Tasya who was undeterred by substandard conditions of a rented postwar summer cottage. She was a country woman and felt more at home in the country walking barefoot, talking simple Russian with village people.

Their home in the city was always full of friends, a glittering crowd of lawyers and doctors, singers and dancers, writers and composers who came to visit their apartment after my grandmother's shows. The worlds of classical and pop music mixed and mingled around my grandmother's table. She wasn't much of a drinker, but she liked a good time and always in the company of men: she was spoiled by their amorous attention, by their adoration of her talent, her charm, her non-Soviet glamour, and her fame. She was equally charming in the company of her children's friends. But because she was so famous, my mother preferred that my grandmother not appear at her school to pick her up with the other children's parents. She looked too different, too bright. My mother admitted to me she was embarrassed by her mother's glamour, her startling Jewish looks, the supple whiteness of her skin, her Hollywood red lipstick perfectly and seductively painted on her lips, her gay green eyes, and her fancily tailored clothes. She didn't blend in with the hopelessly gray postwar crowd. Much more frequently it was Tasya who replaced my grandparents and appeared at most school meetings, to my mother's great relief.

My mother was adorable: plump, according to the fashion of the time, with her mother's almond shaped eyes, her father's soft hair, and her father's long, aristocratic arms and fingers. By the time she turned fourteen or fifteen, she was always in love with boys, and they were always in love with her. Her parents and her nanny were strict, but still she managed to sneak out to go dancing and kissing boys. Her older brother never seemed to spend any time at home, never seemed to study, always went out with girls, but she found out the rules were different for her. One night she came home at some unseemly hour, only to find that my grandfather had been up all night worrying about where she might be. My gentle grandfather's greeting was not very gentle. He slapped my mother's face, told her to kneel and beg for forgiveness.

As expected, my mother was admitted into the Leningrad State Conservatory to study under the guidance of the famous pianist and teacher Nathan Perelman, whose method is still influential today. He said she had talent, and she did, the rare student who under-stands exactly what the teacher is trying to pass on to them. What she didn't have was a desire to work. Professor Perelman called her the devil, born gifted and lazy.

My uncle Evgeniy was two years ahead of her at the Conservatory. They were very close, sharing friends and secrets together. My uncle cared about two things: music and himself. Doted on and spoiled by his parents, rarely punished for anything, he was consistently compli-mented on his lady-killing looks. Even when he grew up, they contin-ued to baby him. He never moved out of their apartment; he liked it at home where the place was always full of people. My uncle loved inviting friends there and introducing them to people who mattered. He always complained about his lack of independence, but he never did anything about it.

My mother was a good girl, from a good family, and now she was a concert pianist, so she was very eligible. She loves to tell stories about all those wonderful boys she used to date: musicians, writers, actors, fascinating fellows in swanky Western clothes that demon-strated black market virtuosity. They entertained her with their bohemian eccentricity or their post-pubescent romanticism. She had no interest in politics, which was just as well given the tenor of the time, but a keen interest in all sorts of music, styles, friends, and fun.

As women did at that time, she zealously guarded her virginity for marriage. It had to do with keeping a good name. No one ever talked about it, but a young girl could hear it loud and clear from both parents. Another thing that was never expressly discussed but implicitly assumed was that under no circumstances were my grandparents going to countenance the marriage of their only daughter to a non-Jew. A goy, even one in love, was a stranger, always ready to insult, attack, betray. It was not a matter of religion, as few Soviet Jews actually practiced Judaism. It was a matter of culture, of identity. Thousands of years of history were not easily forgotten or forgiven. To feel protected, Soviet Jews either stuck together by never marrying outside the faith, or, alternatively, stepped outside their doomed ethnicity by marrying into a non-Jewish family. But either way, for purposes of discrimination, in the eyes of the law, as well as in the eyes of the Soviet community, Jews remained Jews. There were plenty of eligible Jewish boys among the Soviet intelligentsia in Leningrad, but she fell for a boy from Moscow, the city of unsophisticated proportions, boorish generosity, and dubious morality and candor. Big, fat, round, red Moscow was where my parents would meet, choose one another, and fall in love. My mother was visiting her newly married cousin Sopha in Moscow, who declared she was going to set her up on a date. My mother had plenty of dates but could not refuse her hospitable cousin. The blind date, when he appeared on the doorstep, did not impress at first glance. Skinny and bespectacled, his unfashionable clothes hanging on his alarmingly thin body, he was a fifth-year medical student four years older than her, but he looked like a teenager too shy to ask a girl for a date. On the other hand, he was polite, and he looked clean, if a little tired from his just finished shift at the hospital. He had the most peculiar, awkward name: Arkady. It was neither Russian, nor Jewish, and to my mother it sounded like a note which could never be sung right. Nor did things get any better with his last name, *Novikov*, Russian for *new*. He told her that the name at some point must have been changed from *Novik* to *Novikov* to make it sound less Semitic.

As soon as he opened his mouth, however, my mother could see she had never met anybody like Arkady Novikov, and everyone she had known and loved until that evening, impressive as they may have seemed at the time, was no more than mediocrity. Her family did not talk about politics. They weren't blind, but out of a keenly honed Jewish instinct for survival, chose not to talk about the truth behind the propaganda. Instead, they talked about the arts. My mother grew up blindly believing in the idea that the Soviet Union was the most beautiful and strongest country in the whole world. She glided through all those matters without checking to see if there were any questions to be asked. My father laughed at all those notions. He told her about the Hitler-Stalin pact and other historical facts she didn't know.

My mother says that it was not simply what and how much he knew at the age of twenty-five, but the way he spoke. He was scornful, cynical, with a wicked sense of humor. She used to think her beatnik, bohemian friends were cool, getting together in some clandestine apartment with some jazz records, smoking, praising the West, and trying to make a little money selling a pair of used jeans. My father didn't drink and didn't smoke and didn't care whether anyone thought he was cool. She fell for him.

They began to see each other regularly, and to write letters, as people still did then. My mother's letters are chaotic and emotional, while my father's are full of refined passion, boyishness, but at the same time desire to please. My father was slow to propose, and it was his mother who had to tell him not to take his time with this. My radical father understood that there are situations that call for traditional behavior. Instead of going to my grandfather to ask for my mother's hand in marriage, he went to see my grandmother. He could see she was the one in charge. He presented himself at her hotel after her Moscow performance with an obnoxiously enormous bouquet of roses and proceeded to ask her for her daughter's hand in marriage. My paternal grandmother, Anya, fell in love with my beautiful talented mother and her grand family. Every time my mother appeared in Moscow, she would turn her entire world upside down for her, take her to the best cafés and art galleries, and show her off to Moscow society. Life rarely smiled on my grandmother: wars, the loss of her three-year-old Kirochka, care for her sick son, worries about my young father, and my grandfather's rough character took a toll on her health and her looks, but not on her personality. Despite everything she had been through, she loved life, and she recognized beauty when she saw it. She saw it in my mother, and she wanted to hold on to it. One time my mother heard her say to my father: "Just look at how beautiful our Galochka [diminutive from Galya] is." When my parents got married and moved in with her and Dedushka, she had a restored antique baby grand piano waiting in the apartment. Her death just one year into their marriage was my mother's first adult sorrow.

They married in Leningrad, in the midst of winter, on December 6, 1969. The wedding on the English Embankment gathered the elite of Moscow, Leningrad, and Kiev. There exists only one photo of this occasion. With all the chaos of preparations, they decided not to use a professional photographer because my uncle's best friend volunteered to photograph the entire event. When he went to develop the film, it had somehow gotten exposed to light and not a single picture survived. One of the guests took a photo of my parents dancing, and to this day this is the only wedding picture I have of my parents. It is an awkward closeup with my mother looking into the camera, barely smiling. My father, not knowing that he was being snapped, is looking the other way. For the rest of my childhood, whenever I spotted wedding photos of my friends' parents, I thought of it as bizarre and common. At the wedding, my father made a short and timid speech, addressing my mother: "I shall guard this treasure with my life." And he did.

In the decade between their wedding and my birth, my parents enjoyed themselves. My mother was busy with her career, giving recitals throughout the Soviet Union and Europe. My father, who initially was very proud of his new wife's musical career and loved watching her on the country's main stages in Moscow and Leningrad, was less excited about her trips to places in Russia's far east, which involved long rides on dirty trains, lodging in seedy hotels, and fending off the amorous advances of provincial officials.

They both wanted children, but for my mother it was something she was theoretically planning to put into practice at some point in the future. This theory got her pregnant three times, the first before they were actually married or even engaged. She thought it was going to be the end of her life. My father was her first sexual experience, her first real love. To make matters worse, he was in Moscow finishing his residency, while she was in Leningrad, all alone in her tragic state of bodily disgrace, unable to share her dreadful secret with anyone but her brother. Something needed to be done, and my father arranged for an emergency abortion in Moscow. Older, wiser cousin Sopha had to be let in on the secret. It was 1968, and the experience cannot have been a very pleasant one, even though the abortion was performed in one of the main hospitals, and from my parents' correspondence, I read it was my Dedushka who arranged everything in the end. This must have seemed like another disaster; her future father-in law now knew she was about to have an abortion.

In her letters to my father, my mother expressed bitterness and anger. It was all his fault, she wrote over and over again. Far too young at age ten to be reading my parents' letters, I could not understand how my mother's pregnancy could be my poor father's fault. My father's replies seemed understanding, thoughtful, and loving. Devouring those letters, in secret from my parents, I couldn't believe my mother's anger, her unloving tone, her stubborn inability to meet my father halfway even though it was he who arranged everything so neatly and caringly.

After they married, she got pregnant again, and decided to have another abortion, and then it happened again. Each time she told my father it was going to be the last one. Everyone in the family thought my parents were challenged reproductively, no one could imagine that fertility was the least of their problems. When she got pregnant again, she again announced that this would be the last abortion. It wasn't that she didn't like children, she knew she had to have them, they were inscribed into her future in a way she could not escape, in the same way she could not escape her musical career or her marriage to a Jewish man. It was simply that she had no idea what she was supposed to do with them once she got them. She thought that at some special point in time she was going to acquire that special knowledge and only then would she become a "mother". She never bothered her mind about such things, she simply appeared to be surprised to find herself pregnant but not at all surprised to find herself at the women's clinic for yet another abortion. This time, even the doctor there said it should be her last.

There were a lot of abortions in the Soviet Union. As a little girl walking on the streets in Moscow, the sight of a pregnant woman always surprised me because it was such a rarity. The practice was legal from the 1970s onward and surveys indicate the number of abortions outnumbered live births. On paper, the Soviet Union was a feminist paradise, a woman was the equal of a man in the eyes of the law. For every ruble a man made, a woman made the same ruble for the same job. If she decided to have children, she was allowed a very generous maternity package with 100 percent job security, and when the baby came there were public nurseries, kindergartens, and schools so that she could go back to work, because a career dedicated to the progress of the state and to the common good was the highest calling a woman could have.

The state never took away a woman's right to have children and family, but it was up to her to manage that "secondary" part of her life. Women in Soviet Russia got abortions because they had no space to live in, they had no money despite having to work all the time, because their men were despondent alcoholics who habitually beat them or were too exhausted to beat them and instead spent their time in useless idleness.

I saw it in my father's patients' eyes. These overworked Soviet women looked exhausted from being pushed and shoved on crowded, airless, smelly buses on the way to and from work. Their lunch and post-work hours were invariably spent queuing for food. Feminine pleasures like beauty parlors were denied them; there were only a few of these in the capital. They had no time to take care of themselves, they didn't know how, they didn't think they needed to, they were embarrassed, too, even if their feminine nature cried for it. Rearing a child was a feminine luxury many women felt they could not afford.

It may surprise you to know that women in the Soviet Union were utterly indifferent to the ideas of feminism, even as they swept through the West in those days. They did not want to be treated like men; they had been treated like men since 1917, fighting in the bloody civil war, building tanks for Stalin to destroy Hitler, replacing the men in the fields when they died in the war or perished in labor camps on the uninhabitable tundra in the Far East. Soviet women did not want to be treated like men, they wanted to be treated like women.

I learned all this sitting on the arm of my father's chair while he spoke with his female patients. Outside of celebrities and those who dedicated their life to art and creativity, most of them loathed their mandatory employment. Whether a woman was a factory worker or a scientist, her workday was long, and her responsibilities were endless. It left her emotionless for her man, yet at the same time it did not relieve her of her domestic duties. Russian women, like all women everywhere, wanted to be loved and admired and paid attention by their husbands, they wanted to stay young and be beautiful, even as the conditions of their lives were depleting their femininity and making them old before their time. They couldn't quit work, so they got abortions. My mother wasn't most women. By virtue of being my father's wife, she held a special place in that sordid society. She chose abortion simply because it wasn't her time yet to have children. I would have done the same in her place.

The date for the abortion was set. Sometime in February. My mother remembers the never-ending February snowstorms. The gynecologist and the anesthesiologist were my father's good colleagues; they promised to take good care. When she arrived at the women's hospital, a silent nurse walked her down a hollow corridor into some charmless spotless white room with a small stool and a cot.

The nurse commanded my mother to change into a hospital gown (a sad piece of an over-washed material that covered the bodies of many women like my mother) was provided to her instantaneously. The nurse collected my mother's clothes and told her that they would be returned to her in a couple of days, upon her release from the hospital. She then walked my mother out of the white room, marched her down another corridor, which looked identical to the first one, and, finally, deposited her on a metallic chair in front of a tiny child, who was sitting at a cluttered desk scribbling on pieces of paper with a tense expression. The child was dressed in a white robe and had a white hat on, and when she finally spoke, her voice surprisingly adult, hoarse, deep, common, but not unpleasant, my mother realized it was not a child, but a health care worker assigned to her case.

It was only the two of them, and the desk with papers, in that hollow corridor where the light seemed to come from far away. The child engaged my mother in the frankest conversation she had ever had:

"Name?"

"Galina Soulovna Novikova."

"Birthdate and age?"

"February 22, 1946. I am twenty-nine."

"Is this your first abortion?"

"No."

"How many have you had?"

"Two, maybe three."

"How many children at home?"

"None."

"Are you married?"

"Yes."

"Is you husband working?"

"Yes, he is a doctor."

"Is he beating you?"

"No."

"Is he threatening you?"

"No."

"Do you suspect he has a mistress?"

"No, he loves me very much."

"Do you not love your husband then?"

"I love him."

The child stopped writing, looked up at my mother and told her to come with her. The anesthesiologist gave her a wink and asked when the patient was going to be ready, but the child did not reply and walked away with my mother in tow. After that interrogation, she was unable to disobey. They went on a tour of the gynecology ward, where the patients were lying on soiled sheets. These women were young, and yet their physical suffering and emotional helplessness made them look pathetic and old. Even though it was the best women's hospital in Moscow, the equipment was outdated, and things were not as clean as you might expect. All the while, her guide was talking in a low voice about the fertility problems women had after abortion. No one talked about this sort of thing in the Soviet Union; there were no talk shows like you see in the USA. Private life remained private, and things like guilt, shame and sorrow had to be dealt with individually.

The tour was over, and her little guide looked my mother in the eye and said: "Get the hell out of here! I don't want to see you here ever again unless you're here to give birth." She picked up the broomstick resting in the corner and told my mother that she was going to "sweep her out with a dirty broomstick." My mother protested; she felt lost, she didn't know what to do, on top of which all her clothes were locked up together with her purse and her money. How was she to get home looking like that, without her clothes, in this ragged hospital gown? The child smiled, telling her that the cab was already waiting for her; she then quietly took a few wrinkled up notes from the bottom of her shoe and handed them to my mother. "That should take care of your ride back home, mommy to be." On the way downstairs, they met with the doctor and anesthesiologist, who seemed surprised. "Boys, she changed her mind," the child said, and they brushed past them and out to the curb where the cab was waiting. My mother asked her for her name. "It's Marina," said the child. The taxi sped off. My mother never saw her again.

I was born about seven months later, and thirteen months after that, my little sister joined me, also unplanned. The four of us were always together. My parents' lives seemed to glide in parallel to my sister's and mine. My father had this effortless ability to just be. My mother's presence in my life I sensed without realizing it. It was ubiquitous and pervasive. I was never intrigued by it as I was by my father's presence in my life. I never saw her go to work. Once or twice, we were taken to one of her recitals, but it didn't occur to me that her playing that regal looking black shiny instrument, producing those sounds whose beauty always made me weep, had anything to do with work. My mother never had to get up early in the morning, dress in dark work clothes, go to work, and come back home at six carrying bags filled with food. She never had the look of exhaustion and irritation the way other moms did after spending half of their days on line for the most basic food items and most primitive household things like toilet paper or soup. My mother was mostly at home, practicing her piano, going out in her car, which she drove beautifully. She shopped only in places where she had friends, who were only too happy to get all that she needed for a chance to be seen by my father or attend a great concert. My mother never waited on lines for anything. She picked us up from school and when we came home, she had a sumptuous lunch waiting for us, which she always had time to make. My mother was busy with my sister. Her ballet school put her on a tight schedule; her classes ended late, and my mother drove my sister every day from her school to take a class with one of the legendary ballet teachers of the time. In the evenings, however, my mother exchanged her domestic robes for evening gowns. With girlish excitement I used to watch her select pretty clothes. She went to concert halls, theatres, dinner parties, and various other events where both she and my father were irreplaceable fixtures of that society.

The first real music I ever heard was Rachmaninov's second piano concerto, performed by my mother as she practiced it at home when I was very small. The first four bars are exactly the same, almost not music at all, but they swelled into a majestic sea of sounds which drowned our primitive apartment and everyone who lived in it. To this day it is my favorite piece of music.

We too were made to study piano. I had a wonderful teacher, and some aptitude, but, like my mother, no work ethic. Her talent as a performer was not matched by her talent as a teacher, or perhaps I was not the right student, or there was too much intimacy between us and too much expectation on her part so that piano practice consisted mainly of her shouting and me crying. One evening in the middle of my sobbing routine my mother slammed our grand piano's fall board, it fell with a terrible, yet musical crash, and that was it for my relationship with this most beautiful of musical instruments.

Shortly thereafter my mother traveled somewhere to play music. She entrusted us to our father, backed by my grandparents who came to visit from Leningrad for the occasion. I must have been about six years old, madly attached to my father, but my infantile selfishness, my sense of physical and emotional dependence required my mother. I didn't like being without her. She came back two weeks later.

That night there was a blowout fight between my father and my grandmother. I heard it all from the bedroom where I was supposed to be asleep, my beloved voices not only shouting at one another but also gaining new tonalities and textures. The fight was about my mother. My father thought she was working too much; he loved her music, but he seethed with venom that *his* wife had from time to time to go on tours like some common performer and endure the humiliating discomforts of Soviet travel. Each time she returned home she was sick with some new fever, complaining of some sleazy promoter or a colleague doing his best to molest her.

He was prepared to back up his demand. Even though at that time he wasn't a wealthy man, my father was already making an independent living with his medical practice at home. He didn't need his wife to work. Already we had things others didn't have, the private three-room apartment, the housekeeper, the nanny, extra money to buy clothes, vacations to the Black Sea. He wanted her to stay home and stay healthy for him and for their children. He didn't like her state employer dictating how he should live his life. She was employed by Moskoncert (The State Moscow Concert Organization). As a concert pianist she had more flexibility than an engineer or a teacher. As a member of Moskoncert, she had a base salary irrespective of whether she was performing or not. Each recital brought her extra wages. Generally, it was up to her to decide how many concerts she wanted to schedule, or whether she wanted to go on a tour, which always paid very well, but the bureaucracy of the organization and the Soviet dictatorial style with which everything was managed irritated my father to the core. He didn't like her state employer dictating how he should live his life.

I agreed with my father and was glad he didn't want my mother to go away either, but I was frightened by the sound of his voice and by what he was saying. It was an insulting, aggressive attack against my grandmother. I thought of my father as a soft-spoken man, but there he was acting so strong. He was unapologetic. I couldn't help but admire him. He sounded powerful. Usually, it was my mother who had a loud voice, who was so emotional. This was different. My father was suddenly in charge, and I liked it, even though it scared me.

Even more frightening was the voice of my grandmother, fighting with my father like he was her husband, not her son-in-law. In her world, she was the only person who made decisions. She never bowed to anyone. She had no idea what feminism was, and if I were to explain it to her, she would have laughed and made fun of it. She was an individual, a person, who happened to be born a woman, and she was powerful. No one ever said no to her. Until now. And my father's demand was unacceptable to her. She went on the attack: insulting his money and his medical practice, his egotistical ways of treating my mother like a slave and squandering her talent and ruining her promising future. I heard chairs scraping on the floor, voices getting louder, uncomfortable moments of silence and pleas for peace from my mother and grandfather, followed by more conflict. I desperately wanted it to stop, but I was held back by this sticky sense of helplessness bolstered by absolute lack of courage.

My grandmother, like Napoleon, rarely made mistakes, but this time she had underestimated the Russian army and the winter: my father and his uncompromising authority over his own family. That night I understood who controlled my family for real, and it was all right with me. My father's word was controlling not because it was louder than everyone else, but it made more sense.

My mother did not fight for her right to work with the same passionate vehemence as my grandmother. She didn't have the kind of passion, the love for music, the need for applause, that drove Marina. My father understood this, I think, and in the end my mother admitted to herself that she had become a concert pianist to please her parents, and that she might, in freedom, choose something else.

So it was that my mother went to work for my father in the illegal practice of private medicine in their home apartment. She turned out to have a good head for business, and she thought that in matters that did not concern medicine and science, people were going to take advantage of my father's generosity and his easygoing attitude. It was her job to make sure that didn't happen. She held the household together, she made sure my father's patients felt comfortable in our home after their excruciating journeys to see him.

Her greatest talent was as a fixer. She understood who the powerful people were and how to treat them, she was the one who paid special visits to countless administrative offices and brought "gifts" and various forms of acceptable bribes to Soviet bureaucrats in order to secure various favors. My father hated asking for favors, was uncomfortable discussing money. He knew only his trade, loved only to be one-on-one with his patients. My mother, on the other hand, never had a problem with it, she rather regarded it as a form of entertainment. She put on her smile in the same way she put on her furs and her diamonds, effortlessly and bravely, and approached people who were unapproachable. She asked for things with charm, and immaculate politeness, and no one could refuse her. Her manner demanded exceptional treatment, and she always received it.

My father loved how feisty she was, he used to encourage her to be bolder in how she dressed. My father knew nothing about fashion, but he knew about people; he told my mother that whatever she decided to wear, it could not misrepresent who she was: a wealthy doctor's wife. This also was against the unwritten rules of the ruling ideology: everyone was supposed to behave and look the same unless they belonged to the privileged class. People who did not belong to the privileged class, who were hustling for money, were not supposed to be flashy about it. My father despised that hypocrisy. He bought my mother her first sapphires when he could barely afford it, and when she was too shy to wear them, he almost forced her to. They were nothing to be ashamed of, this was not something stolen or illegal. My father was an honest man, but he lived in a confused country run by a deceitful regime. He didn't want my mother to be confused. She always tells me how he gave her the confidence to be sincere about her true status.

She marched into serious offices dressed in fur if it was winter, or sensual sundresses if it was summer, armed with serious gifts and a ravishing smile. It didn't matter to her what sort of line she had to cut, and how stern the look on the unknown bureaucrat's face, man or woman. Once she extended her hand to them and announced with her smile: "I am Galina Novikova, a concert pianist, wife of Doctor Arkady Novikov," all Soviet austerity vanished. The speed and the shock of her approach was so sudden, so stunning, and so entertaining that people on the other side of the table were flattered and didn't know what to do but give her what she wanted. Cheerfully brazen, she dazzled them with her beauty, charm, audacity, seeking favors and bestowing them in return.

In Moscow the traffic police were feared exponents of arbitrary state power—they loved stopping cars for dust on the license plate, or if the person behind the wheel looked a bit too happy. For them it was a form of sport, and the sky was the limit in terms of what they could do to you: suspend your license, penalize you in any amount they wanted, jail you if you dared to argue. Motorists learned to offer a small bribe in order to be rid of them as quickly as possible.

Automobiles in the Soviet Union were a luxury reserved for exceptional people, a category my parents fell somewhat short of, but they had two cars just the same, and my mother had a license in a country where women did not drive. There was no formal law against it, but it was not customary. This made her a magnet for the cops, who weren't used to seeing a glamorous young woman behind the wheel. My mother would smile and chatter with them, making friends, inviting them to her concerts, and most importantly telling them about my father. "Bring yourself, your wife, or your mother to my husband! I know you must have someone in your family who might be sick with asthma or have a heart condition. People wait months, and sometimes years to see him." My father treated them, and all their friends and relations, so that when they saw our car pass by their posts they would straighten up and give us a military salute.

My father had the vision, but it was my mother who handled the implementation. She maintained order among that never-ending flow of patients, made sure they were comfortable after their excruciating journeys, applied the triage so that the sickest and most important of them did not have to wait too long. In domestic and social matters, she built a fortress around all of us, bravely negotiating the terms of our exceptional status with functionaries high and low, in the complex pastry of Soviet bureaucracy. It was a covenant, based on trust and instinct. For no matter how successful he became, practicing private medicine in the center of Moscow was never any less illegal. All his money and powerful friends in the government never guaranteed security, never promised freedom. He knew that the more patients gathered outside of our fancy building, the more envy it caused. We never stopped getting threats from people telling us my father's practice was disturbing their peace, complaining to the building department that the patients might be contagious and were spreading dirt all over the building.

Even Dedushka was concerned that my father was pushing it too far. My mother's parents thought she should persuade him to stop his practice, or at least reduce it. Not wanting to worry his aging father, he promised to look into the situation, or, at times, he treated the whole thing jokingly, putting a humorous spin on it, which tended to worry my serious grandfather even more. In reality, my father knew he was not going to change a thing. He had begun something big and had already risked too much, and he wasn't going to stop now. My mother understood what my father's practice meant to him emotionally, and to us economically.

I grew up with parents who loved one another but who, nevertheless, argued a lot. Their quarrels were loud, disturbing, and they clumsily intruded into my idyllic perceptions of their perfect images. This was my first dilemma because it made me feel like I had to pick a side. I was little, and so I couldn't understand the real context of these quarrels. I always blamed my mother when she got upset. I could never imagine a scenario in which my peaceful diplomatic father could have done something to justify this kind of anger. I loved my father, and I thought that because of my mother's loud, emotional voice he needed protection from her, and my grandmother. I loved my mother, but each time I heard her shout, I was afraid that she was going to provoke something monstrous in my father. There were arguments which led them to not talk for weeks, and then my sister and I had to pretend we were having a separate relationship with each of our parents, who were pretending nothing was wrong.

I cursed my state of being a child, of being dependent on my beloved parents, on their peace, on their love. I could not just get up and leave, and I could not choose to play that shamefully insincere game. Perhaps they felt ashamed as well. When I became an adult and my children watched me quarrel pathetically with my husband, I felt helplessly ashamed of myself: I knew they couldn't choose sides or leave, and yet I was unable to stop.

I realize now, of course, I never needed to worry about my father. He was the stronger one, the real head of the family. The reason he was quiet most of the time was because he knew he had real power. My mother attacked him with her voice because that is what all women have against men, their loud, hysterical voices. These quarrels were bitter and in retrospect, foolish, given how short their time together turned out to be.

Even if it was my mother who started the quarrel, she was always the one to approach him with peace. I think now that it was her ability and indeed her need to make peace at all costs, without even looking at the conditions of the peace treaty, that had her always trying to shield me from reality, as if she could throw a special veil over the bad things in life to keep them away from me. I don't think this helped me in the end. I worked hard at school, but I didn't always do well. Bad grades, a slight criticism, or even a dismissive look from a teacher would demolish my confidence. Instead of just forcing me to deal with my problems, she pretended either that they didn't exist or that they weren't my fault. my mother used to spend hours talking to me, cuddling me, trying to bring me back into life, lying to me that my bad grades did not matter, that it was my teachers' fault, not mine. She used to go see my teachers, made defensive arguments presenting my case before them, always made them reconsider my grade or at least have them give me another chance to take a test. My mother wasn't only my confidant and the most patient listener, she was also the problem solver of constant battles I had with my best and not so best friends. As a young teenager I don't think I ever solved a single dilemma I had with a friend. My mother would pick up the phone, dial my friend's number, and become the mediator. I relied on her to make peace with my friends in the same way I relied on her to make peace with my father. I relied on her to protect me from dealing with things on my own. If I told my mother I didn't want to go to school because I was afraid to face a difficult test, she told my father, who was vehemently against me skipping school, that I was unwell. She shielded me from life's side effects every day, all the time. She still does. I lived in a country where everything was denied to children and adults alike, and yet my mother spent every moment of her existence pretending that my mediocre grades were irrelevant, that difficulties in relationships would either get resolved on their own, or there would always be someone else to make peace on my behalf, that money, which she actually knew nothing about, would never run out, that everyone would always love me and never deny me anything because she sincerely thought there was no one better than I. The only time she spared me nothing was when she told me with the news about my father's death. After that, the veil of blissful ignorance was lifted off my sister's and my faces and we began to see life as it was: nonnegotiable in its sadness, exposed, competitive, insecure, full of adult tears which almost never completely dry out. Such were my Dedushka's tears when we told him of his only son's death. He was ninety with dementia and nearly blind. My mother did not have to tell him, she could have lied to him, we could have all lied to him, made up some story about my father deciding to stay in America for work. We knew it would break his heart, and we were afraid ours would break as well, but we couldn't hide it from him. My mother said Dedushka deserved to know the truth because he was still a human being with a mind of his own, so she told him. For the second day in a row, I watched my mother take the role of the executioner, watched her be honest and brave with the truth that was as simple and unavoidable as it was ugly.

My sister and I watched our old Dedushka swallow his grief in agony. We couldn't recognize him anymore; we helplessly stood there, our bodies convulsing from unstoppable sobbing, watching him go mad. When my mother gave him the news, one of his eyes, the one that could still barely detect light from darkness, grew dark and tense as if he was trying not to see but to hear with it. He moved his arms trying to find my mother's face, her eyes, her wicked mouth which spoke those foul words. "What? What are you saying to me? My Aka? Arkasha? What happened to him?!!! Say it again! Repeat what you just said!? My Aka!!!" She did. He began to wail. "Aaaaaaaaaaaaahhhhhhhh! My son, my son! Aka! Ahhhhhhh! He is my son, it cannot be! Galochka! Kill me now, take my heart, take my heart, I don't need it, my Aka...." His blue blind eye had no tears, only anguish.

III.

My Stubborn Little Ballerina

WHEN MY SISTER WAS BORN, I WAS JUST A YEAR OLD. LIANA was the name my Dedushka picked for her. Compared to me, she was a quiet baby, my new little plaything. She only got annoyed when I snuck up on her to undo her blankets or to take her soft toy out of the crib, or to tickle or pinch her.

As little girls we were read the same books, watched cartoons together, we loved our Russian ice cream, soft and creamy. I was not that much older, but my sister always seemed a lot younger than me. It was like she was born too soon and needed to finish baking. She was willful, nobody could tell her anything, and we were all a little afraid of her intensity.

I liked school and was eager to learn how to read, but when the time came for her to join me at the very best school, she wasn't yet ready to enter into the social contract with classmates and teachers. The rules said she was seven, so she had to go, but she refused to answer questions or engage with her classmates. The Soviet school system was not particularly wise or enlightened, but one thing it knew how to do was force a child into submission. Individuality in a small person was a sign of trouble, and a little girl who refused to eat the school lunch was an insult to Soviet principles. Everyone had to eat the school lunch. Her class mistress, a tall and imposing woman, declared that unless Liana finished her lunch, the other thirty or so children would not be allowed outside for recess. My sister gave her a tough stare and again refused to eat a bite of that food, some porridge or sausage with potatoes. All the other kids were upset. The nice ones were pleading with her to eat, the mean ones were threatening her, but she was steadfast in the face of their pressure. "What would your Majesty prefer then?" the teacher asked her. "I only eat food prepared by my mom," said Liana, as if it was a real question. They marched her back upstairs to the classroom, carrying in her hands the plate with her untouched lunch, in front of everyone from the littlest kids to the high schoolers and of course me with my whole class. I felt my friends' sticky fingers poking at my back, pointing at my sister, gossiping in worried tones. I don't know if the rest of the class got to go outside to play that day.

It was at about that time we were taken by our mother to see *Coppelia*, a popular ballet with a large number of child dancers in its corps-de-ballet. After the performance I was elated. The music, the choreography, the spectacle of it all made me drunk with excitement. I was happily looking forward to a lovely afternoon of dancing in front of the mirror. My sister, on the other hand, said she hated everything about the ballet and wanted to go home. All the characters were ugly, and she never wanted to step into a theatre like that again. But the next day she asked my mother to sign her up for dance classes.

Russians love to dance, and there were countless classes and clubs in Moscow. My mother took my sister to the Palace of Young Pioneers where they taught all styles: folk, classical, jazz, pop, ballroom. My sister had to pass a little audition to get into one of those groups, and she attended one or two sessions before announcing to my mother that this was not what she had in mind. She wanted to be a ballerina, like those girls on that big stage in the real theatre.

That was when my mother got worried. She thought my sister wanted a hobby, but ballet was a vocation, a change of life trajectory not only for Liana, but also for my mother. She stalled for time, hoping she'd forget, but every day Liana begged her to take her to the Moscow State Ballet Academy, that special school where they teach you to become a professional ballerina. My mother knew that ballet was the sort of path that required ultimate sacrifices: intense physical conditioning, strain on the growing body, a high likelihood of injury, long-term health issues, early retirement with limited career choices, constant adherence to diets and weight watching, not to mention the other little ballerinas with their rivalry and competition.

Weakening in the face of Liana's constant pestering, my parents went to seek the advice of an old ballerina, a former Bolshoi dancer whose name I no longer remember. The old woman checked out her form, her ankles, her knees, her legs, her spine, her rotation, the arch of her foot and the width of her shoulders, and then tersely announced her verdict: "The girl is not fit for ballet." She explained that my sister did not have a ballerina's body, none of her body parts stretched far enough, her limbs were either not thin enough or flexible enough, or jumpy enough; no amount of coaching could change things like the width of her shoulders or the shape of her knees.

My mother affected disappointment but was secretly relieved, thinking this obviously expert opinion would be the end of the discussion, but Liana refused to give up her desire. My sister was rather small for eight, with dark curly hair and big sad eyes. When she danced, she was more expressive than musical. She went to bed and woke up with one idea only: to become a ballerina. Her teacher, Natasha Revich, stretched Liana, she sat on her, she pulled her little muscles and ligaments, she made all of us do the same to her at home.

My sister hated our school. It was a mirror of the official philosophy of the system under which we all lived: the principal was chief dictator while the teachers comprised the politburo. Each student should obey orders from above and be, if not the same, at least not different from the others because that is how sameness is achieved. My sister, the individualist, was the class goat, always in trouble with the teacher, engaged in an academic boycott. My sister didn't fit in. She couldn't fit in. It wasn't in her nature. It didn't make her brilliant, necessarily, but it did make her disagreeable, and there is nothing Soviet educators hate more than disagreeable children. The approved method is to break the spirit of the offender by harassing them with bad marks, calling in their parents, or most cruel of all, organizing the other students in public boycotts against them. As her sister, I was regularly called in by her teacher to be informed that my sister once again did not learn her lesson, refused to talk, and her backpack was a mess. I was only nine at the time, and obviously the idea was to humiliate me as well. Every day I made sure I avoided that big-boned woman's eye by taking longer than usual in the bathroom or just losing myself amidst my noisy girlfriends.

I hold a picture of Liana's class in my hands; she is about seven years old in it. Almost all the faces of her classmates are crossed out, and there is a big hole in the middle of the photograph where she had violently carved her face out with a sharp object.

Liana's escape plan was to join the Bolshoi Ballet Academy. It was the most elite school of the most elite art form, way more prestigious than our privileged English school. Every day I saw my sister in the hallways telling her classmates how she was going to become a ballerina. I think she did not know what failure was, let alone imagine it could happen to her, crafting her body in the image of the great dancers. She collected their pictures, read books about them, went to see performances of the same ballets over and over again.

It was nearly impossible to be accepted at the Academy. Russian Ballet aesthetics, which are the world standard, originate in a mathematical study of body proportion. If children at the age of nine corresponded to those specifics, they were granted admission. This being the Soviet Union, certain less than perfect specimens got in because of who their parents were. Gorbachev's granddaughter, for instance, was a student, although when his political star fell, she lost her place. Some of these fortunate ones were talented, others not so much. Family and pedigree, even bribery and special connections could get you in, but you couldn't get to the very top without talent and a high degree of professionalism and desire. Soviet audiences were discerning and demanding, their taste and understanding of the art profound and highly particular. The country needed only the best; even to be in the corps de ballet was an honor. Every couple of years there were examinations where some people washed out, and the class got smaller until nobody was left who couldn't cut it at the very highest level.

Initially, my father was not excited about my sister's ballet fantasy. It was a world remote from his experience. Perhaps he was embarrassed by its shameless naked beauty, by its apparent frivolousness. He could see her choice to dance was not a girl's fantasy but a fanatical desire which if not satisfied would impair her ability to learn regular subjects as well.

There were twenty people on the committee, but Madam Sofiya Golovkina, the head of the Moscow State Ballet Academy, was the only one that mattered. The empress of the Bolshoi had graduated from the Academy in 1933 and been a principal dancer until 1959, when she became the much-honored director of the Academy, where everyone treated her like the queen she was. Her position and her power were analogous to my grandfather Saul's. This was the person my father would have to persuade, otherwise his dancing girl would be so terribly disappointed it was difficult to predict what would become of her.

He liked a challenge. He knew Madame Golovkina was a ballerina, with an entire entourage of special Kremlin doctors. To her, he would be a nobody, some Jewish doctor whose daughter wanted to be a dancer. He needed to make a bold stroke to pierce Madame's impervious heart.

One evening, while I watched, my Father dialed her phone number, which he had acquired in some mysterious way, and in a slightly mischievous, yet gallant voice introduced himself: "Hello, Madame Golovkina" (on the other end of the receiver I heard a voice saturated with theatrical nervousness and matronly hysteria: "Yes, yes, who is this?"); then my Father again: "Madame Golovkina, this is none other than your secret admirer . . ." There was a slight pause, and you could feel the utter shock at the other end of the line, for no one spoke to anybody like that in Soviet times, let alone to an elderly married lady. Her husband was a retired general with lots of medals, but she was one of the most powerful and revered people in the arts world of the entire Soviet Union. My father quickly ended the pause with a light laugh and disarmingly re-introduced himself as Dr. Arkady Novikov, a friend of such and such, and the father of Liana Novikova, who desperately wanted to dedicate her life to professional ballet. I could barely decipher the rest of the conversation, for most of it consisted of laughter and half-finished phrases. I sensed with my stomach muscles that my father had touched the old woman deeply. After all, she was only a woman, who must have been starving for a man to talk to her this way, humorously, lightly, flirtatiously, without losing touch of who she really was. She invited him to meet her in person in her grand office at the Academy.

My father smiled serenely as he hung up the phone and went to tell my anxious mother that Madame Golovkina was a very charming lady. After the first meeting followed the second meeting, then a third and a fourth. Sometimes she invited him and my mother to her beautiful apartment where they drank tea and discussed the state of the arts, contemporary medicine, whatever Madame wanted. The subject of my sister and the chances of her getting into the Academy never came up. To every meeting my father came bearing gifts, more extravagant every time. Everyone gave her flowers, her office was like the pavilions of the Botanical Gardens, so my father, ever resourceful in the procurement of beautiful things, brought her expensive perfume, jewelry, extravagant scarves, and finally, as the third audition approached, a nineteenth century teacup and saucer with an image of Napoleon, light as a feather and exquisitely painted royal green with some gold ornaments. It was a family heirloom, preserved somehow from the vicissitudes of Russian history. No one was ever allowed to touch it except Mother; the most we could do was caress it with our clueless eyes, and breathlessly admire it from afar. Napoleon's rosy face stared back at us with narcissistic indifference, through the glass of our china cabinet, until he went to live with Madame Golovkina that spring.

In the fall, my sister began attending the Moscow State Ballet Academy. Having seduced Madame Golovkina, my father remained devoted to her. It was not just business, nor was it all friendship. It was a uniquely Russian bond of loyalty. Russians don't play by the rules, even when imposed by the Soviet Union. Officially it was a bureaucracy of infinite paperwork where personal relationships were not supposed to matter, but in fact having friends you could count on was the only key to success. Sometimes Russian people get this feeling about one another, which they may call friendship and at other times love. Russians don't like defining things, especially not themselves; ambiguity is what gives them their power and inner freedom. Clearly, Madam Golovkina felt strongly about my father. She may never have named her feelings, but, obviously, she was flattered by the attentions of such a charming and handsome younger man. They understood each other: she respected his courageous, honest way, his manner of doing things; he respected her for the way she responded to him. Whenever my mother worried about my sister's future at the Academy, my father always assured her: "Don't worry, she will never betray my trust." And she never did; even when he died, my sister was not discarded, the way some other kids were when their circumstances changed.

When in September my sister came to visit me at our old school she was like a swan. All her former classmates flocked to her, even the girls who had been so mean to her before. She stood there in the school yard timidly smiling at them all, quietly refusing to satisfy their nosy curiosity. I was proud of her, and yet I thought she should not be so proud and so distant, she should forgive and forget their cruelty and bullying and content herself with telling them all about her ballet classes and her magnificent school, the slippers, the tiny skirts, and all those other mysterious items every dancer can't do without in her graceful profession. But she walked away. We got into my mother's car, and she waved them goodbye.

The actual experience of the Academy was a humbling one. Most of the other girls were perfect in their body shape, their form, and their preparation for their first year. They already knew how to do the exercises, while my sister was a complete novice. Irritated by her ineptitudes and deficiencies, her main ballet instructor, Margarita Alekseevna, paid her minimal attention. Students generally anticipated to be either praised or screamed at, slapped, or even kicked out of the classroom for not following the instructions, mocked for breaking into tears. But being paid no attention at all meant that you were a nobody in that school. This was a professional school, and if you couldn't take the instruction as it was offered, you should go home. Professionally, my sister had a gigantic mountain to climb.

Margarita spoke the same way to my mother, evidently hoping that both of them would get the message and go away. My mother might have taken the hint, but Liana woke up every morning and got on with it, driven by a kind of courage made up of passion and stubbornness. She had burned all her bridges behind her. It was inconceivable to her that she should go back to that awful English school. She loved the Academy, she had friends. From the age of ten or eleven, they were allowed to take part in real ballet performances on the stage of the Bolshoi Theatre. On those nights they shared the same changing rooms, the same makeup, they breathed the same intoxicating air as the ballet stars who danced next to them.

My sister, already shy, had found a refuge where she could be separated from everything but her art. The Academy was a world unto itself, they taught everything there: math and science and French, literature, history, fine arts, esthetics, and etiquette; a dancer must have perfect manners. They danced for hours every day, until their feet bled. I remember her red face with droplets of white sweat above her upper lip and her wet ballet clothes laying all over the apartment. Every night she came home physically and mentally drained and she still had to finish her homework, wash her ballet clothes, and prepare the many elements of her ballet kit for the next day.

Liana held herself aloof from her schoolwork, as if it existed outside of the realm of who she was. I had to help her, that is, do it for her. I wrote essays, completed other assignments while she was busy with her ballet things for the next day, or dressing her bleeding toes.

I was tired, too, and I had my own homework to do. I let everyone know I resented it, and then I did it anyway. Once I was done, she would casually walk over and take the paper with a timid gratitude that was very sweet. She never seemed to notice my resentment; she only saw in me her older sister who wrote essays for her that came back with good grades on them. It made things easier for her with teachers, as well as with her friends. I knew she admired me for that, and I should have helped her more, and I should have never been angry or bitter about it. She never had any free time to play or watch TV. Her day began at seven-thirty in the morning and at three p.m. when classes were done, she would go and spend hours with her outside ballet teacher.

Officially the rule of the school was no outside teachers, but unofficially, everyone had one. Liana needed help more than anyone, and so my parents found her the greatest teacher any classical dancer can hope for. Marina Semenova was a legend in the world of classical dance. She was a prima ballerina, the favorite student of the great Agrippina Vaganova, who developed the world famous Vaganova method incorporating the teachings of the old Imperial Ballet School. Semenova graced the stages of the Kirov, Bolshoi, and other world theatres in every famous role, even after her husband, Lev Karakhan, an old Bolshevik and a Deputy Foreign Minister, was purged by Stalin in 1937.

Somehow, she managed to survive as the prima ballerina for twenty years even after the murder of her husband. She never said anything, retreated into her art, and this only added to her mystique.

At the Bolshoi, they greeted her like a queen, with reverence, adoration, love, fear, trepidation. She held her head high with her green eyes glaring straight at the person she was conversing with.

She lived in an apartment of imperial proportions, filled with treasures like I had never seen. We'd been introduced by a patient of my father's, naturally. Those who dedicated themselves to the most prestigious arts in return were coddled in luxury by the state. The living room was cleared for dance, a worn wooden ballet barre with a huge wall mirror behind it, because this was the home of a working ballerina.

She was well into her seventies, tall and imperious with a formidably straight posture; she was famous for her beautiful back. Semenova scanned my sister, not quite ten, with her piercing green eyes, immediately detected all her imperfections and just as quickly, it seems, decided they didn't matter. "Whose idea was it to have you study at the Academy, yours or your mother's?" My sister gave the right answer. It might have been the only thing she said the whole time. Semenova admired her well-proportioned head, her big eyes on her pale face and the way her dark wavy hair was pulled back in a neat bun. What touched her was her expressiveness; she felt she could work through the rest. She didn't need her ballerinas to be perfect, but she looked for a certain harmony, for substance, and I suppose she saw it in Liana because at the end of that very strange audition, in which scarcely a word was said, Marina Semenova asked my sister only one question: "Girl, do you want to work with me?" My sister nodded, and so she became the student of the great ballerina.

Naturally, my parents asked Semenova what sort of financial compensation she would be expecting for the honor of lessons. She got offended and told them never to raise the subject of money with her again. This was my father's way with his patients, but I think it took him a long moment to understand that for Semenova, the very idea of money encroached on the nobility of her art and the dignity of her calling as a teacher.

She gave my sister a sense of herself as an artist and a future woman, the confidence to be a ballerina, to be feminine, irresistible, stunning rather than indistinctly beautiful. My sister had striking features; sad, puffy eyes and a pale face framed by dark curls. A very Jewish look, not at all Russian, people used to say when she was little. To Semenova, as to my father, my sister's features were a work of art, and they were both proved right when as a young woman my sister Liana became a most extraordinary beauty.

Semenova's teaching technique was different from that of other teachers, more pristine, simpler, and yet still more sophisticated. Watching Semenova with her students, you didn't need to be a dancer to understand this was a great master. She rarely raised her voice, but her remarks were caustic and shrewd, her eyes worked like a green X-ray machine. She detected mistakes that seemed silly at a first glance, but once corrected, it made all the difference. Once I saw her explain a difficult pas, and then execute it flawlessly, even though she was well into her seventies.

Semenova understood that my sister's decision to become a dancer was a decision she had imposed upon herself and knew this noble dream came at a price my sister did not yet know she had to pay. Although nature had already made her strong, she was learning from her teacher to be even stronger; this was a professional strength.

There were constant diets, abridged vacation schedules, very different relationships with friends. On a holiday, when everybody went off to the beach or to the pool, my sister had to go to some desolate studio where she would practice twice a day to keep herself in shape so as not to lose form before the new semester began.

In the year of Liana's examinations, we spent every vacation in the company of Marina Semenova. She demanded from Liana the same attention, the same level of responsibility, the same focus as her adult students, but she was also kind. She knew what she had to go through every day when she faced her perfect ballerina friends at her perfect Academy with its unyielding, militant teachers and their humiliating methods. Sometimes, after a very long and exhausting day at school, my sister would appear in the heavenly apartment with a sour expression on her face and a bad professional attitude, but Semenova knew how to handle her. "Okay, Lenka," she would say. (In Russian, the -ka ending is called the familiar; only family and good friends will talk to you this way.) "You must be tired, aren't you? All right, get changed quickly, and we shall have some tea together." Tea was served in an exquisite set made by the Imperial Porcelain Factory. My sister was expected to sit down, with perfect manners as she'd been taught, and enjoy her teatime without haste. Meanwhile, Semenova was having her conversation with my mother, and she left Liana alone with her tea, recognizing that a nine-hour day of physical activity, competitiveness, loneliness, self-doubt, and actual hunger required a bit of tea and solitude. That entire tea ceremony dedicated to my capricious, vulnerable sister never took more than twenty minutes, but in that time, Semenova was able to change her little student's entire momentum. Semenova knew she needed my sister's full mental and bodily focus for the class.

It was only because of Marina Semenova that my sister became a ballerina. She taught her the secrets hiding in between the letters of the ballet alphabet, opened to her its countless nuances, showed her the power of imperfection which is true art as long as there is harmony in it. Artistic harmony is not taught in schools. It's rare. Only great artists possess it, and not all of them can communicate it to their students. My sister had harmony within her. She was a silent artist. She spoke little, felt a lot, and there was no mask, no buffer, no compromise between her outward brevity and the depth of her inner life.

After the third and fifth year there were examinations to decide the fate of every third- and fifth-year student in the school. This fearful panel consisted of Madame Golovkina, the entire teaching staff, and choreographers and ballet coaches from some of the main theatres in Moscow. My sister needed to be in perfect shape for her third year, end of the year examination: her bodyweight, her technique, her artistry couldn't be as good as the other girls with their perfect forms; she had to be better than all of them. She was eleven and a half at the time. The pressure was crushing, but at the same time, Semenova worked her steadily and my sister was ready. It was her chance to perform, to show off her professionalism and innate artistry. Then, the bizarre, unforgiving thing happened: She wasn't careful running down the steps of her academy and broke her ankle just a couple of months before the examination.

Ever the stoic, she concealed her injury until she got in the car with us, waved to her friends, smiled, and told my mother to drive away. As soon as we were out of sight, she let out a terrible scream, and we took her straight to the hospital. The doctor confirmed her ankle was broken and would need to be in a cast for at least a month, followed by another month of recuperation.

My sister was inconsolable, but Marina Semenova inspected the cast, sized her up with her green eyes, and said: "So Lenka, you've messed up, haven't you? All right, girl, no tears, we are going to go see my doctor." *Her* doctor was a very big orthopedic surgeon, a specialist in traumas. All major dancers, gymnasts, and figure skaters went to see him. He had been Marina Semenova's doctor for over thirty years. He thought the cast could come off in two to three weeks and my sister could resume training a week or two afterward, in time for the examination. She never quit training, working everything but the bad ankle. She passed her examinations, the committee was unanimous, and she was promoted to the next grade.

Liana and I were always very different. In her early days my sister was shy to the point of solipsism, not at all interested in having friends or being the center of attention. She used to follow me and my friends around, but usually all she did was make trouble for me. Nothing gave her more joy than to interfere with some game I was in the middle of with my cronies, get involved and then mess it up by disregarding the rules. I hated it and pleaded with my mother to keep my sister away from my friends who, unlike her, I wanted to have. I needed people to like me, and I was ready to play by the rules, up to a certain point. My little sister's presence irritated me, and I did my best to exclude her from the society of my friends. But whenever the game got rough, my sister would jump to my defense immediately, like a fierce and loyal dog. She never allowed anyone to insult or injure me. She lived in the world of ballet, surrounded by her ballerina friends who she intuitively knew were really her rivals. I was her only equal who she didn't need to impress, from whom she did not seek approval, who she didn't need to fear, with whom she could squabble all day long about the most trivial things and never worry about making up. The peace process between us occurred as spontaneously as our little wars stated, everything was organic, nothing needed to be explained, no big words needed to be used; we just moved on with our life the way nature moves on with its state of being after some big calamity. We were equals, and yet I also could see that my sister admired me. Everyone at the Academy had heard of me: the "beautiful older sister." I didn't think of myself that way, quite the opposite: clumsy, matronly, already fully developed at twelve, devoid of any sylphlike qualities whatsoever. Yet, when I met my sister's ballerina friends, they all seemed to think of me as she did, the "beautiful older sister."

I never saw my sister feel sorry for herself once. She rarely complained about how she felt, or about her friends in school the way girls her age usually do. At the same time, however, I can never say that she had a happy spirit. My sister accepted very few people into her world, only those who could create a sense of equilibrium for her, a sense of balance, like Semenova or my mother. She had a profound attachment to our mother, but she never expressed any feelings for our father. Her coldness to him used to turn my heart upside down with sadness and anger. When she was little, she would not jump into his arms, she refused to play with him, to respond to his jokes, even to talk to him. Every morning, he tried to entertain her morbid mood with his funny remarks, but she replied to him either rudely, or with cold indifference. She had little if any sense of humor. To my father, my sister was a little marvel; a tiny thing with strange sad puffy eyes and dark curls falling all over her pale face. As with me, he joked about her, sang songs about her; wanted to play with her, this curious, fascinating elf from some fairyland.

My mother, on the other hand, did not see her as a marvel. She detected her vulnerabilities and guarded them against the world. She understood that my sister did not think anything was funny. They never talked much, but my mother had a key to her heart, and my sister instinctively allowed herself to be unlocked by that key.

Since my breathing depended on my father's heartbeat, I feared one day he would die of a broken heart from my sister's indifference and so I did my best to help him. I quarreled with her, I called her names, I wept, I complained to my mother. She never said she didn't love him, she never said she was angry with him, but, equally, I could see that her heart was neither bothered by his presence nor by his absence. Usually, my father laughed it off, but sometimes he even asked my mother why his little Liana, or Lianochka as he called her, didn't seem to like him.

My sister and I had plans together for the future we imagined. We would always be together with our parents, perhaps we would buy a beautiful place for them and all be happy together forever. But how could she prepare herself to be so happy with father at some time in the future yet be so cruel to him now? I couldn't understand it. I thought she might become kinder, more loving with time. Adults on the whole are kinder than children. I never liked anyone my age; you never knew what to expect. Adults always smiled—maybe someday she would smile at our father.

And indeed, as she turned twelve, something warm seemed to move inside her. One day we were dropping her off at the Academy, and he gave her a bar of dark chocolate to take with her, told her to have a bit whenever she felt she was losing energy. She was always on a diet, so it felt illegal, clandestine, conspiratorial, my father's specialty. She quickly hid it in her bag and kissed him on the cheek. He was so happy. The rest of the way to my school I was afraid to say anything to him, like any spoken word would shatter his bliss.

A few months later we were in the car again, on the way to the Otradnoye spa resort. Our parents were going to America, without us. After that, they would take us to Europe. Our father was driving, our grandfather Saul solemnly sitting in the front seat, and the two of us together with our grandmother in the back glaring at the month of June through the car's newly washed windows. We didn't want them to go, but we couldn't really say so out loud. I was afraid to look at my sister in case of any trace of sadness in her eyes. I was the sad one, she, the stoic one. Everything in the country was so green, its warm scent all around. When we finally arrived, we checked out the accommodation while our grandparents took care of the luggage and father was delegating powers and duties to any number of people. I wished he would stop talking to all those superfluous people. The day felt slow, the summer had barely begun its reign but was already sprawling in its oppressive warmth all over. I leaned against it, waiting for him to come and say goodbye. He walked over to me, with a slightly guilty look, inquiring whether I thought the place was good enough. He could see I was unhappy, and my sister must have looked so aloof. My heart was bursting from guilt, pity, and love for him.

I embraced him, and as I put my arm around his neck, I remembered how wet the collar of his shirt was; he was hot from all that running around, trying to make us all happy. My sister walked over to him; he lowered his knees to make it easier for her to hug him. She wrapped her arms around him and glued herself to his chest without uttering a single word. She held him that way until it seemed like time had stopped. I overheard my mother tell someone later how taken aback he had been by her sudden sentiment. She made him happy, just like that time in the car.

I don't remember where Liana was when our mother told me about our father. I went to my mother's room one day and asked her how we were going to live. My mother thought her absent-minded, romantic, innocent Anya was talking about grief. I clarified that I meant money and only money. I knew how tactless I sounded, how desperate and scared I was. I stood there, waiting for my mother to respond to me, as if she were a student and I were a teacher, challenging her to give me the only acceptable answer. If she had said to me that we would have to live a little more modestly, and spend a little less money on some things, but in general still live a wonderful life, I would have never been able to accept it. No, I wanted her to lie to me, and so she lied: "Anechka, I promise, you and Lianochka will always live in the way you lived when your father was alive." I felt like I could breathe again. Our life was never the same again, but in the darkest moment of my life, seeing nothing before me but abysmal dread and utter helplessness, when I was convinced that life with its silly pleasures and occasional cloudiness was never going to return to me, my mother's unequivocal promise that everything was going to be beautiful once more, and I was going to be happy again, gave me the courage to hope.

For a month or two, all we did was walk around the apartment bumping into things. My sister was a ghostly shadow, walking from room to room collecting my father's clothes and holding them close to her chest. So great was her sorrow that I felt ashamed to be in her presence. To look into her eyes, to approach her, to embrace her, talk to her about our sorrow for our father, I could not do it because I was ashamed. She understood, and I know she felt the same way, but we had no comfort to offer each other, nor could either of us receive any from our mother. The source of all our strength was gone and without him, my mother and my sister Liana were just as weak as I was.

Our parents always promised us that the next day was going to be better than the one before, and they were always going to be there for us, loving us, protecting us; and we believed them. Death was just a rumor, but in that ominous resort, counting days to our parents' arrival, we sensed in our hearts something was not right, something was being hidden from us. We were afraid to say to each other, "Do you think something happened to our parents?" We lived with this worm in our minds for weeks, and when everything finally became simple and real, when our father's death exposed us before the world, my sister and I, instead of embracing each other, turned away from each other in shame.

Perhaps it was me who walked away from my sister, feeling ashamed and embarrassed. Now hope was gone, and it was an ugly dirty reality. We were privy to each other's shameful, disgraceful secret, two little girls intuitively figuring out what everybody tried to hide from them so neatly. I continued to avoid my sister for many weeks after our father's funeral, and she avoided me. We almost never talked about our father, perhaps, only in passing. We understood each other very well, I think.

One or two days before our departure for America we sat on the park bench by the stream not too far from our apartment building and planned our future, like two grown-ups. We felt no regret about leaving our past behind, only a sense of relief and a teasing curiosity about the future in a strange country. Because of how obsessed I was with my own destiny, because this very obsession had blinded me, it was impossible for me to know that neither America, nor our promising future in it, could ever separate us from our Russia, or from our past.

IV.

In the Land of My Father's Dreams

It was 1990–1991. The situation in Russia at that moment was much worse than I suspected. The Union of Soviet Socialist Republics was beginning to crumble. Those who were sensitive could feel the tremors, certain types of businessmen, those connected to the government, could smell the opportunity that comes with change, even chaos. My father surely felt them, and with all his friends in the right places he might have ridden out the storm and prospered in the new Russia, or we might have emigrated. It was hard to see what we should do without him and his vision for the future. My mother would have to do the best she could.

Fortunately, he had left a good deal of cash behind, and that was what we lived on. The Soviet banking system was primitive, ordinary citizens were not supposed to have money anyway, so people kept their money at home. If it came down to it, we could sell our paintings, our antique furniture, my mother's diamonds.

Initially we lived as we always had, perhaps even more grandly as my mother tried to soothe us with tasty things. My mother also had to support our Dedushka and his housekeeper and supply him with his medications, which now were becoming even more expensive. She had to make sure his standard of living was kept up and he wanted for nothing, because that was how my father had done things. Soon, though, the money started to run short, and my mother saw that our beautiful apartment, the oasis my father had created for us, was not going to protect us from the metamorphosis the country was about to undergo. Unless we thought of something quickly, the new reality was going to swallow us.

The year after my father died, Boris Yeltsin was elected President of the Russian Federation in the first direct presidential election, while the old Soviet leadership of Mikhail Gorbachev who was the Soviet President and the General Secretary of the Communist Party at the time, tried to hold on to power. Gorbachev's glasnost and his economic reforms did not agree with hardened communist bureaucrats of the party. The loss of the Easten European States and the upcoming USSR's new Union Treaty meant the disintegration of an empire, and therefore the end of their power. The treaty was supposed to decentralize the central Soviet government's power and distribute it among the fifteen republics which made up the USSR. The discontent within the party was the cause for the coup of 1991, when, on August 19, top hardliners of the party formed the special committee (GKchP) and, with the help of dispatched KGB agents, detained Gorbachev and his family at his holiday estate. I remember the tanks and the soldiers passing under our windows, the anxious looks on people's faces. Yeltsin condemned the coup and demanded that the military not take part in the overthrow of the government. We watched on television with the rest of the world how he climbed up on one of the tanks that surrounded the parliament to make a speech. The tank commander was faced with a dilemma: whose orders to obey? Who was the good guy? In the end he didn't shoot Yeltsin, or the thousands of protesters who had gathered in the street and the coup was averted. Gorbachev was safely returned to Moscow, but he did not come back as a hero leader of one of greatest powers in the world. He came back to Moscow a wounded animal. A soon to be new tsar was waiting for him upon his return. The coup signaled the collapse of the old order, which indeed ceased to exist in December of 1991, when Gorbachev announced his resignation as President and the Union of Soviet Socialist Republics passed into history.

Yeltsin announced radical economic reforms called "shock therapy." The goal of these reforms, recommended by Harvard economists responding to this unprecedented opportunity, was to transform the world's largest state-controlled economy into a market-oriented economy overnight. Liberalization, stabilization, and privatization were supposed to open up competition, free the market, and create conditions for capitalism where none had existed before. This would require major sacrifices, like super double-digit inflation, which fell hardest on the poor and elderly, causing them to suffer a severe drop in their living standard, which was not high to begin with. People's lifetime savings were wiped out, as the value of the rubles they kept at home fell to nothing. Our formerly financially stable friends were barely scraping by, many were emigrating, others began venturing into business activities that made some rich, but others went broke, or worse.

Any business in Russia in those days was dangerous because by default you got yourself tangled up with criminals. It was no place for a widow with two teenage daughters to explore her entrepreneurial talents. Soon, almost every business in Russia, from curbside vendors to huge oil and gas companies, made payments to organized crime for protection, called *krysha,* which means "roof" in Russian. Contract killings were commonplace. Nobody could open a business, not a bakery or a bookstand, without paying off some sort of "roof" entity, or another intermediary. Under such circumstances, one either needed to be a man, or married to one, and my mother fell into neither of these categories. All we wanted was to live a quiet life, but since my father was gone and there was no great demand for concert pianists, it did not seem possible.

We needed to change our life completely, at its root, pulling it out of the only soil it had ever known and transplanting ourselves into a new place where we stood a chance of thriving. America, the country of my father's dreams, seemed like the only way out, but it was nevertheless a daunting project. My mother spoke no English, she had no special skills, like medicine or mathematics. There was no offer of any sort of job, no special immigration status, no bank account. She did have relatives in America, but none of them were much help. But in the days after my father's murder in New York, while she helped the police with their case against the killer, she met a friend who would change her life. His name was Mark Vaserman. Everyone called him Marik.

When my father's death was first announced on the news, people gathered in the apartment where my parents had been staying in Queens to pay their respects. They all had the same expression of sorrow, the same questions and sighs, until my mother felt she couldn't breathe. Some were long-lost relatives and friends who had immigrated to America back in the 1970s, others were strangers with a tangential connection, and one of these was Marik. He had a head of messy hair atop a small agile, wiry body, and he told my mother he was a friend of my father's from his medical school days.

My father had told her about Marik, who had been a prodigy back in medical school: he got his degree in physics from Moscow State University while he completed his training at Moscow Medical

School #1, receiving the Red Diploma both times. Physics was his passion, and he only went to medical school to please his mother.

He was different from the other people who came to the apartment; he did not come bearing grief. Before he appeared, my mother sat in the apartment in one position, surrounded by a wall of mourners who either spoke too much, or not at all because they were too afraid. She felt numb, unable to move her head or her feet. Unlike the others, he spoke about my father and his youth, and my mother found herself wanting to know all about it, what they did, how they studied, who they dated, how they misbehaved. Marik wasn't my father's closest friend, since he was in pursuit of two degrees at once, but he said they "got" each other when it came to political and social issues, they knew they were on the same side.

Marik lived in Manhattan, unlike other Russian immigrants she had met, who all seemed to reside either in Queens, Brooklyn, the Bronx, or Staten Island. Some preferred New Jersey or Long Island. He asked her if she wanted to get out of that apartment. She really did, so they got in his car and went driving into the city. She liked it so much he did it every day, driving his beat-up Toyota back to Queens. He let her talk, he asked questions, and he listened. He listened a lot. She explained to Marik how we weren't a regular Soviet family, that we couldn't just emigrate, and live in a strange country with no money. She told him everything about the way we lived, my father's practice, the apartment, everything. My father's dream had been for us to come to America, to New York, but now it seemed cold and unreachable, and she had no idea what she was going to do or how she was going to live.

In those three weeks in America, he never left her side, until he fell in love with her, either despite her tragedy or because of it. It came without warning, without explanation, just because he could, because he wanted to, because nature told him to. It's a mysterious thing, love. He told her she was going to live in America. Everything Arkady would have done he would do for her. She looked at the streets through the windows of his car and heard him say, "Don't you worry, this is your city, this is where you shall live."

Marik had been a Refusenik; that must have been another reason his name came up between my parents. In those days, Israel welcomed well educated and highly skilled Russian Jews, who were happy to trade their second-class status in Russia for a new life in Israel. The Soviet government let them go reluctantly, subjecting them to bureaucratic harassment and clipping them for every ruble they ever had on the way out. At the visa office, Marik said, the hours were very limited; there was nowhere to sit, and the bureaucrats were rude. It was designed to make you feel inferior and unwanted, because just by being there you were making a statement against the state. As soon as you filed your petition to emigrate, you immediately lost your job or your student status. Your friends shunned you out of fear, and even your family might disavow you. Marik's parents refused to sign a form saying they did not object to his emigration, and he had to threaten to forge it and risk prison until they relented. Once his petition was approved, Marik had a month to leave the country. He had to sell such belongings as remained to him and settle his affairs, such as they were. He told us he lived only on oatmeal, bread, and water, with some fried fish, and what kept him alive was love of science and hatred for the Soviet Union.

Marik saw terrible things: people arriving at the airport, thinking their overloaded yellowish folders full of paperwork were in order, turned back by the authorities, standing there with their families while customs officers searched their pitiful luggage with a razor blade to make sure no one was sneaking anything of value out of

Russia. People stood there sweating, answering humiliating questions, afraid to say the wrong thing, to look the wrong way and so lose the chance to leave their hopeless past behind and enter a free but indefinite future. Marik was by himself, he had nothing left for the guards to steal. He arrived in Israel with nearly empty pockets, and never saw Moscow again. "I traveled light," he said, and this was his approach to life ever after.

He lived in Israel for a number of years where he worked as a scientist, then moved to Paris to teach at the Sorbonne. He learned to speak fluent Hebrew, then fluent French, then fluent English. He had a talent for languages, his secret was total immersion. He was a bachelor all his life, loved being independent and having light, uncommitted relationships with women. He loved to travel, loved to eat, and knew all about wine.

I'm not sure how he ended up in New York City, but when he got here it turned his head around and he discarded his easygoing bon vivant ways and became a striver. Most of his friends in America were doctors and chained to life by the bonds of marriage and financial responsibility, something Marik used to poke fun at. Yet he could not help noticing what nice houses and cars they had. Working as a physicist was not going to earn him the life he wanted here. Fortunately, thanks to his wise Jewish mother, he already had a red diploma from the Moscow Medical School and all he had to do was take the boards and then do a few years of residency.

He worked at one of the busiest hospitals in New York. There were gunshot wounds, drug overdoses, and suddenly Marik found himself responsible for making life and death decisions on the spot. This is part of the physician's training, but by now he was past forty years old and it wasn't as easy for him to stay up for a forty-eight-hour shift. The other residents, much younger, often outranked him, his language was not perfect, and he felt he wasn't as quick or good as was consistently required of him.

For all his brilliance, his facility with languages, his photographic memory, his formidable intellect, he had no instinct for healing others. When comparing my father to Marik, as I often did during those days, when it came to medicine, everything my father was, he was not. When he finished his residency, he went into nuclear medicine; this powerful new diagnostic tool was one of the most lucrative fields in medicine at the time and it was all about machines, which he liked. He was trying to save money to open up his own practice, but the machines he needed were expensive to buy. He was working at the hospital, saving his pennies, when he met my mother.

My mother told us about Marik when she got back to Moscow. We intuitively guessed what he was to her, or maybe we didn't even need to guess. We needed a Marik in our life. My mother needed to travel back to New York for the criminal trial. I was frightened every time she had to take the trip, convinced something bad was going to happen, even though I knew she was staying with Marik in his brownstone apartment on Third Avenue and 17th Street.

Her trips to New York were lengthy, and I hated when she was gone, but by now I knew from my conversations with my mother and what she had told Marina and Saul that she and Marik were a couple and that she needed to build a life with *him*, because *his* plan was to build a life with us.

I was relieved and even happy that she was not alone. Marik's presence seemed to make her feel and look stronger and happier. It was good that he was not a complete stranger: he knew my father, he came from our old, familiar life, and he seemed to like me and my sister. Yet, I resented her trips with him. Each time my poor mother had to leave us with our grandparents I became hysterical. I threw tantrums, I yelled, screamed, I accused her of every sin under the sky. I threatened to harm myself. Was it jealousy, possessiveness? At thirteen and fourteen I couldn't reconcile those feelings intellectually. I simply wanted to go with her, I didn't want to be left behind. I wanted to own my mother's attention on my terms, the way I always had when my father was alive. In my previous life, my sister and I had some control over our parents' lives, or so it felt. Now life controlled us. When conditions changed, and my terms weren't acceptable anymore, even to my mother, my character struggled with it ferociously, exposing for the first time the traits of my personality I would become familiar with as an adult.

My mother kept repeating to me the same thing: "You will understand when you grow up." I grew up and I understood. I have become a very understanding person, and when life changes its terms on me, I try to adjust.

Marik was not making much money at that time, but because of the exchange rate, his American salary helped to improve our Russian standard of living. Our finances were dwindling, but Marik knew our troubles and occasionally he helped us out with cash.

At this perilous moment, we received the amazing news that the new financial reforms actually allowed people to become owners of their apartments, which under socialism had belonged to the state, just by paying some administrative fees to the government. My mother realized she was sitting on a rare treasure, a renovated apartment in central Moscow. Marik recommended she not waste any time. My mother ran off with stacks of paper to some office where she worked her customary magic with officialdom. She returned in just a few hours, as the owner of property, a concept we could scarcely grasp. Now, as Marik, more experienced in the ways of capitalism, explained to us, we couldn't say we were without money anymore. We could rent it out and move to America.

She decided she would never rent to a Russian, because she believed that a nouveau riche Russian would never be able to cherish her beloved apartment in the same way. My mother was patient, and finally found her perfect tenant. He was a beautiful, sophisticated Englishman named Sam Bales, the president of an American company in Moscow. He walked into the apartment and gasped: "Now, this is what I am talking about!" He was smiling with his beautiful teeth, so delighted with the Western conveniences. He was shocked to hear about my father, and he promised to take good care of the place because he could see what it meant to us. He was so obviously sincere and after some negotiation, his firm paid the three-year rental fee in advance, way above market price at the time.

We landed in New York on August 3, 1992, and entered through customs at John F. Kennedy Airport. This was my Ellis Island. To this day, whenever I land at JFK, I look at it through the prism of that humid summer day. I remember my mother's anxiously excited face, my sister's timidity, which some could have mistaken for indifference. As for me, I was gloriously excited to have finally reached the land of my father's unrequited dreams. Marik and his friend Fima were there to greet us.

As we walked outside, I looked up and saw the sky. It was just like the Russian sky, as uncheerful and uneven in color. It looked down upon me with the same indifference as it did on all those other immigrants and visitors, cared nothing for how special I was. I got into the car, and we drove off toward our future. There was traffic. The outer boroughs were not inspiring like Manhattan, dull working neighborhoods with messy streets, garbage bags hanging on the trees as if they were Christmas decorations, homeless people talking to themselves and shouting curses at God himself.

On that first ride through the streets of Queens I couldn't help comparing it to the magnificence of Moscow and Leningrad, but I pushed that thought away because my dream was to love New York without looking back. Manhattan was beautiful, and my life there was going to be beautiful, too. I had already made up my mind to fall in love with the city. It was all mixed up in my mind with my childhood fantasies and my father's vision for me.

Our new place on First Avenue and the corner of 90th Street had a doorman. Respectable looking people walked in and out. The apartment was big as New York apartments go, and from our window on the twelfth floor the view was of rooftops, fire escapes, and water towers, with the Triboro Bridge in the background. If you tilted your head and squinted your eyes at these utilitarian structures, there was romance in them. It wasn't a great apartment, nor in the best of neighborhoods, and my sister and I shared a very small bedroom, but I made a home of it, arranging the books I brought from Russia on my shelves.

My mother couldn't wait to finally show us her favorite streets and shops on the Upper East Side, especially her beloved Madison Avenue, where she used to spend many lonely hours while waiting for Marik to return from work. We walked uptown and downtown, from east to west, south and north, until we knew where we were going. I thought the city was smiling at me.

I was ready to accept Marik as our new man. Actually, I had already accepted him as such a while back. He was never going to be my father, he was not planning to replace him, but he was going to play the role of a normal man. In my view a "normal" man was a male who upon finding himself in love with a woman who happens to have children will be expected to protect her and her children from the bad memories of the past, as well as from the unknown present in the new country. I had prepared myself to love him.

Liana did not take to Marik. Everything I liked about him seemed to irritate her. She thought he was coarse and insensitive, and to be sure his personal habits were somewhat crass. He ate onions the way most of us eat apples; ate herring with his hands and then tapped my sister's shoulder with the same finger.

Marik, on the other hand, found my sister very interesting, unusual. This was a pattern with her and men. The more she ignored him, the more fascinated he became. Marik accepted what he took to be her challenge; he loved to ask questions, and he always asked them in a slightly humorous and cynical manner. I found it clever. My sister found it irritating. She could barely stand it when our father tried to be funny with her; she wasn't going to start accepting jokes from a stranger. He could see he wasn't getting anywhere, yet he persisted. He was a little tone deaf when it came to people.

Also, he wouldn't shut up about Russia. He loathed the place and any Russian who didn't have the guts to get the hell out of there. I couldn't agree with everything he said, but I was fascinated with the way he said it, his boldness, his elegant Russian, his unapologetic tone. His disdain for Russia notwithstanding, he spoke and thought like a true son of his people. No one dares to express themselves with as much passion, venom, and ambiguity as a Russian.

My sister loved Russia, she missed Russia, and she wanted to go home. She cared nothing for politics. Her entire world was culture, the ballet to which she had dedicated her life embodied Russian culture, respected and admired in all times, throughout the world. He told her she ought to get into modern dance. Martha Graham for example, was what the world wanted to see. This was an ill-informed opinion that showed he knew absolutely nothing about ballet. He didn't even pretend to care what she thought, and Liana decided after that there was no point in talking to him at all. In her usual manner, my sister never displayed any visible hostility or bad manners toward him, but on the other hand, she openly dismissed everything he used to say to her: her blank stares and her rigid shrugs said it all. His opinion was unimportant to her. Although we never intended to leave, we had not come to America officially as immigrants, but on a six-month tourist/business visa. My mother was unable to open an American bank account: she had no social security number, no credit card, just cash. She had to give it to Marik to put in his account and give her the money whenever she needed it. I'm sure Marik was an honest man, and nothing funny ever happened, but it wasn't good for their relationship for her to have to depend on him like that. In addition to being her interpreter and her most trusted advisor, he became, of necessity, her banker. When he asked to borrow some money for his business, she said yes. After all, we were a family.

My mother's first priority was to organize our lives, our schools, my sister's interrupted ballet training. Curiously, she sent me, the one who spoke English, away to Staples High School in Westport, Connecticut, where I had been a Russian exchange student the year before. (This was not my first trip to America. In the fall of 1990, our school in Moscow traveled to Westport for a month. About twenty students from my grade and ten teachers joined the trip. Each one of us lived with an American family, and then a few months later we had a group from Staples High School visit us in Moscow for about four weeks.) There, I lived with an upstanding American family from Sunday evening through Friday afternoon. The school itself cost nothing, but my mother paid my living expenses to the family.

The family didn't want to take the money, but my mother insisted. Marik paid with my mother's money but with his checkbook and they admired his suave generosity.

It ended up being a disaster. It was all supposed to be about my education, but I couldn't forget that I had left my mother and my sister all alone in a strange city where they didn't speak the language.

The School of American Ballet, the only place for a dancer like my sister, was not an academy, just a ballet school for a few hours a day after school. My mother called a very old acquaintance from her days in Leningrad named Mikhail Baryshnikov, who was kind enough to introduce her to a respected Russian teacher, Svetlana Krasotkina, and the whole thing was easily accomplished in Russian.

High school presented a bigger challenge. The new school year had begun, but my sister was still not at school. She needed to learn English; without it, she was completely isolated. Every day she prepared her backpack and slung it on her back like she was going to school, but she wasn't. Really, my mother needed Marik, he spoke English and had the "know-how," as they say here, but he was too busy with his new medical practice to help her.

One day in September on the way to work he dropped my mother off on 68th Street and Second Avenue, in front of a building that looked like a penitentiary. "Here is high school for Liana. I am sure they have English as a second language here. You are a big girl; you can figure it out!" Then he drove away. My mother took a look at the guards in police uniforms, the bars on the windows, the full body scanner at the entrance like they have at airports and walked away. On the way home she turned down 78th Street between Madison and Fifth Avenue, and there were the words "High School." Since these were some of the few words she knew how to read, she went inside.

This is how we learned about the scientist, philosopher, and spiritualist Rudolf Steiner (1861–1925). His fusion of science and spirituality he called "Anthroposophy," love of humanity, and his educational philosophy focuses on the inner development of the child. Steiner's writings are esoteric and difficult to grasp, and my mother didn't quite understand it all, but it was a pleasant-looking private school in a great part of town, ready and willing to accept my sister.

Marik didn't see the point of spending money on private education. Public school was free. Liana's ballet lessons already cost a fortune. I thought with his keen cynical view on life he must have seen that a big jail of a New York City public school was no place for someone as sensitive as my sister. Anyone who knew her and cared for her could see that, so maybe he liked the idea of throwing this proud Russian princess into a den of American wolves. This thought led to the next, that he simply wanted my mother's money for himself and that he didn't love her. This was perhaps too harsh. He loved my mother, but he was thinking like a practical immigrant about money, as a means to an end, to build his business, buy property that would appreciate in value. This is how one becomes rich in America. Ballet lessons and private schools for spoiled silly girls are not something immigrants can afford. He thought spending money on beautiful clothes was a waste, but splurging on good wine and food was not, because he liked to eat and drink. I think he was just cheap. Many cheap and selfish people spend only on things that are important to them, while economizing on things others consider essential. In the end, it didn't matter, because it was my mother's money, and Liana was her daughter, not his. Mother made the decision, and my sister went to the Rudolf Steiner School.

Their relationship was going sour. Marik's friends used to call him a "classic" or "old" bachelor. They were all shocked when he fell in love with my mother and committed himself as well to her two teenage daughters. It is not a Russian way, to burden oneself with that much baggage, and when family life began for real and my mother started to adjust things to her liking, when he found some things like responsibility and the high cost of children were non-negotiable, it was not easy.

Still, he kept saying they were going to get married. My mother wanted to marry Marik because she loved him, because she needed his warmth, because he helped her in the most difficult time of her life. Last, but not least, he had a green card that could help us to legalize our status in America. A couple of months had passed since our arrival, our visas were aging rapidly, yet each time my mother mentioned marriage he avoided the question, even as he opened his private practice in Brooklyn with my mother's money and loans from the bank. He had very few patients, but he went into the office every day.

My sister was having a terrible time; she began to hate America and wanted desperately to go back to her Russia. Liana was utterly lost without English language skills, unable to connect with teachers, classmates, even to read the books. She was always quiet and shy, but now she felt like a deaf mute. English came slowly to her, and she resisted it at every step. Her tiny school didn't have a formal English as a second language program, there were perhaps two people in the building who spoke Russian. Some kids extended their hand in friendship to my sister, others didn't know what to say to her.

Some Russian speaker succeeded in explaining to the very large lady managing the front desk that she had to let my sister out the instant classes were over because she had ballet class on the other side of town and had to be there at exactly three p.m., all changed and ready for class. This lady, like small functionaries the world over, was a petty tyrant. She demanded proof of enrollment at SAB—this was submitted, but she was still not satisfied and unsympathetic. Perhaps she detected arrogance and insubordination, which Steiner educators didn't like any better than their Soviet counterparts. One time my sister was running late and went to leave without signing out, and the woman angrily blocked the door with her enormous body, towering over Liana, who, unable or unwilling to explain herself in English, pushed her hand away and ran past her.

The only class she liked was French, which she had studied it at the Academy. The teacher was Eleonora Pavlovna, a Russian Jewish lady of considerable erudition. The Steiner intellectuals adored her, but I thought her mediocre by Russian standards. Americans are often easily overimpressed by Russia and Russian personalities. Liana loved her, so relieved to have a teacher who spoke Russian and seemed to understand her and like her. Eleonora was friendly with our mother, and she became good friends with Marik, who spoke fluent French. Our family became something of a Russia fix for her, and she helped us to acclimatize to the US.

Then, a terrible thing happened. There was an important test in French, and Liana was studying very hard, wanting to impress the teacher, all of us, even herself. She was not doing well in any of her other subjects because of her language handicap, so French was her only chance to succeed. She was well prepared and finished with the questions rather quickly. She put her pen down, and then she wanted to confirm one of her answers.

My sister's French textbook was breathing in her direction just a few inches away. Liana waited for the French teacher to turn away, she then discreetly lifted the cover of the book, picked with her nail the very page that interested her, glanced at it and with lighting speed shut the book. Almost simultaneously she heard a young female voice: "Excuse me, Miss, but Liana is looking up answers in the book!"

Here is the difference between Russia and America when it comes to school. In Russia, cheating was not about honesty or competition, but about loyalty and relationships among friends. The teachers were on the other side, the side of the government, so if you had a friend, you let her copy off you, or use a cheat sheet, and you never, ever snitched because everyone knew a snitch was a traitor. In America it's all about competition. Your test answers are your private property, and even helping your schoolmate complete his homework falls into the wider definition of cheating here.

Liana knew the rules by now, she should have turned her paper over if she wanted to pick up the book. The teacher was on the spot, she had to enforce the rules or else be accused of protecting her pet. She took her red pen, made big red lines across the page, and chastised my sister in both English and Russian in front of the entire class in accordance with the rules of the school and the code of honor, and perhaps to show the rest of the class she didn't play favorites. My sister felt no guilt and no sense of having done anything wrong, only rage at her betrayal by this sly Russian immigrant who had been pretending to be her friend. I don't know if she felt any anger toward that girl, the snitch who had ratted her out. Knowing my sister, she might have thought it was beneath her to consider her at all, the way she felt about her classmates in her old English school in Russia.

It was a hard time for us all. My mother spent her days walking around Manhattan. She had no friends in the city, knew no one. She took a crosstown bus to the West Side and waited at the Café Mozart for my sister's ballet class to finish. She told me later how she used to sit there at the café looking at people coming and going, barely understanding a word they were saying to each other. She had no plan for what to do next or how to accomplish it.

I didn't know how lonely and scared she was. It was never in her nature to parade her sadness in front of us. Russians in general do not talk about their problems in the same way Americans do. No one expects anything to be resolved by it; intuitively they know that they have to live those issues through. That's why therapists were never popular in Russia. But even if she said nothing, I could see when I came to the city for my weekend stays that she was not happy. While she suffered in New York, I was deeply unhappy in Connecticut.

The girl whose family was hosting me now was the same girl who stayed with me in Moscow when my school was involved in the exchange with the school in Westport. Her name was Kate. She was two years older, and we made cozy friends.

Kate was amazed at our beautiful apartment, we had to explain that most Russians did not live this way. She was even more impressed by my mother, who was beautiful and glamorous and not at all what she had heard about Russian femininity back home. They took to each other at once. Kate was funny, exuberant, friendly, generous. After a day, they didn't even need me to translate for them; they found their own language. They could talk about anything: men, women, relationships, sex, clothes. Kate loved my mother's wardrobe. In those days my mother smoked cigarettes, and Kate asked if it was okay for her to smoke. My mother had no problem with that. Kate winked and said: "Just don't tell my parents!"

During that visit our apartment was always filled with people. My father wasn't alive anymore, but that was exactly the kind of thing he would have loved. I always had my small group of friends, but I was never popular. It bothered me that some people were magnets who attracted almost everything and everyone. I always wanted to be like them. When they all came to my home not once but many times, I felt my whole body had that magnetic pull. My Russian schoolmates joked and curried favors with me, the American kids couldn't wait to see me in America as one of their own at Staples High School. Every time I saw their huge smiles and heard their *"Whoa! That's Great!"* I thought the entire galaxy was smiling at me. I thought to myself I was going to love it there in Westport with my new friends.

It wasn't nearly as much fun at home with Kate's family. Martha and Bob Robertson were good and honorable, but too conservative, in my view. They didn't talk to their kids about sex, restricted their television viewing and looked askance at any song with naughty words. There were rules for me, too, mandatory attendance at meals, a set time to use the shower. In my family we never had time for rules.

At school, all those people who had partied at my house in Moscow didn't seem particularly happy to see me. No one tried to make friends. Everyone had their own group of friends, their circle, their life. In Westport everyone drove cars, students were independent, and no one was going to plan things with some new foreign student with a strong Russian accent.

The school was much larger than my school in Moscow, with 2,000 students, all of whom looked and behaved the same, just like in Russia, although I didn't see anyone compelling them. I almost never saw Kate; we had different schedules, and she had her own group of friends. Everyone was obsessed with sex, or at least with getting themselves a boyfriend or a girlfriend. Kate spent all her time gossiping about sex and trying to get a date; but she had to do it all in secret from her parents. Sometimes she would share with me some of the secrets of her rebellion, but I couldn't be the fun co-conspirator she wanted. At sixteen, coming from Russia, I was on a different planet when it came to that subject, and besides, things had turned serious for me. I was not a tourist anymore, nor was I an exchange student. No one was amused by me anymore; few were interested in me. I was just a foreigner, an immigrant, living among strangers. I spent a lot of time in my room doing my homework and obsessing about getting into college.

There was another reason why I could never love pretty Westport. I was already in love with New York. I visited New York every weekend. People recognized my face in the shops, the doormen knew my name, it was easy to walk on the street and not feel foreign or strange. On Sunday nights on the way back to my prissy Westport, I used to watch through the car windows as the city was about to enter its night life. Everyone was just about to start living, they were all dressed up and ready to begin their night, while I was being taken away into cold, dark suburbia. I found I had overestimated my own courage, in fact, I had no courage at all. I was not cut out to live without my family, not even when they were forty minutes away from me.

Every day I felt more out of place in that provincial, small-minded town. How lonely was I going to be today? I counted the minutes for the day to end. People would talk slow, pronouncing their words deliberately, as if I were deaf or mentally disabled. Eight years of English instruction in Russia had seemingly taught me nothing that was useful in America, and now I had to pass the Test of English as a Foreign Language to get into college. Russians are expected to be geniuses at math, but it was never my subject, which caused me no small embarrassment.

When I called my mother every night before bed, my throat and every cell in my brain was swelling up with tears. I was reluctant to admit to her my misery, but I couldn't hide it when I was home on weekends. I also saw my sister's doomed indifference to her own situation, and Marik's indifference to all of us.

All the way up the highway he would go on to my mother about the benefits of my Westport education. This was an opportunity, one of the best public high schools in America, and I should make the most of it. An immigrant has to be tough. Tears started to pour down my face. He didn't understand my sorrow, away from my family. I was just a girl.

Marik once said that immigration was a form of illness, and it is true. It is a humiliating trial that exposes your most unflattering characteristics and your deepest weakness, in my case a lack of courage and absence of willpower. It overpowers you at first, and eventually you get over it, but it leaves a mark on you that never comes off. I had it easy in some ways compared to him, but I paid a price just like he did, and I have the marks to prove it. There is no such thing as immigrating with no consequences, and the most unsettling thing is that you never know at which point in your life you will be presented with the bill.

Suddenly, my quiet sister raised her voice: "Why must I live here without my Anya?! I don't want it this way! She must live with us!" Emboldened by this outburst, I expressed the same desire: to leave dull Westport and move to New York where I could go to school together with my sister. Marik was against it, no doubt he was thinking of that second private school tuition, but my sister and I would not be denied.

One evening at dinner, I wearied of the conversation and felt the need to go upstairs to continue my studies, so I excused myself from the table. To my shock, Kate's mother, Martha, told me that I could only do so after dinner, since they had company. I was taken aback. Hadn't I asked so nicely, and didn't I need to go study? It all felt like jail. A little clump right in the middle of my throat began to flutter like a caught butterfly. Once it settled, I asked for permission to use the phone. Once I heard my mother's voice, I uttered in Russian "Take me away from here now!" My mother responded: "Yes, Anechka, I will bring you back!" I could hear my sister's elated voice in the background: "Anka is coming, Anka is coming, I told you she should be living with us!" They were a good family and looking back, I know it might have been my ignorance of American customs and tempestuousness of a young immigrant girl that led to such bitterness on my part. But there I was, rebelling for the first time in my life, ready to quit suburbia and to take on Manhattan.

The next morning, they came to get me, and that fall I entered the Rudolf Steiner high school. I knew my life in New York had begun. I would give America another chance, and maybe it would give me one back. I loved it there on East 78th Street: the smallness of the space, the intimacy of the environment. Unlike the kids in Westport who paid me no attention, the Steiner students were open and friendly. It was such a relief not to hear anyone talk to me as if I were hard of hearing, to be able to express my opinion and not worry about my accent. There were perhaps eight other kids in the class, and according to Steiner practice they had all been with each other since kindergarten, but they all treated me as if they were my older siblings.

I won the Shakespeare competition, reciting Sonnet 62, and one of Juliet's monologues from memory, beating the guy who was unbeatable since grade school. I suspect they let me win because they were very nice and they liked me, and if it was a mercy win, I accept it even today. I felt like I was walking in a dream, the Upper East Side on one side, Central Park on the other. There was nothing that could disturb my equilibrium of happiness. It also made me like myself, at least temporarily. I was never the popular one, never the star of the show. Frequently I found myself to be in love, even if no one had ever fallen in love with me. Memorizing other people's grand thoughts, being the conduit of someone's else's genius turned me into something I believed other people could truly fall in love with, the actress I had wanted to be as a girl.

My classmates were talented, funny, aloof, and charming. They already had "real" boyfriends and girlfriends, nearly all of them smoked pot on a regular basis. On our senior getaway trip, we all went to the Virgin Islands and one of the girls brought her twenty-five-year-old boyfriend along, without objection from the teachers. Every evening, we gathered at the beach to just sit around, sing, play guitar, and chat. Then they would all smoke a joint. Nobody ever pressured me to join in; they just let me be.

In the city I could lose myself by feeling anonymous but never lonely. Walking in New York made me feel free because everyone around me looked so busy. I was a stranger no more to those Manhattan streets and avenues, to their neighborhood grocery markets and restaurants whose aromas and happy crowds were seducing my innocence. I decided I would never abandon this scrumptious island.

My sister and I were together now, too, walking to the same school hand in hand every morning, speaking Russian to each other. From First Avenue we crossed west over 90th Street, then we walked down magical Madison Avenue all the way to 78th Street, looking in the windows of the shops. Every morning, we would notice some small change to the window displays.

Mother and Marik were dancing their last variation. Marik came home from his office rather late, often with a bagel, watched the news and went to bed smelling of onions and fish. My mother no longer got annoyed when he came home late. Marik too made fewer comments about things and acted more like a college roommate than a lover or husband. It was my first glimpse into an unhappy, broken relationship. My parents used to argue vehemently, but it seemed to me their quarrels had purpose, they were about important things like love or jealousy or money. My mother and Marik didn't argue at all. I guess after he made it clear he had no intention of marrying her, she didn't think she could change his mind.

My mother had never broken up with anybody in her life, she had always been married, but she needed to do it now. How does it work in other countries? Who leaves whom? Who stays in the apartment? What will become of her antique furniture which she could barely get out of Russia and was now still in transit? She did her best to shield us from the situation, but it was right there in front of us, all the time.

The answer came from an unexpected quarter when another man entered the picture. One night, out to dinner with my sister, my mom and Liana ended up at a place on Second Avenue and 88th Street called Cronies. My sister was enjoying her cheesecake when a very good-looking middle-aged American man walked over to their table and began a light unassuming chitchat. He had a drink in his hand and a cigarette, very nice and easygoing, and it turned out he was the owner of the place. He invited them for dinner there the next night.

A couple of nights later he asked my mother out again, this time to a different place; and then he asked her out again. By the time I arrived in New York from Westport, this new man, whose name was Ed McCauley, had fallen in love with my mother. This was unexpected. She came from a traditional society and going out with one man while living with another was not part of the script. But since Marik was not treating her right, and since she had always been a self-respecting woman, she wasn't going to sit at home and suffer. I think she was going on instinct.

Despite the language barrier, he understood my mother was not some destitute immigrant widow but a glamorous Russian lady living on the Upper East Side with two teenage daughters in private school. Very quickly and very elegantly he asked her if she could lend him some money for his business, and she agreed. He charmed me and my sister as well, taking us all to fun, delicious places. There wasn't a restaurant owner in the city who didn't know him, and we got VIP treatment everywhere we went. I still remember my first Japanese food experience in 1993 on top of the World Trade Center. He taught me how to use chopsticks.

He was a dashing gentleman, everything Marik was not: clean, neat, tall, well dressed, with a charming southern accent and impeccable manners that he had learned from his mother, who when I met her was a considerable woman. He lacked Marik Russian sophistication, erudition, and cynicism, but that was wearing a little thin anyway, and when one day Ed invited my mother to move in with him, she said yes. He lived on Third Avenue and 85th Street in the famous building that was the exterior set for *The Jeffersons*, whose theme song went "Moving on up, to the East Side." It was a deluxe apartment in the sky, as the song says, a spacious two-bedroom with a balcony, and we would all love it.

When Marik learned of all this, he began to feel sincere regrets, as men will. He tried to pay better attention, came from work early, offered solutions, spoke with less cynicism, became more plastic, flexible, and adaptable. I felt terrible for him, because I liked him, and I didn't want to move. I have always hated change, and still do. During the winter break mother approached us, wanting to know whether we wanted to move and change our lives again. To go live with this other man, whose name was Ed, or to stay with Marik? My weak character and my innate laziness were whispering "stay," while my awakening sense of pragmatism and womanly instinct said "run." I went with the most honest appraisal I could offer: People don't change, I told my mother. Marik would go back to his old ways soon enough after we agreed to stay and live with him again.

My mother took my advice, and we left Marik a few weeks later. Ironically, the people who said he was not the marrying kind, including my mother, me, and Marik himself, were proved wrong when he became really good friends with my sister's treacherous Russian French teacher Eleonora Pavlovna and, within a year of our departure, had married her.

To my mother, Marik will always remain an antagonist. She has almost nothing good to say about him. He betrayed her. As her daughter, I stand by that verdict. Yet even antagonists, either despite or because of their difficult and unusual character traits, are capable of making great changes in someone else's life. He helped my mother survive and not go mad from sorrow after my father's murder, he gave her hope when she had none, and for better or for worse, he was the catalyst for bringing us to America. He pushed her away and forced her into the whirlwind of an American life where she had to learn many things from the beginning. With each day after we left him, she gained more strength and wisdom. Some would say she should be grateful to him for that. Yet, in my mother's mind, as well as in my own, he will always remain a very interesting man who went back on his word to be our king. He ran away from his responsibilities toward the freedom of his lost youth. Does that make him a bad man or simply a weak one? The two traits are related. I think that weakness in a man inevitably erodes his virtue. Only weak men are capable of betraying their women.

We all moved in with Ed. He was a straightforward American, and when he said he wanted to get married, he meant it. He took us down to Birmingham, Alabama, to meet his mother, who was thrilled her Eddy was finally settling down. Back in New York there was paperwork to be filed and lawyers to be hired and Ed, whose signature was required on everything, was not the most punctual or reliable person, tending to sleep all day after closing the restaurant in the small hours of the morning, so things moved slowly. In retrospect it was not such a long time, but things always seem to take forever when one is waiting for them to happen.

Liana went to the Professional Children's School, established in 1914 to cater to kids who were professional dancers, actors, musicians, and the like. It was as rarified and custom-tailored an education as it is possible to get in New York; among the alumni are Yo-Yo Ma, Darci Kistler, Uma Thurman, and Vera Wang. It was only a few blocks from the School of American Ballet, and the curriculum included English as a Second Language.

We all hoped to see a smile from my sister, some sign that she liked her new situation. Weeks passed and then months went by, but still she had not mentioned a name that would make any of us believe that she had made a friend. Finally, the principal called my mother in, arranged for an interpreter, and related how, after a holiday, she had asked Liana how she was doing and whether she was happy to be back at school. My sister replied "No." This was the truth, but it betrayed a negative, un-American attitude and this was a concern for the diligent headmistress. She asked my mother some very American questions: "How do you think your daughter is doing? Do you think she is happy? Do you talk about things at home?" The woman meant well, of course, but my mother was taken aback. In the Soviet Union teachers and principals did not ask questions about anyone's feelings.

Liana could never understand that in America the "How are you?" question is not the sort of question that expects an honest answer; it is merely an invitation to conversation. In America no one wants to hear about your problem, they want to know you're fine and then get down to business. You have three seconds to respond in the affirmative, because this is a culture of positivism. If someone is not fine, that is a question for specialists.

Even with New York City, everything she liked about it was either abstract: the arts, ballet, fashion, or inanimate: old mansions, French cafés, fancy desserts. She loved to shop, especially with our mother, she knew what matched with what time of the day and for what occasion. When she sat down to eat, it mattered to her how the table was set, no matter whether we ate at home or at a restaurant. She could not stand American mass culture, but she recognized and enjoyed New York's exquisite style and the luxury of the Hamptons.

She had learned some English, yet she pretended not to speak it. She would say a few words when she desperately needed something, but never encouraged people in conversation. Her friends, if you could call them that, were mostly Europeans, a few bohemian Americans who managed to be taciturn and cynical at the same time. She read books in Russian, becoming an avid reader and introspective scholar, more out of loneliness and boredom than anything else.

Once, at a big charity event, they played the Star-Spangled Banner to open the program.. When the band struck up the anthem, the audience rose, as is customary, and my mother was experiencing a feeling a patriotic emotion until she looked to her immediate left and saw my sister had remained seated. Looks were exchanged, but

Liana refused to get up. My mother told me later she felt the roots of her hair turning white.

Ballet was Liana's biggest frustration in America. At the School of American Ballet, George Balanchine had created a new, unique, and brilliant choreography, based on the Russian traditions. When Balanchine was alive, he taught the Russian method, but since his death they had been teaching something else in his name. This opinion is not original with me, it is shared by the majority of Russian-trained teachers and dancers. My sister found herself having to re-learn everything she had been trained to do since she was a little girl.

Everything the great Marina Semenova taught her was now put into question. What was it all for? Her Russian teacher in New York, Svetlana Krasotkina, was a good teacher and understood American demands. She was prepared to continue working with Liana and prepare her to audition either for the New York City Ballet or American Ballet Theatre, which was more in line with the European tradition, but her American ballet path was anything but certain. She saw older girls not getting into any companies at all after years of training, never tasting the *pyl szeny*, the dust of the stage.

She wanted to go back to Moscow. It took her a while to formulate the idea, but once she figured it out, that was all she could talk about. She came up with a plan: to go back and finish the Academy and join the theatre, preferably the Bolshoi. Even if she didn't make the Bolshoi, she would have ended up in the second best, or even third best theatre, because that was how it still worked there: ballet belonged to the Empire, and the Empire took care of its servants. This was the deal they made with you when you were nine years old. A ballet professional who finished at the best academy in the country was not going to be left without her vocation. She was not scared about living in Moscow in the dorms of the Academy. After all, it was her school, her friends, her native city, her people who spoke her own language.

She would wait until her green card came through, so she could come back to see us without a visa, and then she would quit this land of freedom and go live in a pseudo-free Russia. That was Liana's plan, and she would not be swayed from it, even if our mother and I were staying here.

The green card took some time, but once it came, having failed to dissuade her, we were all sitting shoulder to shoulder on a Soviet made plane, barely able to control our trembling hearts, peering into the darkness of the Russian sky as we landed in Moscow. It was January 1995, four years since we had left. I often think of the words spoken by Elizaveta Prokofyevna at the very end of Dostoevsky's *The Idiot*: "And all of this, all this life abroad, and this Europe of yours is all a fantasy, and all of us abroad are only a fantasy . . . remember my words, you'll see it for yourself."

Russians, outside of their natural habitat, always look and feel displaced, proud, yet still inferior, ill at ease with the rest of the civilized world. As a matter of fact, the more inferior they feel, the more pride they exhibit about themselves to the outside world, about who they are and where they come from. In a way, their pride protects them from that perpetual gnawing pinch known as the Russian inferiority complex. To a Russian, the world outside Russia is either a nightmare or a fairytale, but either way it is a fantasy. Those who can't accept this fantasy either don't survive immigration, or return to Russia. America is supposed to be all about realism, and yet for those who immigrate to America, it is a land of chimerical promises.

No one explained this to my sister, but I think she felt it more than most. She understood she would have to become somebody else, even if all that was required of her was to learn English. She refused to adapt to America, to participate in the fantasy that it offered if you put on the mask of an immigrant. Liana felt ridiculous having to even try it on. She was the most honest, sincere, real person I've known, and if someone would have asked me: "Do you think your sister Liana should live in a fantasy?" I would have replied "Yes, because with time, perhaps she would have been able to adjust to this fantasy and flutter in it like a butterfly."

Instead, she chose Russia. Our Russia. Some would argue that her Russia was also a fantasy. But one's motherland is never a fantasy; it is the most real thing there is, just like one's parents. The Russia we had come back to was a country with a ruined economy, confused politics, aggressive corruption that permeated every sphere of the society, and unabridged freedom of speech. Crime seemed to be everywhere. I remember how dark and dangerous the streets of Moscow were. The passageways underneath the huge avenues, which during Soviet times were clean and safe, were dungeons and hideaways for prostitutes, drug addicts, and homeless people. Social ills like these, identified in past with the Western world, were now a Russian problem as well, and Russia had no way of dealing with them.

That winter break in Moscow was the last time Liana and I were together as we always knew each other: intact, remembering the same past, still wanting the same things despite having different goals. We still openly loved each other, we knew how to be happy with one another, we were on the same wavelength with life itself. We spent our days in that cold, snowy Moscow going to famous street markets for crispy homemade pickles, Russian candies, chocolates, and cookies, seeing old friends who interviewed us about America.

My sister and I were too excited to notice the dire state of affairs when we went to visit our friends in the same nice apartments they had always lived in. We didn't notice the alarming scarcity of food, the way their parents looked so nervous and exhausted. Russians are known for their hospitality, ready to spend their last ruble to impress their guest, their tables overflow with homemade meals and sinful alcoholic beverages, but not now. They had just enough not to embarrass themselves. We went to see other friends as well, who by luck or talent, had become part of the new oligarch class and were thriving. My sister and I were so blinded by our nostalgia and the lavish hospitality of these friends that we were more entertained than frightened by all that decay surrounding us.

As the time drew close for us to part, my heart began to beat faster and tighter. When I was little, my sister used to follow me around, admiring me, wanting to be with me. Now she was leaving me. She would come and visit me again in America, but she was never going to be an immigrant in this country again. And so we parted, and I came back to my strange America, this time without my Liana. Liana was unstoppable in her obsessive desire to be in Moscow. There was no future for her in New York, but here she saw her entire professional future, and therefore her entire life. The Academy dorm, where she shared a room with a few other girls, most of whom she knew, was like a high class *kommunalka*, but my sister was happy again, drunk with the excitement of being back in Moscow at her school. My sister got along with people by never getting into any gossip and by sharing everything with everyone: her food, her money, her spare ballet slippers, her ribbons, her clothes, her warm sweaters, her makeup. She began to go out. She was eighteen, after all. Suddenly she was a young lady in charge of her own life, in control of her time. In those days we spoke on the phone a lot. She used to tell me how she spent every free hour of her time getting to know Moscow, falling in love with it, embracing its unfriendly, dark soil with her stubborn arms, demanding that it love her back.

V.

My Broken Heart

MY FIRST REJECTION LETTER WAS FROM NEW YORK UNIVERSITY. It was my safety school. I thought I was doing them a favor by applying. I had never experienced a rejection letter, those polite, unapologetic words with the power to decide my life. It was a late winter, and I didn't know how to go on living after reading those words. I put the letter away, saying to myself I had many more letters to look forward to: Harvard, Yale, Columbia, Princeton.

I was so hopeful as I went on the rounds of interviews. I was planning to double major in theatre and natural sciences, hopefully at Harvard. I had come here to be the best, so of course I would go to Harvard. I discussed my plans openly with everyone. People must have been amused at my immigrant optimism. When I went to Cambridge for an interview, the admissions lady was so lovely in her genuine interest in my story, her questions about my Soviet education, her curiosity in everything I had to say. At the end she gave me a long embrace, one of those heartfelt American embraces, which I mistook for a sign that everything was going to be all right.

The letter came. I took it into my room with the early spring flirting with me behind the window and opened it to find the same polite but firm words of rejection. A sharp pain in my middle was preventing me from taking another breath. In what strange, unfair world was I not supposed to anticipate my acceptance into Harvard?

I had a clear vision of my life going down the drain. I was not going to get the best education, either in the classics or sciences, nor the social standing that comes with a Harvard degree, nor be part of the "right" crowd, destined for success and fulfillment, to which I thought I belonged by default. And that smart, enchanting, promising young man who was waiting to fall in love with me there in the Quad? I was never going to meet him. The rejection letters came thick and fast after that. One or two were generous enough to put me on a waiting list. Despite my talent, my belief in the American dream, my mother's unequivocal faith in my special path, it was clear I had failed. I wanted to be chosen. Instead, I was overlooked.

I did not perform well on standardized tests, not having the advantage of American children in elite schools who start learning to color in the right little balloon in first grade. After my first encounter with this American phenomenon had gone badly, my mother threw her hands in the air and exclaimed: "After just a few months in America you can't be the best at everything!" This was obviously true, but no excuse if I wanted to get into Harvard. I was not always the best student, but mother told me not to worry about teachers' criticisms and mediocre grades, that I was better than most. Obviously, this was wrong, and it was irresponsible of her to worry about my nerves and baby me and, honestly, herself, instead of insisting that I study harder and learn to play the piano. In her role as my father's fixer, she got by on charm, but I couldn't do that at my Soviet school, and still less in America. My mother's powers of persuasion did not work as well here.

It was a rough introduction to reality, to have a bunch of strangers tell me that whatever my mother thought, I was not "better than most."

My college advisor came to my rescue. We gathered all my documents, my essays, my test scores, my transcripts and I applied to the Lincoln Center Campus of Fordham University. I was interviewed and I got accepted.

Fordham was kind of like going to college in an airport. Anodyne buildings, anodyne furniture, people looking bored. No brick buildings or green lawns like at Harvard. Nevertheless, it was college and I decided to do my best. The classes were interesting, the other students were intelligent, but it was still Fordham, and I was still dreaming about Harvard. I failed to appreciate Fordham for what it was, a college for the children of immigrants who couldn't get into the club at Harvard even though they were smart. Somehow, I did not want to be part of it myself, even though there was no denying it had been made for people just like me.

Fordham was a commuter school. There was no campus life like the one my friends who had gone away were talking about, no "college experience" of fraternities, sororities, parties, one-night stands, meetings for various causes and associations, special friendships lasting a lifetime. I heard about all these things from other people. I saw my classmates in class, and that was it.

All I needed from Fordham was an education. I was planning to go to medical school, so I took science courses. People in my classes were friendly enough and the professors knew a lot. The Rudolf Steiner School, I discovered, had been an intellectual luxury, a featherbed where I felt like I was almost never wrong. My thoughts, doubts, mistakes were all indulged in the interest of spiritualism, I suppose. At Fordham no one had time to sugarcoat things for me, even in my theatre classes, which I took to keep the flame of my first ambition alive.

I was shy, and my first friend was another shy girl named Dana. She was a second generation Chinese American and lived in Brooklyn with her family. Clever yet modest, with a dry sense of humor, she was a real science girl, a great lab partner. Her face was wide, and she wore glasses. I thought she was much smarter than me. We went to lunch together because we were shy girls, habitual, casual friends, we never felt we needed to explain anything to one another, we never had any obligations toward one another except those relating to our schoolwork. Afterward, life threw us in different directions, and we lost track of each other, but for a while she was my best friend.

Dana dressed for school as if she had decided to stay home on the couch, and then changed her mind. Other girls tried to make themselves look attractive, but she was overweight and never at ease with herself and maybe she felt she was beyond repair. She always dressed in the same men's flannel shirt on top of her jeans, her long black hair pulled back in a ponytail that she seldom let down, and a deadpan expression. Dana had a warm, vivid smile, she was a sensitive, bright young girl, but nobody but me took the time to find out. It was easy being friends with her because she had no other girl-friends, and no boyfriends. She was a virgin, like me, but we never discussed sex, for we were both hopelessly shy and insecure, comfortably stuck in our state of maiden stagnation. To make ourselves feel better we joked about the girls we saw flaunting their voluptuous and not so voluptuous bodies all over campus for the inspection of random guys.

The truth was I was lying to myself and to my friend, for even if I didn't want to look or behave like those girls, I was curious about what they felt. I wanted to be wanted by someone. Who could it be? What was my problem? I did not have a strict family, neither my mother nor my grandparents ever hindered my personal freedoms.

My new stepfather Eddy thought I ought to be having fun in college. He always hinted about parties and boys. He was so excited for me it was like he was the one who was going.

Wild Eddy liked a good time. He was so charming and funny, he even made Liana laugh from time to time.

Eddy had made the scene back in the disco seventies at Studio 54, and he made fun of me for not being young and wild and free. He thought I was too serious, barricaded into my room with my books and my classical music, but he didn't understand. Love seemed safer if all I did was read about it in books. I dreamt about love all the time, wrote poetry full of mystical contradictions. I was a young girl brooding while I waited every day for something wonderful to happen to me.

Eddy, with his experienced eye for the ladies, could not help noticing that I had become, for all the world to see, a young woman of eighteen years. He would roll his blue eyes and shake his head with a smile. I, however, was appalled by my new body, especially my large breasts which felt heavy and clumsy on me, yet curiously were much admired by others. Other girls told me I was "lucky," but the fact that no boy my age ever seemed interested in me I attributed to my unfortunate physique, which continued to grow at an alarming rate. The only looks I got were from middle-aged men, who were not ashamed to look straight at my chest.

I wanted to vanish, but this was not possible. Like all girls I looked at the fashion magazines and adored what I saw: slender, gazelle-like nymphs like my sister's friends, the ballerina sylphs, smirking at me in their fancy clothes. They were the ones everybody said were pretty, even if they were mean, but I wished I could be just a little like them, graceful, athletic, with long legs and small, logically shaped breasts.

If only I could look like that, I thought, I wouldn't be humiliated by those lustful looks I was getting from men in the street.

Like anyone, I wanted to be paid attention to, liked, maybe even loved. I was flattered by the attention I received, even if I mistrusted it. The problem was I had no idea what to do with it. I was invited to go on dates. They were all older, reliable, and Jewish, the kind of man you should marry when you get old enough.

I was flattered when this wonderful young lawyer Alex, who was about twelve years older than me, began inviting me out. He did some legal work for my mother and became her piano student. He was the first one to comment on my blue eyes. I was easily bought. For so long I wanted someone to mention my eyes and since he noticed, I agreed not only to go out with him but also to like him. Later I noticed he was staring at my chest, but at least I was getting his undivided attention. When he went to kiss me, I couldn't do it, even though I knew it was expected. Finally, I did, and I hated it. He really was very patient the way he tried to become my boyfriend. We even went to Russia on his dime, and he respected every inch of my tiresome virginity which I preserved throughout our acquaintance.

My problem was that when I wasn't next to him the idea of him ignited me with feelings I read about in good books. When I saw him, and he tried to kiss me, there were no feelings. Once I went to get out of his car without a goodnight kiss. I thought he might overlook it. I'd been avoiding the subject of romance the whole date, but he had other plans. He stepped out of the car and demanded we kiss properly. "Okay," I said to him, "let's do it, but let's do it fast!" He got offended, of course telling me that we didn't need to do it all.

Later at home, when I had some time to think about it, I felt bad. A nice man wanted to kiss me, but what was wrong with my heart, my mind, my mouth? I was free to do things, and yet I felt no freedom within me. I grew up on Bunin, Guy de Maupassant, Chekhov, Nabokov. They shamelessly dress and undress young girls, women, old maids, only to show us how desperately all these heroines want to expose their bodies and therefore their hearts to men. They all do it so that in the end these men chose these women to be *theirs*. I frequently imagined myself as one of those sensual creatures, coming of age, like little Olga in Bunin's short story "Light Breathing," seduced by an older friend of her father, with a handsome forked white beard. It ends badly for Olga: the young officer she has promised to marry kills her once he finds out about her and the older man, but the seduction scene is dazzling. It made a profound impression on me when I was twelve. That was what I wanted for myself, so effortless, so irresponsible, and yet here all these men were willing to play the other part and I felt nothing but embarrassment and emptiness. I had none of that heroine's will to freedom, none of her feminine sensuality. Like a turtle I hid my head inside my shell as soon as someone tapped on it to get my attention.

Next, I dated an Israeli guy, Noam, who was as Jewish as you could ever want, but almost primitive in his traditional masculinity. He saw my Star of David and decided I was the girl for him. His approach was direct. I noticed how he was looking at me from across the library from where he was sitting. I liked it. Then, he got up and walked over to talk to me. I liked that, too. He was of medium height, thin, yet athletic. He had heavy black eyebrows and large dark eyes that held me in their gaze, both embarrassing and tantalizing. Alex hadn't looked at me like that; he was either too nice or not brave enough. Although he wanted to pretend he was a "bad" boy by talking about his past romantic adventures all the time, he had never put the moves on me the way this guy did.

Noam had been in the Israeli Army. I was rather smitten with that part of his biography. He was the first authentic Israeli I had ever met, and I was dazzled. Since I was little, I'd identified Israel with my Jewishness, and so Israel's people, especially its men, were all Davids, all Solomons, all Sauls to me. I was prepared to fall in love with them all.

He was a virtuous, Persian Israeli immigrant, the first in his family to receive a graduate education. He was getting his MBA. He was the only brother with three sisters, the family's golden child. He studied very hard. Noam was very proper. When he used to pick me up, he always came upstairs to pay his respects to my mother. He was always a little too well-dressed, even on a Saturday night. Perhaps it was because he was an immigrant, and he wanted to show respect, or present a more confident image. One time he asked me to go change from my cool jeans into something dressier. I had spent a lot of time picking out my outfit that night. I was irritated, but I put on a dressier top. I was a good girl who didn't want to upset a nice guy at her mother's house. Sometimes Eddy, with a cigarette in his mouth getting ready for a night at the restaurant, would make an off-color joke, which Noam would studiously ignore, with an uncomfortable smile. We found out later that Eddy was high on cocaine a lot of the time. My mother could never understand what that white powder was on his night table.

Noam tried hard to be romantic, taking me to nice places, giving me flowers and asking me such painfully trite questions as "What was the most adventurous, daring, or romantic thing you ever did?" He desperately wanted to have sex with me, and he desperately wanted to introduce me to his parents, in that order. I found this desperate pushiness aggravating, and then repulsive. He may have thought I was leading him on, and maybe I was. I thought I might come to like him more, perhaps even fall in love with him, because he seemed like a good person, if a bit staid and dull. I waited patiently to fall in love, but it didn't happen.

My grandmother Marina, who had come with her Saul to be with us in New York, told me I needed to relax. She was a woman of great experience, married to a lovely man her whole life, but someone was always in love with her, and she was not a saint, either. She wanted me to experience life with all its tastes and flavors as she had. Every time I got back home from a date, she used to look at me like she was expecting something.

One fall day I was sitting in my organic chemistry class with the sun shining brilliantly through the window, thinking of my doomed youth and sizing up the potential of every male I saw to become the One. With another part of my brain, I was enjoying the class. It reminded me of a jigsaw puzzle where everything made sense; molecules were supposed to match up and make up new molecules, they were naturally attracted. Our friendly professor used multicolored chalk on the green blackboard to make it all less confusing for us. We were about to take our first quiz when a handsome young man walked into the classroom late. He apologized and took a seat in the back of the classroom. He was excessively tanned, dressed in a horrible black leather vest over a spotless white T-shirt that tightly hugged his well-muscled body. He carried a motorcycle helmet. I had never seen him before, and we had already had about five classes. He did not seem to be the One, so I went back to my quiz. He was so hopelessly late, he'd missed so many classes already, why bother take the quiz at all? He was awfully full of himself, with his vest and his helmet, but to my surprise he got up within fifteen minutes of sitting down, submitted his paper and left the classroom, quietly, but with a slight air of cockiness. Everyone else, including me, was still deeply engrossed in their quiz, because organic chemistry is a hard subject. I felt quite at ease with all my formulae and my chemical reactions, but my mind kept wandering back to motorcycle man. *So stuck up, probably thinks everyone is in love with him....I wonder if he is a virgin... unlikely!*

The next class, the quiz grades were back. He was on time. I was so curious to see his grade as I picked up my sheet with the 79 percent. Surely, he had failed. He had been so arrogant. He was polite, said hello to the teacher, found his work and as I squinted, I saw his name and grade on the paper: Daniel Roitman, 99 percent.

My heart skipped a few beats at this negation of all my assumptions, and I felt delightfully intrigued. This Mr. Roitman was apparently a very brilliant fellow, in addition to being Jewish. He was in several of my classes, where he arrived late, left early, took his tests, and generally seemed to excel. He held himself a bit aloof, was casual and polite with everyone. Everyone called him Dan. He was about twenty-five, a little older than the rest of us. He had returned to college after a few years off and was doing his premed requirements so he could apply to medical school. I often saw him outside the building, smoking. He smoked a lot. I considered taking up the habit just to make friends with him. I didn't know how to approach him because I was shy, afraid of boys, and didn't know how to flirt. Meanwhile, I craved to see him every day, even if to simply observe him. From hearing him speak with other people I detected he had a sense of humor. He was funny but not silly, he was caustic, but not at all offensive. He was light. The one time I managed to maneuver myself into a conversation with him, I was utterly tongue-tied and barely made any sense, at least to myself.

Dan became the leader of a small study group. It seemed like he could tutor for hours, he simply wanted those who came to him for help to understand. He made a very peculiar, concerned grimace that made him look like a child. He spoke very little to me. We had so little in common, and yet I felt comfortable sitting with him for hours and laughing at his witty comments. I also aced my exams in organic chemistry that semester.

One day he invited me to come to the gym with him to the famous Vertical Club, the hip gym of the day, just a couple of blocks away from his tiny apartment on the East Side in the fifties. No one else in that place looked like me: Everyone there was toned and tanned in stretchy outfits which left nothing to the imagination. I was wearing my everyday oversized sweat suit which made me look larger than I was, but I didn't care, because I was in *his* presence.

Then he invited me to dinner to an Irish place in his neighborhood. He didn't talk much. Was it because he was bored with me? Was it because he didn't have much to say? Was he shy? Was he studying me? I became aware that I was filling the silence with my nervous chatter. Because he never interrupted me, I thought he was fascinated. I managed to leave the man speechless, I thought. I must be good at this game, I kept thinking as my ego kept outgrowing my heart. He walked me all the way home to Eighty-Fifth and Third. When he said goodbye to me, I opened my mouth again, but he stopped me: "Hey, Anya if we, you, and me, I mean, both of us are going to do this, I got stuff I want to say as well." That was it. No kiss, just a little hug.

It wasn't like in the book, and it was all very strange, but for the rest of my life he defined for me the meaning of falling in love, the essence of passion, and the lonely murmur of heartbreak.

It was late afternoon, and the youthful month of May was smiling at me through his dirty window while we sat on his cheap sofa bed and watched *Seinfeld*, which I thought so funny. Then he began to kiss me. He didn't ask my permission. My left shoulder and the left side of my neck didn't mind because they had waited to be kissed like that for a very long time. He guessed it and continued kissing me like that for a very long time. It tickled a bit, and I tried hard not to laugh, but he noticed, and he turned his head toward me and began kissing me on the mouth. For the first time in my life, it felt right, neither cheap, nor fake. Was it because of his lips? He had perfectly shaped lips, and they pressed against mine effortlessly and unpretentiously.

His hands were all over my breasts, my stomach, and my thighs, and instead of burying myself in shame I began to find tingling delight in his touches and his kisses. I just didn't want him to get bored, I wanted him to continue. I knew what the next thing was going to be, and I was both curious and nervous. Dan was free with me, kissing me everywhere. No one had ever done this to me before. He managed to do all that keeping my clothes on, but then, slowly, he began to unzip my blue dress and to undo my bra. He did everything smoothly, without any awkwardness, but when I was almost naked, I began to feel a bit embarrassed. While I was considering how best to tell him I was a nineteen-and-a-half-year-old virgin, he began getting undressed, and suddenly there he was, naked like Adam. I pretended to be cool, but I had never seen a naked man before. Not in real life.

Now was the time to tell him I was a virgin, so I did. It came as a surprise to him. He took out a cigarette and smoked it, sitting in his bed beside me, staring at me. He smoked it with such devotion, with such hunger, as if it was the last one he would ever enjoy. He finally put it down, laid beside me, smiled and offered me a free anatomy lesson. He was clever, and his sense of humor was seductive, and I laughed and surrendered to him. I had no idea how to have sex, but it had to be done, and now. I knew I was never going to find anybody better than Dan to help me get rid of my virginity. He was going to be my One. He then undressed the rest of me, and there I was for the first time lying in the nude alongside another nude male body. He then proceeded with the most ancient deed of all.

He was definitely not a virgin, but I was the first virgin he ever had. I bit my lips, I tried to appear serene, but it hurt. Nevertheless, I was determined to go through with it, and I craved his attention and his closeness. He promised me that eventually I was going to enjoy it. It was strange, messy, painful, and I felt his presence everywhere. When everything was finished, I felt light and free. While still making love I asked him if he was in love with me. His answer surprised me. He told me he wasn't planning to be my boyfriend. My ego felt a bit bruised, but I was so proud of being able to have sex without it making me feel sick that I didn't dwell on it much at that time. Besides, I saw the way he looked at me, his hands adored me, his lips were in love with my mouth and my whole body, and in his eyes, I read the words I did not need to hear.

I spent the next few years in the ecstatic state of being in love with him, and he was full of passion, but he never gave me a chance to love him the way I wanted to, because every few months he would break up with me. After all, he was not as light as I thought; he had internal conflict, childishness, and struggle. In retrospect, I can see I never loved him but was rather in love with the feeling of being in love with him.

Love cannot be measured, it can't be explained, but it justifies mistakes and beautifies the world. It is bigger than any one person. It is too big, too generic, too ubiquitous of a feeling. Sometimes love can be confused with a habit. We love what we are used to. We can be married to the same person for sixty years, think we love that person, meanwhile it is just a habit of living next to the same dear face, touching the same soft hands, understanding each other's language,

not love at all. Loving each other is safe but it doesn't give you butter-
flies. Only falling in love does. I never loved Dan. I only remember
being desperately in love with him. Being in love means to never
have peace of mind, to always have a knot in your stomach muscles,
to always wonder, to always tremble with anticipation that if he sits
close enough and bits of his clothes touch your exposed skin, he will
then begin his game with you. Being in love means to never be tired
of his cruelty, of his moods, of his exhausting unpredictability. There
is no safety net with falling in love, that's why they call it "falling."
It's an abyss over which the one who is in love hangs suspended
until she or he falls. If the person lands safely then the "in love state"
turns into regular love, and they live happily ever after, forgetting all
about their dangerous passion. If the person who was in love lands
unsuccessfully, it is the heart that breaks.

In the periods between breakups, I got to know Dan well. He
was back in school after having spent the last few years recovering
from a drug addiction and had severe psychological problems as a
result. For a while I couldn't understand the reason for his abrupt
mood swings or his chain cigarette smoking, for his strange way of
being silent and simply staring at me. I had never had a man in my
life before. I never knew what a man did at home on his own, how
he ate, what he drank, what shows he watched, how often he read,
and how he relaxed, how much time he spent in bed, and how often
he made love. I found his smoking to be interesting in general, and
his smoking in bed very sensuous. He drank a lot of beer, and the
taste of beer mixed with cigarettes made my mouth feel cold, and it
excited me.

He had sessions with his therapist a few times a week and he was
dependent on those sessions. He regularly attended his AA meetings. His loyalty to the group could not keep him away from his beer.

He invited me to go with him to some of those meetings, and I went, happy to be included in his world, even if I was bored. I went into Barnes & Noble looking for a book on what it meant to date someone like him, on whether it was a sign of a promising future being invited to an AA meeting by a boyfriend who changes his mind about everything every few hours. On the one hand, it seemed like he was someone from a good family: obviously brilliant and on his way to being a doctor. On the other hand, he'd been addicted to cocaine.

Dan, the child of teenage lovebirds who gave him up for adoption, landed with a well-to-do Jewish couple from Scarsdale who gave him a loving home. I saw his family album. I could tell by the smile on his kind face and by the way he kissed his grandmother. He had a proper bar mitzvah, he went to Israel, he went camping with his family and did well at school. As an adolescent, he got himself involved with the wrong crowd and with all sorts of drugs, especially coke. He ran away from home, lived in all kinds of places, with all sorts of people. He went to college, dropped out, tried to start again. His parents paid for college, and for various treatments and rehabs, none of which did him any good until he overdosed but managed to survive. Finally, it was the Hazelden Rehab Facility in New York City that saved him, he said.

When he told me about it, I wanted to run away. How could I let this person touch me? How could I, brought up with such wisdom and such care, end up with someone like that? I couldn't run, even though the door was closer to me than the bed he was sitting on. I ran into his bed instead.

He was the first man who made me feel regal. I don't remember what it was, the way he talked to me, the way he looked at me, or how his hands, the tips of his fingers touched my face or my neck. Often, I would fall asleep feeling like a queen and wake up to him telling me that he "wasn't ready," because he "couldn't," because he needed to see other people, because I "deserved better." Sometimes he would ask me to come over because he felt lonely, and I would rush to him, breaking commitments with my other dates and my friends only to find traces of perfume in the air, forgotten earrings, mascara in the bathroom. The last time we really got back together was right after we graduated from college. He really wanted to be with me; he even said those heavy, adult words, "I love you." We drove his parents' fancy car to the Hamptons, behaved like adults, spoke of the future, listened to music, spoke of literature, he had read everything. We made love.

In the car on the way back to New York, stuck in a mundane Sunday traffic, he announced he couldn't do it, the thing he thought he could do the day before. I felt as if I was choking on something. It must have been my own tongue because I couldn't speak for some time. The worst part of it was that I was stuck in the car with him, and we were going nowhere. I couldn't understand why he couldn't wait until we got back to the city but now, I understand. He couldn't wait. The desire to be free was bigger than anything else. He needed to let me know he was free right that minute. Freedom can't wait. Many years later I had come to understand the feeling well.

Of course, I was devastated. I was no different than anyone else who had ever been desperately and hopelessly in love. I listened to my mother and to my wise Marina, but they couldn't make me feel any better. I had become physically and emotionally dependent on my Dan. Without Dan in my life, even my recent college graduation did not make sense to me anymore. What would my next step be without Dan by my side? How could I let any other man ever approach me, look at me, touch me, joke with me? They all seemed so simple-minded and trite, so inept, not like men at all. I lost my ability to smile, to be happy, even to be unhappy, because to be unhappy one needs to feel some happiness from time to time. I just felt nothing.

❧

One day I resolved to go to him. I thought I simply needed to tell him once and for all that I loved him. I needed to tell him I was in love with him and beg him to love me back. It was right before Thanksgiving. Rainy. I took a taxi. That charming neighborhood, that sweet street. I buzzed, and miraculously he let me in. He smiled so beautifully when he saw me. I broke into my monologue, pleading with him not to break up with me, reasoning with his mind, hoping to beseech his heart. He was half sitting on his bed, smoking, I was sitting on the floor, holding his hand, kneeling before him, sobbing. I don't remember his exact words, only that they were sweet, heartfelt, kind, but still his verdict was "no." My dazzling, passionate Dan did not choose me.

There I was, broken up with, unwanted, living with my mother, who had also recently become single. Our dashing Ed McCauley had turned out to be an alcoholic and a coke addict, unable to hold on to his cash or his business. He owed money everywhere, and one day some men came to his restaurant and put big, heavy locks on his door. It took a lot of money to get him out of that one, and my mother helped him, but the business was drowning.

It was an unhappy time. Eddy was a very proud man with a big ego. Nothing hurt him more than asking for money early in the morning while his hangover was exacerbated by the memory of the fight he'd had with my mother the night before. Either because she loved him, or because she didn't trust him, she began spending all her evenings with him at the restaurant. She took up smoking and she did not let him have a peaceful existence, watching him like a hawk and giving him a piece of her mind at frequent intervals, especially for his unrestrained flirting with anything in a skirt. Poor Eddy. He had never been married, never had any children he was aware of, and consequently he had never had to answer to anyone, never had to hide anything. He lived the way he breathed: openly. For him, getting married was a heroic mistake.

Eddy had been on the New York scene since the disco days, drinking, doing drugs, and chasing women. He was what is called a "high functioning alcoholic," but I never saw him as a drunk. The Russian fondness for vodka is a cliché, but when I was a kid no one in my family or in our circle of friends drank regularly or to excess. Drinking is not a Jewish thing. We would see drunks in the street, those wasted, clammy, foul-smelling, toothless, bruised up, stuttering creatures; my father told me they were sick.

Our Eddy wasn't like that. Clean, dashing, well dressed, sharp, witty, smelling of expensive cologne, he ran a successful business, knew everyone important. He was kind to his immigrant busboys, always a generous tipper. He opened his heart to us and took us into his home. Some people said we made him look good, but I thought we all looked good together. If he needed us, we also needed him at that time. But as well as he held his liquor, it began to tell on him.

One evening we had some people over for dinner, an English couple. My mother was very excited to receive them, and she cooked a Russian banquet: potatoes and crab salad with sweet peas in special mayo dressing, white fish in tomato sauce, Russian herring with apples and eggs, liver pate, gravlax, homemade caviar blinis, followed by a fish dish, and then a sweet and sour stuffed cabbage. We sat down to eat, and everyone was having a nice time, complimenting my mother on her beautiful food, but Eddy wasn't eating. Sweet

Ginger McCauley, Eddy's beloved Doberman Pinscher, was making the rounds in anticipation of a treat and Eddy, seeing her, took his plate, filled it up with delicacies and set it on the floor for her.

This affront overwhelmed my mother's respect for the rules of etiquette in front of strangers and in her bad English she gave Eddy hell right there and told him everything she thought. How could he give her food to a dog! Our friends calmed her down, told Eddy off, and insisted he apologize, and he complied. We still had a whole dinner to look forward to, there was her apple charlotte for dessert, the aroma of my faraway childhood. Everyone pulled themselves together and we ended up having a nice time, but she never forgot that fight.

They lived in a perpetual state of emotional trouble. In America people call it "toxic." Eddy was a chain smoker and since my mother spent all her time with him, she became one as well. There came a time when she began to consider quitting for her health, she wanted to look young, and the color of her teeth and skin mattered to her a lot. She always had the most beautiful teeth. Out of spite he told her she was never going to be able to quit. When she heard him say that, she was in the midst of enjoying her cigarette. She took it out of her mouth, put it down, and never touched another.

Even when Eddy tried his best to behave himself, my mother still suspected him of mischief, which he blamed on her lack of understanding of Anglo-American culture and she blamed on actual events. Once when we had just moved in with Eddy, we were startled one night by the sound of an unfamiliar female voice shouting abuse, and then the sound of things breaking and smashing and sweet Ginger barking. We rushed out of the room to see a very tall, attractive woman in her early fifties smashing the glasses off Eddy's face, which she proceeded to rake with her fingernails, ripping his shirt. I was shocked to see a crazy woman invade our home and attack our charming man, but it turned out she was not crazy at all. She was his girlfriend, a well-to-do lady who lived in the building. Her name was Brandy and he had neglected to break up with her before he met another woman and moved her and her whole family into his apartment. There was nothing wrong with her, she was just a woman, vulnerable, helpless, justified in her jealous attack as far as I was concerned.

The end came one afternoon when my mother's piano lesson with Alex was interrupted by a process server. This woman banged on the door, thrust legal papers into my mother's hands, and then barged into the apartment pointing at items of furniture and demanding to know who they belonged to. She introduced herself as Eddy's attorney, but my mother recognized her as one of the regulars at Eddy's restaurant. Alex, who was a lawyer, introduced himself and told the lady she was in violation of the rules of professional conduct. Any lawyer could see he was right, so she left when he told her to get out. The papers contained a big fat lawsuit demanding alimony and rights to our Moscow apartment, ridiculous demands. Eddy evidently wanted to use my mother's ignorance in legal matters, her limited English, her overall innocence to his advantage, hoping to scare her into an easy settlement.

In the midst of this, I came home from school. I'd never seen my mother in such a state. She looked humiliated, lost, frightened. I was filled with anger at Eddy for doing this to her. It felt good to be angry. I took the elevator down, walked briskly through the lobby, and then I ran, heart pounding like an Olympian, through a misty rain a few blocks to the restaurant. Eddy was at the bar, a drink in his hand, chatting with one of his new waitresses. Like an eagle, I flew over to him, smashed the drink right out of his hands, grabbed him by his shirt, and with my girly voice in heavily accented English full of hysteria, told him to never dare treat my mother like that again. I felt like I had committed something heroic and unpunishable. I felt everybody was gazing at me, mostly the waitstaff who had known me up to then as a very sweet, polite girl. Fear and doubt overcame me. I ran home.

Legally speaking I had done the wrong thing, and it allowed Eddy to get a temporary restraining order against me and my mother for threatening him. The next thing that happened was he locked us out of the apartment, which was still in his name. We had to go to court to get our toothbrushes back, and a judge gave us a few weeks to find a place of our own.

My mother took this all very hard; it was the notion of divorce itself, the stigma of it. Her entire life she had been a married woman, accustomed to squabbles and infidelity, but divorce was something different. People got divorced in the Soviet Union, but a divorced woman was an abandoned woman. Unless she left her husband for another man and succeeded in marrying him, she was a failure as a woman. People would say: "She should have never left her first husband!" She kept repeating to me: "What would people say?" In our old life in Russia, it was customary to explain oneself to family and friends, one's behavior, feelings, deeds, and misdeeds. This was nothing to do with the USSR, it had to do with Russian culture.

Really, it didn't matter what anyone thought, because this was America, where people get divorced all the time. What my mother really needed was a good lawyer. Alex introduced her to a friend of his, and in the end, Eddy never got a cent from her. The question of "what will people say?" came to have less importance and eventually got resolved on its own.

Eddy was not very popular with the management of the building because he never paid rent on time. But the lady from the real estate company, Rose, had always liked my mother. She knew everything about Eddy's sketchy history with money and women. Officially, there were no apartments available in the building, but when she heard the story about Eddy changing the locks, she took two sets of keys out of her drawer and told my mother: "You pick." America, Russia. Certain things are always the same across the globe. People love a smile, they love charm. It's all about relationships.

My mother and I moved into the new apartment. It was 1997 and I had about four more months of college left. My sister had finished a year dancing for the Kremlin Ballet and was thinking of transferring to her ultimate dream company, the Bolshoi Ballet.

My mother bounced back quickly after her divorce from Eddy. I was there to make sure of it. I would not allow her to spend even one evening at home. She got invited to many parties, she met very respectable men, who invited her on dates—politicians, businessmen, doctors and lawyers, university scholars, all very eligible. Like a hawk I watched these invitations come in and I always made sure she accepted. Soon, as expected, my outgoing mother got back into the swing of things.

Even though Eddy was the cause of a lot of turmoil and unhappiness in our lives, it was he who introduced us to New York City and to lots of people who became our friends. One of the closest to my mother was Denise Rich, a singer-songwriter and one of the most passionate and successful philanthropists of her time. Denise's daughter Gabrielle had died of leukemia when she was only twenty-seven. Denise founded Gabrielle's Angel Foundation for Cancer Research, which has awarded $35 million to over 300 of the top physician-scientists in America. She threw the most fantastic parties, in New

York, the Hamptons, London, in St. Tropez with famous people like Michael Jackson and her very good friend Bill Clinton. At one point, Denise asked my mother if she could use her contacts in Russia to bring someone important to her board, and she got her friend, former President Mikhail Gorbachev, whose wife Raisa had died of leukemia just a few years before. Denise has been our friend for over thirty years, and her personal warmth and kindness have always been a source of support for my mother and for me, first when we knew almost nobody in New York City, and then, later, after my mother's divorce from Eddy. I have seen many society ladies in this glamorous city, but I consider Denise one of New York's truly great ladies.

My mother stopped trying to justify her divorce to other people when it became clear to her it really wasn't such a big deal here. She went on living in the same building as her ex-husband and his ex-girlfriend Brandy, greeting one another occasionally in a very civilized way. In a fatherly tone, he always commented on how thin I was allowing myself to get. When he was too drunk, he even remarked on the disappearance of my large bosoms. He didn't care if the elevator was full of strangers. Sometimes, if we happened to run into Eddy too early in the day, he was less friendly than in the evenings, but we knew by then his disposition depended on his alcohol intake. Eventually, he lost his restaurant. More time passed and we learned he was married to some Polish woman who gave birth to a girl. No one knew for sure whether it was his daughter or not, but he was devoted to her, he took her to school and brought her back home. He must have been in his late seventies then.

The last time I saw him was a few summers ago, on a very hot day, in Midtown on the east side, with a walker. He was barely recognizable. Because I stared at him for a very long time, he looked back and stared back as if trying place me in his memory. His gaze frightened me, and I walked away, clasping my older daughter's hand. He died in New York City during the grim COVID summer of 2020.

At twenty-two, the world seemed to be twirling around me and that included boys. I encouraged their interest. I thought it was shameful to be without male company, I felt lonely and less feminine sitting home alone. I never learned to pick up guys because I never learned how to hang out at bars, didn't like clubs or noisy parties. I met people either through friends, or through my mother.

One sunny morning on Park Avenue, a guy in his early thirties began a friendly conversation. He told me he was a writer, and I wasn't surprised when he commented on my accent and asked me where I was from. The air smelled of dry wind and the sun was showing off its might to the indifferent folk rushing to work. He told me he lived on 13th and University and only came to my "fancy" part of town because he worked as a personal trainer at some exclusive gym on Madison Avenue. He asked me for my phone number, and I hesitated for about five seconds, but I gave it to him.

I knew I wouldn't be an old maid, because the curse of virginity had already been lifted, but I thought I would age before my time without a man in my life. I was not thinking about marriage, but I was thinking of not staying single for too long. His name was Eddy. I didn't like the name, not only because it belonged to my mother's ex-husband, but because it sounded edgy, childish, and flat. It didn't fit the person who was doing his best to charm me. But I wasn't going to get all picky about names. I really wanted someone to start paying attention to me again, and it began to feel like any guy who would smile at me would be good enough. He was nice, polite, he knew how to smile, and he was Jewish. In a couple of weeks, we began to date.

Eddy #2, as I took to thinking of him, had a widowed mother who lived in Westchester, in the same house where he grew up. She was old and sick, walked with a cane and had a handicapped sticker on her car, and kept her children busy catering to her every need. I wasn't a doctor, but I didn't think there was anything wrong with her that losing 100 pounds wouldn't have cured.

Eddy #2 held a master's degree from Columbia University in something having to do with literature, and he lived in a tiny studio which he neglected to clean, like his mother. He told me he had no time to keep things neat and tidy because he was busy writing a play. He even had an agent. To make money in advance of his big break, he worked as a personal trainer to rich people, all of whom he resented except for one very rich fellow named Charles, who was his patron and benefactor. A charming Englishman, he adored the arts and had an enormous family horse farm estate somewhere near Baltimore. Eddy would house-sit for him while he was traveling.

Eddy #2 had a problem with money and social status. Other people had these things, and he didn't, and he resented it. He had a headful of Marxist ideas that had no coherence. If people stood socially above him, or if he decided they did, they became his enemies.

He talked about art and about his soul and the nobility of his position as a starving artist, and yet he was full of materialism and resentment over his lack of financial success.

I did my best pretending to enjoy his work. It was obviously autobiographical, angry characters always lamenting the death of a father, going to Columbia to study writing on a scholarship, confronting the agonizing dilemma of choosing art over money, involved in some trivial love triangle. I didn't think there was anything wrong with the story itself; the irritating part was the dialogue, which sounded dead to me.

When he told me his favorite writer was Dostoyevsky, I was not impressed. Americans love Dostoyevsky because he writes page-turners in the Western style, more accessible to the Western mind than the works of Tolstoy, Turgenev, or Gogol. I had read Dostoyevsky in Russian, but my new boyfriend with his master's from Columbia never asked me what I thought.

I knew he wanted me to see him as he wanted to see himself, but even he knew he wasn't what he pretended to be. His first love was live theatre, of course, but all the money was in television. He swore he was never going to change his style of writing to make it more saleable.

He was vain, whiny, and not very attentive to me, but I decided to ignore all that. I was looking for a repeat of my experience with Dan. Dan was insatiable, both sexually and emotionally. He was genuine in all his spoiled wants, none of it was an act. Somehow, I thought everyone was going to be like that. With time, I had to admit to myself I wasn't falling in love with Eddy #2.

His art-money conflict meant very little to me at the time. I loved the arts, and I grew up with money, and he resented me for it. He thought people with status and money had no right to love and understand the arts. Except for Charles, who caressed his insatiable ego and paid his bills, and in whose case Eddy #2 overlooked all bourgeois defects.

In America, boys who don't want to deal with girls of any complexity call them *high maintenance*. I love the term because it's humorous and vague, so it is almost impossible to insult anybody by referring to them as such. It is almost flattering, as if you were a sports car. He never told me I was high maintenance, but he would have loved to adjust a few things in my behavior so that I did not irritate him so much by resembling my mother, whose contempt for him he sensed, or wrinkling my nose at his dirty apartment.

Now that I think of it, he called me his flower. Even that sounded fake coming out of his pretentious mouth, and certainly he did little to water or care for me. One nice day I came over to his studio, all hot for him. I had on my silky yellow with blue flowers sundress, cute sandals on my feet, and my toes were painted bright red. Everything seemed so light, so happy, so effortless, as I came sashaying into his studio. He was writing. I waited for him to finish, impatient. When he was done writing, he said he wanted to eat. I don't remember now whether on that evening we ordered in or went out to eat. Mistakenly, I thought he would find me sexy, throw his dry burrito away and demand that I make love to him. Instead, he turned on the TV and began his daily catch up with sports. Somehow, I was unable to distract him. He must have seen how adorable I looked in my dress, he even complimented me. We went to bed, watched a movie, I even kissed him timidly, and he said good night.

I thought of the greasy burrito, of the street, and the heat and sports channel, of the fact that I wasn't even in love with him, and I began to feel sick. Without any courage in my voice, I had asked him: "Eddy, do you still like me?" He replied: "Yes." "So, why aren't we making love, why haven't you made love to me tonight? I see you only once a week, and I have to leave tomorrow morning." Instead of a reply, he went to sleep.

In the morning, I tried to smile and be happy, but he barely looked at me. I asked him what the matter was, and he told me he was disgusted with my behavior, and he couldn't even look at me after what I had told him last night. I felt like I had been doused with freezing water: for just a few seconds it numbs your entire body, but then it coats it with security and warmth. I got angry and it felt good. I grabbed my bag and left his place. Yes, I was very high maintenance.

New Year's Eve 1999 was coming, and like all good Russians, my mother and I were planning a big celebration. Karl Marx called religion "the opiate of the masses," and so all religious holidays were canceled; new holidays came to replace the old ones to promote the state's propaganda, so naturally all the joy and humanity was taken out of every celebration. New Year's Eve was the only holiday at which the Soviet citizens had the right to be human. Every family's festive table was overflowing with all kinds of foods. People celebrated all night long, eating, drinking, dancing, singing, joking, laughing, thanking the old year and welcoming the new one. People wore their best clothes, children were allowed to stay up and do all sorts of unforgivable naughty things that children do when adults finally pay no attention to them, and for a little while, the abused citizens of the Soviet Empire would forget about whatever humiliating shortages or Stalinist repressions the year had seen. It was a grim country with grim people, but at New Year's you could see those people sparkle.

My mother, as usual, was going to get all dressed up in her most beautiful clothes and cook her most delicious dishes. She invited Eddy #2 and his older brother Kevin to dinner, and I made it clear they were expected to dress up. Kevin took my request seriously, but Eddy #2 showed up in dirty jeans and a moth-eaten whitish sweater. My mother was dressed like a queen in a long golden gown, Grecian in style, made of some ethereal material. With a grin, Eddy #2 complimented my mother on her outfit, telling her she looked like Cleopatra. He ate my mother's delicious food from her best English china with a terrible appetite, disregarding the extra silverware, squinting and making strange grimaces, hoping to get a similar reaction from his brother every time my mother raised a glass to drink a toast. Kevin sat there eating politely, Eddy #2 couldn't wipe the grin off his face. He must have thought it made him look like one of the sexy characters in his play. My mother played the piano, and Eddy

#2 told her that had he known it was going to be such a glamorous evening he would have dressed appropriately for it.

Obviously, he hated us and everything we represented to him. It had very little to do with us, all we were doing was enjoying our lives as they were. It was ideological. We were class enemies. In the Soviet Union, this term was applied to aristocrats, bourgeoise, clerics, business entrepreneurs, who were accused of being anti-proletariat. It was silly to think of us this way; we were not capitalist oppressors and Eddy was not a worker, he was, like Marx himself, a scrivener with a wealthy benefactor.

One morning he told me: "I know your mother wouldn't be okay with you ending up with someone like me. I don't have the money. I don't mind having more and all that, but what I have now is enough for me. That's how it's going to be. I am not going to sell out." He was right. The more time went on, the more my mother resented him until, after the New Years episode, she only tolerated him because of me. My mother saw him as our *class enemy,* and we were his, but really this was all Eddy's problem. His unsatisfied ego rebelled against our ability to live with pleasure.

Finally, I got a job working at the cash register at the Rizzoli Bookstore on 57th Street. I made six dollars an hour. Rizzoli was a magical place, full of wonderful books. Celebrities came to shop there, and we were expected to behave in a very cool and aloof New York manner with them. My co-workers were eccentric, charming, brilliant, well-read; they all looked like they were born inside that store holding books in their hands, which is why they were working in a bookstore. Americans loved to see a piece of Europe in it, while Europeans saw something of an older America.

I loved it there, but I couldn't turn it into my future. I wanted to be the one buying those beautiful books, not selling them. Working at Rizzoli wasn't what I wanted from life; I needed to go further, even though I had no idea where and how.

I went to a headhunter, gave my speech, and got an entry level job at Morgan Stanley, "a global leader in financial services." It was 1998, and the first tech boom was underway. Morgan Stanley was very generous. I worked in the creative services department, turning the handwritten research of the financial analysts into presentations for the decision makers. That place worked like a conveyer belt, and I was a key link in the chain. There was no room for slip-ups and everyone I dealt with was always stressed and wanted everything done five minutes ago; part of my job was to calm them down. To many analysts I was just a puncher, a nameless face, but others smiled at me, knew my name, talked to me. I pushed their work to be done first. Empowered with a false sense of influence and genuine feeling of gratitude for their kindness, I marked their jobs with my big, fat, red "PRIORITY" stamp. I got promoted at Morgan Stanley; now I was working directly with analysts in their research, and organizing various corporate events. There was more money, and my co-workers were better educated and more polished, but I found investment banking to be dull and ungratifying.

Eddy #2 resented my new job as he resented the entire capitalist society, the rich and the privileged—with the singular exception of Charles—corporate America, my mother's acquaintances, his accurate perception of her view of our relationship. The more he talked, the less desirable I found him. I got bored pretending to be interested in his work anymore, and he detected my indifference. I stopped asking him to allow me to read his pages or for any news from his agent. Some network was interested in one of his works, but they wanted him to make some changes. He was fuming for weeks. His agent did his best to find a compromise, but this was not possible, so the deal never happened.

I wanted to free myself from him. But I had never broken up with a boyfriend before. He wasn't just a date whom I could suddenly stop calling or give a lame excuse about a sudden and indefinite trip to Russia. He was in the process of finishing something big just then, with the promise of an off-Broadway production, and he was nervous. One very late night, after I was finished with my shift, he asked me to come over. When I arrived at his apartment, I noticed that, for the first time, his studio looked immaculately tidy. Even his desk was cleared of all his paperwork; his pencils neatly placed in a mug with the proud label of Columbia University. The kitchen area bore no traces of food. Any cleaning in his modest abode had typically been done by me; I guess he wanted to demonstrate to me he could do it all by himself. He then silently pointed to the bed, which could only mean that he wanted me to sit there. Without looking at me and with a smirk on his face, with half pressed lips, he broke into a monologue about how it was time for us to break up. I was not the girl for him. I was not there to support him in his endeavors, didn't care anything about his feelings. I couldn't believe it. He had beat me to it. I was thinking how best to make my exit when I heard him say something about sex. I must have heard him wrong, but no: he was asking me to have sex with him, just for old times' sake. He had that insincere grin on his face, like some slimy character from one of his plays. I told him he was a very funny person and left.

Outside on the street, I felt exhausted but happy. This entire Eddy #2 situation was something I'd wanted to be rid of for a long time, and suddenly with a strong wind, it was gone. I got a cab back home, feeling tired but not ready to go to sleep. The city was winking at me from every direction, as if approving of my newly found feminine autonomy.

VI.

I Meet a Good Man

Growing up in Russia, I always imagined my life as a sequence of fun and beautiful events in which every person was going to be like a character in some book I had already read. I thought of my future as something as safe and familiar as my sheltered childhood. And when my father told me I would need to rely on myself, especially if I ended up living in America, I decided not to take it to heart. Even when my grandmother Marina, from time to time, in her unapologetic tone, would declare that I had to prepare myself for anything, I laughed and teased her in response. Instead, I chose to believe my mother, who passionately believed that my life was going to be cloudless, not only because of my talents in which she so blindly believed, but also because she promised me that both she and my father were always going to be there to guard my safety and my dreams.

I did my best to become a doctor, as it had been my father's dream for me. I applied to medical schools all over the country. My grades were good, I had done well on organic chemistry, which is known as the class they use to weed out the weaker students. The premedical school committee gave me a fine recommendation, I wrote a good personal statement, but I tripped over the Medical College Admission Test. I could do quizzes, I could write essays, answer questions orally. I had a good memory. Yet, when my knowledge had to be narrowed down to one out of four bubbles, I found myself lost. I took the Stanley Kaplan prep course that everyone takes, practiced taking tests, but I made little progress. Perhaps I didn't know how to study, I focused on the wrong things, and I spent too much time feeling inadequate and petrified of the test and of failure. My scores were not high enough to get me into the school of my choice, or even my second choice. The only one that accepted me was the American University of Medicine in the Caribbean Island of St. Maarten. I refused to go there. In general, Caribbean medical schools do not have good reputations because of the high dropout rates due to a less selective screening process. This meant they tended to accept less prepared candidates. This stigmatized a school like the one I was accepted into, and I knew it was going to create difficulties with job placement in the future.

I could have tried again, but that would have meant an entire year doing the whole application over again, and worst of all, retaking the MCAT. The truth is: I hadn't gone beyond myself to do my best. I was only doing the minimum; I was afraid to give my studies the maximum push because I was afraid that even then, I might not get a high enough score, might have to come to terms with the notion that I simply wasn't as brilliant as my father.

That was the hardest part about giving up on medicine, allowing myself to give up on my father's faith in me. He wanted me to become a doctor. He was convinced I could do it. I watched him work with his patients for years, learning the things they don't teach in medical school. He talked to me about medicine, about his patients, about their illnesses, things he never discussed with his students or with other colleagues.

Maybe if he had lived, he could have helped me overcome the disappointment of my first failure. It was only a test. Any test can be passed, as I later proved with the bar exam. But without him, I was all alone with my fear of inadequacy. Every rejection I took as a personal insult. I felt, discouraged, belittled, the uselessness of my college degree made manifest. Perhaps my experience was not all that unique, but it felt unique to me and not in a good way. It felt lonely. I decided to stop trying.

Much as I thought I wanted it, I must not have wanted it enough. Giving up on medical school caused me to shed many tears. I knew I was betraying my father, disappointing my mother. She told me I was wonderful, but the test told me I was not good enough, and the world believed the test, not her. I had to accept it, and I had to make my mother accept it as well. The notion of giving up on something was painful, but at the same time, as I realized later, I wasn't lamenting that actual *something*. It was hard to admit it to myself, but I could live without becoming a doctor.

As a matter of fact, I had changed my major to art history from natural sciences in my junior year in college. It was just at that time I hadn't made up my mind about medical school yet. In Russia, art was everywhere, my eyes never distinguished it from anything else I was surrounded by. In New York, eccentricity was everywhere, but that was not always art. Art you had to look for. I had always loved museums and galleries, they were part of my early training as a cultured Russian person, but I wanted to be more than just an idle lover of the arts.

I thought with a master's degree in art history I could get a job curating collections at famous galleries and museums. I mentioned that idea to one of my mother's very practical friends, and he poured a bucket of ice water over it, even going so far as to tell me it was childish. He said I was never going to get a job like that and even if I did, I was never going to make any money. If this was what I wanted, he said, I should have thought about it in college, gotten myself an unpaid internship at some gallery, made friends and connections in the art world to get my foot in some door. None of this had occurred to me. He painted a very dull picture of my artistic future which led me to conclude going to graduate school would have been a complete waste of time and money. I tried to get my foot in a door, like he said, but everywhere I went I was politely told I had no experience. Where I was supposed to get that experience was not explained. Was I supposed to open a gallery in my apartment?

Becoming an actress, the dream of my childhood, also seemed out of reach. When I was a little girl, someone old and wise told me that I belonged on stage. It stuck with me. I loved attention, and my body quivered every time I came up on stage to recite a poem, act, or dance. I belonged to various theatre clubs, I won contests and competitions back in Russia. But I didn't just want to become an actress, I wanted to become a star. This was vain. When I came to America and found out that I would have to wait tables to support my passion, I had no spirit for it and decided to give it up. I was weak, or, unlike my sister with her ballet, I just didn't want it enough. After the medical school debacle, I found myself, for the first time in my life, without a goal. My friends all had jobs and internships, they were starting their careers, but not me.

I always worked whenever I could. I was living at home with my mother and always felt guilty if I couldn't make even a little bit of money. I wanted to be helpful, and I also wanted to be like everyone else, but I never liked the actual act of doing work as such, and I never liked being a "rabotnik," an employee. In Russian the root of the word "*rab*" or "rabot" originates from the word *slave*.

When someone says "work," I think of supervision, power of authority over me. Work, jobs, employment, responsibility, authority—those are pious words, and I have always despised them. Work without supervision pleases me, but it rarely pays. Supervision takes away freedom. It matters not whether one's collar is white or blue, because if one has to obey authority in order to be paid, one is not free. Making money is an obligation because without money one cannot survive, so one is obliged to work, which at base is an agreement to exchange time, which everyone has in equal measure, for money, which some people have more of than others. The time and freedom to do what one wants can only be bought. This is the paradox. Some people resolve it better than others.

My mother was no help at all. She thought I was the embodiment of perfection and could not have cared less whether I had a job or not. She knew that eventually I was going to land something great; she blindly believed in my star. Her constant praise of my small achievements made me feel even more undeserving than I already felt I was. Maybe she was just waiting for me to get married. Her friends might have helped me, but I was too shy to ask. My mother had no problem asking on my behalf, but that meant we would have to be grateful to those people, and I desperately wanted to stay clear of being grateful to strangers. This was wrongheaded of me. Nobody gets ahead without help, and people like to work with people they trust, friends, family, friends of the family, and the family of friends. This is how it worked in Russia, and my mother understood it is how it works here, too. People did favors for her, and she did favors for people. She had learned the skill of saying "thank you." I, on the other hand, had no idea how to be grateful to people. I wanted to be free. This was a misguided notion, but my mother did not press me on it.

I'd abandoned my other dreams, but I didn't have a new one. Perhaps I was not imaginative or bold enough. I began to think about law school, perhaps as a substitute for a dream. My contemporaries at Morgan Stanley with fancy graduate degrees, especially law degrees, seemed to have more options. People told me I was a good public speaker. I was argumentative, and I had opinions. It might be a little like being an actress, although I suspected a bit duller. I knew nothing about the law, but law school became my answer. Law school was going to save me. Three years of law school was going to buy me time, like an extra-large bandage which I could apply over my innate flaws. It could become my cave for the next three years while I considered difficult and abstract questions.

In the summer of 1998, I was still going out with Eddy #2. My mother could barely stand the sight of him and had come out in the open about it. She had a friend by the name of Aaron, a nosy but kindhearted fellow, and as old people have done since the beginning of time, he played matchmaker, telling her about this nice young man he knew. He invited my mother to a meeting of the New York Toastmasters, a very American organization all about self-improvement and overcoming your shortcomings. When she came home that evening, she couldn't stop talking about Samuel. Samuel was a businessman, a striver, in his early thirties. He came from a very respectable traditional Jewish family on Long Island. She said he had an open face, was courteous and very inquisitive about her daughters, especially the older one. He had suggested we all meet up within a week and go out to a nice club.

In Yiddish, they call this a *shidduch*, an arranged marriage, and I was having no part of it. I knew my mother meant well, but Eddy #2 was my bad boyfriend. I'd found him myself, and I would decide on my terms, my own way, when to dump him. "I am not asking you to fall in love with Samuel," my mother said. "Just keep your eyes open, go out, have fun, he seems nice."

One Thursday night Samuel called me up from some noisy place. He was with a bunch of people, including his friend Joel, and did I want to come out? I declined. He insisted, in a joking and gentle way that was charming. He said to bring my sister, who was visiting from Russia. I relented, and once I got all dressed and ready to go, I felt ready to face the world with my eyes open.

The place was somewhere downtown. Once we got inside, I recognized him right away, or perhaps he recognized us. He had a trustworthy, virtuous face, I remembered hearing my mother's words somewhere inside my head. He was very tall, about six foot four, taller than anyone I had ever dated. He was wearing a gray suit, with a shirt and tie, already loosened up by the time we got there. When he spotted us, his gray eyes began to smile and his long arms started to make waving gestures signaling to us his welcome. He had kind eyes, and my mother was right, he had an open, honest face.

Samuel was striking to look at. He was a Jew of Austro-Hungarian descent, with deep set gray-blue eyes and a thin face with high cheekbones. He was only in his early thirties, but his hair had a lot of gray in it already, making him look a bit aristocratic. Nothing was hidden beneath that handsome face; everything I needed to know was right there where I could see it. I immediately felt at ease.

As was usually case with me, his good looks and flattery prompted me to switch on my charm. For about an hour I forgot all about my brooding boyfriend back in his apartment. I wanted to dance, and so we danced. I am a good dancer, always have been. Samuel danced enthusiastically but without any logic, swaying his long limbs in all four directions, happily stomping his feet on the floor, letting his tie do its own dancing around his neck. He looked very happy. We sat down again and talked some more. I couldn't hear very well because of the noise but I learned he grew up on Long Island, in New Hyde

Park, a middle-class suburb with good public schools and a strong Jewish presence in the Shelter Rock Jewish Center. Everybody knew everyone else in that tight community; thirty years later he was still friends with the same guys he had gone to school with.

Samuel's family on his mother's side had been in America for four generations, his great-grandfather had a candy stand on First Avenue and worked around the clock, except when he went home to observe the Sabbath. His grandfather had built a successful scrap metal business from nothing. Grandpa Benjamin had been the patriarch of the family, and I heard many stories of his honesty, work ethic, loyalty to family and faith, and unwavering support of the State of Israel. Samuel's father's side of the family had a wicker furniture business with a store in Midtown, which his father, George, continued to run. His mother, Esther, worked as an advertising manager for *The Garden City News* while raising Samuel, his older brother, and younger sister.

After graduating from Hofstra University, he worked on the New York Stock Exchange, and by the time I met him, he was trying to develop his own business in promotional marketing. It was a little difficult for me to understand what he did, but it sounded good.

He seemed almost too good to be true, not at all intimidating, and I decided to play with him a little bit. When he asked me what I was doing the upcoming weekend, I blurted out I was hanging out with my boyfriend. I hadn't mentioned that useless Eddy #2 because I didn't want to spoil my fun with this nice Samuel. I had noticed a long time ago that many American men stop trying to woo you the instant you mention to them you have a boyfriend. Most Russian men, on the other hand, will not be deterred by the competition, even if it is a husband. Most American men want to play it safe; they might take calculated risks when it comes to business, but they rarely gamble when it comes to personal life. Their excuse is that they don't want to waste time; time is money. In America everything is money. I may even agree with that, but some women are worth it. Love is worth it, even if it betrays you in the end. In my view, a man who waits for a woman to break up with her boyfriend or with her husband before he can claim her and own her is only half a man, so I was encouraged when Samuel laughed it off and told me it was not a problem. I felt a little foolish, but still intrigued, so about one week later I called him at the number he gave me.

Generally, I am a traditionalist. A Russian traditionalist. A man should be the one to ask a woman on a date. A man should always make a first move, be it kissing or more. A man should always be the one who pays for a drink or for dinner. This is how it's always been. Rules can be altered very carefully sometimes, just to add some spice to the game, not to change it. Every time a woman changes the game, she appears desperate and ends up humiliating herself. Men love the chase, and it should be left to them. A woman should never chase.

I had this self-centered habit of throwing huge birthday parties for myself. My father always made a big deal about my birthday, and since he'd been gone, my mother and grandmother had kept up the tradition; they cooked a royal feast and we invited everyone we knew. It was very Russian, people made speeches, my grandmother played the piano and sang and the Russians all laughed and felt like they never had to leave, and everyone felt wonderful, especially me. I was excited to have Samuel come to my party that year, but his grandfather was dying, and he couldn't make it.

He always seemed happy to hear from me, and I enjoyed an occasional day with him; we met for lunch or for a walk in the park. Often, he carried his basketball with him, he liked to play with his friends. He kept it light; we talked about anything I liked.

Then, I didn't see Samuel for a while. Eddy #2 had dumped me before I could do the same to him, and I enjoyed my newly found freedom. I went on some dates, but nothing seemed to click. I wanted someone good, someone reliable, someone I could get married to at some point.

All this being said, I dialed Samuel's number. For the first time in my dealings with men, I didn't feel nervous at all. My instinct was telling me he could still like me, and indeed he was elated to hear my voice. Encouraged, I proceeded with my questioning; was he dating anybody special. He wasn't. "You must have been waiting for me," I replied. We laughed, then arranged for our first date. It was March, college basketball season, and his friends were gathering at some bar to watch the game. Afterward, we could have dinner together.

Samuel was so kind and so attentive to me, so light and easygoing. I didn't drink anything, but I enjoyed smoking my cigarettes, the only bad habit I had. That was the bit of Dan I took with me; each time I inhaled I thought of him, but only for the first drag. Samuel almost avoided flirting with me, which I found a bit disappointing, but liberating at the same time. On the one hand it was a date, but on the other hand I felt free to talk, smile, and flirt with whomever I wanted. I did not yet belong to anyone, but at the same time I felt secure in knowing I was already admired by at least one person in the room. The basketball game was finally over, and we headed downtown, together with his nice friends.

At dinner, he put his arm around me a few times, touched me a little, and it made me happy. We left the place, and it began to rain. His friends seemed to disappear into the darkness. The moment of awkwardness was approaching. I found myself at a loss. He wasn't going to make a move. He wasn't going to take me in his arms and kiss me without my permission. A simple kiss was waiting for its grand entrance, and no one was opening a door for it. A first kiss is something that needs to be overcome, survived, and endured. Sometimes it is tender, sometimes it is clumsy, and most often it is both. My shyness and impatience were eating me alive as we were walking in that warm rain. I followed my intuition and turned my face toward his and kissed him. He kissed me back.

We began dating. It was easy. He never played any dating games with me. He introduced me to his family: the old folks, his sister and brother, a multitude of uncles, aunts, and cousins. They were all very close and I was invited to an endless succession of summer barbecues, Thanksgiving dinners, Jewish holidays at home and in the synagogue with the entire shul *mishpacha*.

His father was quiet and modest, economical with words as well as with his opinions. His mother, on the other hand, always made sure her voice was heard. They were good-looking people, all tall with those clear blue eyes, and they all smiled at me openly without reservation, inviting me into the family.

At one cookout in their perfect suburban backyard, a lawyer friend of the family began to cross-examine me. I think Samuel was a bit nervous, but I always loved attention and I sensed that his family wanted to like me. There was nothing not to like about me, especially when I was in a good mood, and I told my story well. I was aware they were sizing me up as a potential bride, and I felt confident because not only was I Jewish, but I was also Russian Jewish. Eventually they met my family, and everyone got along so well it felt like I was gaining a new family, even though Samuel and I were nowhere near that serious.

For a very long time I could not get used to the fact that Samuel just wanted to be with me. I kept waiting for him to break up with me the way others did, but he stuck around. Our dating was remarkably peaceful, free of turmoil, squabbles, and fireworks. I liked his straight-forward way of thinking, his almost one-dimensional approach to things. It didn't bother me that he was not a poetic type. He didn't care for classical music or for the arts. He didn't mind going to a concert or attending an exhibit, but his peaceful heart remained at peace with or without the sounds of Verdi's *Requiem*. He didn't read things I read, and he didn't like to argue. Back then it didn't matter to me. I had already dated a few capricious self-absorbed bohemian philosophers.

No one called him Samuel, he was always Sam. So, I began to call him Sam as well. He wanted to be everyone's friend. He talked to everybody, waiters, doormen, bus and taxi drivers, homeless people, rich businessmen, mothers with strollers, anybody who agreed to say more than "hi." At first, I used to think it was charming, entertaining, a breath of fresh air, truly American. He gave people advice on how to run their small businesses, pubs, restaurants, bodegas, shops, which was not always kindly received. He told me it was good for his business, although I didn't see how.

He was always working on building his business. He didn't have an apartment in the city; he was living on Long Island to save money. He was very careful with money. My traditional sensibilities were offended when we had to split the tab at a restaurant, but I knew he needed to save for his business, so I chose to close my eyes on it.

Sometimes when his grandmother went to stay in California for a few months, she would ask Sam to live in her magnificent apartment on Sutton Place, where the doormen wore white gloves, and cheerful elevator men pushed buttons to get me to the apartment and back to the ground floor. I loved the luxury of it all. Whenever his stay on 54th Street came to an end, and he would have to retreat to Long

Island, I would get sad about the status of our relationship. It felt strange, unreal, almost childish.

Sam wanted to be independent. He didn't want to work for anybody, not even for his family. He never wanted to be an employee, which was something I sympathized with, having inherited a visceral loathing of authority from both my parents. But I couldn't quite understand the nature of his business, or why it didn't seem to be making enough money that he had to ask me to split the tab and make me feel like I was half a woman. Because I liked him, because I didn't want to lose him, I didn't press him, but I wondered: was he broke, or just cheap? Either answer would have been problematic, so it was easier to pretend none of those questions existed and even if they did, that it didn't matter.

Most working American girls my age would not have been bothered with these questions. I have seen many Americans, so I should have been used to it by now, but I wasn't. I was not an American, even after years of living in this country. The entire philosophy of equal financial responsibility between men and women not only irritated me on a theoretical level but it made me feel less of a woman. While I do believe in everyone's freedom of choice, I simply do not believe in equality between the sexes.

Men and women are not equal because they are made differently; biology once and for all had determined the difference between female and male psychology, their emotional state of mind, their free will. I don't argue against women's right to choose, or the right to have an equal opportunity with man. They should, if only to prove to themselves and to the world that they are not as good as men in many things they so brazenly claim to be. The same rule, theory, applies to men as well. No matter how many hours an average woman spends at the gym perfecting her strength, or working on her muscles with some guru trainer, she will never be as strong an athlete as an average man, because she was born with a different physique. Two female hormones control women's life: estrogen and progesterone. While on the one hand estrogen increases the brain serotonin levels, which are responsible for happiness, it is also wickedly linked to mood disruptions that come to us either in the form of PMS, postpartum depression, and depression linked to menopause. It is not a matter of opinion but a matter of fact that estrogen plays such a dominant part in a woman's sexual and reproductive system and is a major player in regulating moods, because it plays one of the major roles in the brain, which controls our emotions, a woman's emotions. An average woman lives her life in between three physical realities, all of which are deeply connected to her hormonal cycle: premenstrual reality, postpartum reality, and menopausal reality. Ninety percent of women experience premenstrual syndrome, which in some cases is so severe that it interferes with their quality of life. Countless women with postpartum depression have been known to either take their own lives, the lives of their children, or both. The same female hormone even affects the psyche of women who are about to enter menopause. A woman's entire existence on Earth is governed by this chemical. After this, how can women claim that they are equal to men? Aristotle was correct in believing that men and women are not only different physically, but also mentally; that women are "more mischievous, less simple, more impulsive . . . more compassionate . . . more easily moved to tears . . . more jealous, more querulous, more apt to scold and to strike . . . more prone to despondency and less hopeful . . . more void of shame or self-respect, falser of speech, more deceptive, of more retentive memory [and] . . . also more wakeful; more shrinking [and] more difficult to rouse to action" than men. Aristotle knew nothing about hormones, or about the ratio of estrogen in women versus men and how it affects the brain and body of both sexes. Should women be given a chance to explore their insanity, capriciousness, and perhaps, their skills, gifts, even genius? Yes, absolutely. Very often however, when a woman goes on her expedition thinking she is ready to win over the world on par with her male counterpart, she is soon disappointed. Her biological needs, her intellectual wants, and her emotional hysteria provoked by consistent hormonal imbalances often cause a lot of dissatisfaction and resentment throughout her life.

Most women know they will have to produce a family, and what's more unsettling is that most women know they will want to produce the family almost as much or even more than they ever wanted to prove to themselves and everyone else that they could be equal with men in the career race. It is only a matter of time before even the most ambitious, most talented, most special, most progressive women begin to adjust their formidable careers because their hormones tell them so. Some women self-righteously demand that the entire industry adapt to their maternal needs, some simply decide to reluctantly part with their career recognizing the impossibility of prioritizing without going completely crazy. At home, educated, and, what's more, talented women frequently fail in dedicating themselves equally to their home and to their beloved careers. Whenever you split anything, you never take the full benefit of the whole, and you can never dedicate yourself completely to either. Choice and opportunities, and especially the most manipulative claim that this ability to choose will make women equal to men, has turned women's existence into agony. Most women want a husband, most want children; their body prepares them for it since birth; women not only want to give birth to their babies, but they also want to care for them and give them their whole soul. A man does not have to make that choice. His manhood is in his professional success everything else is a sweet, yet unnecessary addition to his personality. It is very different for a woman. If we are talking about a woman who at some point had set out to do something extraordinary or prove either to herself or to the world that she is as good as a man, she will have to change her nature, not the environment.

I don't mind having a choice, I don't mind other women having one either. As a matter of fact, I always enjoy doing whatever I enjoy doing at any given moment, but this freedom, this ability to choose, this opportunity to be equal to men does not and will never make me equal to the male sex. I hope that when a man goes to bed wanting to make love to me it is not because he finds me equal to him but because he finds me unequal to him in everything and because I stimulate in him nothing but his old-fashioned male desire. Women would have much easier time being women if they understood the scope of their boundaries. The same is true of the opposite sex.

I grew up in a society where women were educated on par with men, and where they had no choice but to work and nobody had any money to go out, but even so, it was unheard of for a man to offer to split the bill. In the Soviet Union, despite being deprived of makeup and beautiful clothes, women never seemed to lose their femininity. In America, on the other hand, while striving to achieve equal education and career opportunities with men, women forgot, some purposefully and some unconsciously, about their feminine privilege. American men don't have to try as hard; they don't seduce as elegantly but it doesn't cost so much. Cheap is cheap.

One day as we were walking to his grandmother's home on Sutton Place, Sam asked me how I was planning to pay for law school. Objectively speaking, it was not an unfair question, but I felt as if I was being tested. I was midway through the unpleasant process of admission and had already taken my LSATs. I knew how expensive law school could be, but surely it must be worth it, for the degree that symbolized your worth as an individual and entitled you to charge for it. My education had always been my mother's responsibility and I assumed this would continue because nobody in my family ever questioned the value of education. My father hired tutors, who bored me, but he insisted, and I obeyed. He said the only thing worth spending money on was knowledge. I couldn't understand why Sam, my boyfriend, my lover, was so concerned about such a boring issue.

The question of "how I was going to pay for law school" interested me far less than the subject of how I was going to get into law school.

I applied to very few law schools. I applied to New York Law School, Cardoso Law School, Hofstra, Pace Law, and perhaps one more. They weren't fancy law schools, but a law degree is a law degree. I remember the day I received a huge envelope from Pace Law School. I knew all about the sanctity of large envelopes, and the wretchedness of small ones. I had a date with Sam that night, so I waited and opened it in front of him and read him the words that I was accepted. In a couple of days, another large envelope arrived, and then another one. It was a new experience for me to have my pick, and I picked Pace Law School because it was the first one to say "yes" to me and I immediately accepted before they could change their mind.

My mother was going to help me pay for my first year; I was also planning to take out loans, like most people applying to law schools and medical schools. Everyone I knew was doing the same thing. Sam was perplexed. "How are you going to pay it back? Are you sure?"

"Sam, how is everybody paying it back? By getting a job! I got into law school! Have you any idea how difficult it is?" If he didn't, he should have, he'd driven me to the test, seen what a wreck I'd been about it, but now finally, it was beginning to feel like my immigrant dream was taking shape. I was beginning to feel that I could straighten my back, take a deep breath, and press a "go" button. With law school, my healthy family, and my solid boyfriend, things were looking up for me.

Samuel was sweet and there was no doubt he cared very much for me, but sometimes I felt that he neither understood me, nor the things that were part of my small universe. His hobbies were playing and watching sports, he was inspired by stories of famous athletes and how they overcame adversity. He liked motivational speakers, especially Tony Robbins, known for his infomercials, seminars, and self-help books including *Unlimited Power* and *Awaken the Giant Within*. I had no idea who Tony Robbins was. Samuel attended his seminars, during one of which Robbins walked on hot coals.

Sam's reading consisted almost entirely of self-help books, biographies of athletes and famous business figures. Sometimes he would cut out a phrase or a tag line from an article and put it on his wall. All those one-liners sounded strong and heroic, straightforward and positive, but they felt vacuous and superficial because these were other people's words, like Eleanor Roosevelt: "No one can make you feel inferior without your consent." To understand the meaning of Eleanor Roosevelt's words, you have to understand her life as she lived it, one of the most skillful public personalities of her day, yet full of self-doubt and insecurity.

So much of what Sam admired was about overcoming human weakness, achieving strength, and winning. Everything was about people's superhuman ability to be human. When things go wrong, inspirational quotes are not much use. What about human vulnerabilities? People cannot forget mistakes; it is only because they remember the pain caused by their mistakes that they are able to learn their lessons, if at all.

It took me years to be able to see this.

This was another thing I chose to ignore. In the early stages of our relationship, I found Sam's approach to things amusing, sometimes a little bit childish, but never frustrating. Samuel was peaceful, he was kind, he wanted me, he was not interested in anyone else. Was Samuel then the one for me? Yes, in those days I thought he was. My inexperienced eyes saw no one else.

I was warned that law school was going to be hard, but I had no idea how hard it would be when I began in the fall of 2000. It was the most humbling experience I had ever had, and it made me ask myself whether I had overestimated my intellectual and emotional abilities when I decided to apply.

The first thing they tell you in law school is: this is where you learn to think like a lawyer. Things I learned in college, philosophical concepts like the notion of truth, my personal opinions, were of no consequence and had to be discarded. I had to learn how to read all over again, to figure out what was relevant and what was a distraction that could confuse the case and damage the outcome. The law was taught with real cases, either correctly decided or not, and within those cases we learned to identify and distinguish facts, issues, the letter of the law, and the courts' decisions about how it should be applied. My law experience consisted of what seemed to be infinite hours of reading and analyzing cases on property law, torts, criminal law, constitutional law, contracts, civil procedure, all in an effort to train our minds to think like lawyers.

Many people do not survive the first semester. No secondary education prepares you for the monumental amount of work, including the intimidating Socratic method, awaiting you in law school. Some of my fellow students had perfect 4.0 GPAs in college, others were street-smart middle-aged business owners tired of spending money on lawyers, all smart people, but I remember their lost, indignant faces every time they got told they were wrong.

Few people make it through law school without joining a study group. It was all about survival, like trying to jump onto the last car of an accelerating train. It was up to me to speed up, not for the train to slow down. In that meticulous, grueling routine one learns about friendship, as well as about oneself in the most prosaic and in the most poetic way. At first, I found it impossible to be in a study group because I was so far behind everyone else. When we gathered to read from the outlines, the only thing I understood was that all the others understood one another and could see things I could not in the material. They tried to help me out, but it was hopeless. Three weeks before my first finals, sitting in that room, their voices stopped making sense, words became indistinguishable, everything became muffled. I couldn't even tell whether we were covering torts or criminal law. Hopeless tightness in my throat forced me to get up, and I left my study group. Out on 57th Street it was a beautiful day, and people all around me looked unforgivably happy. Tears were rolling down my face.

I survived my first semester of law school. My exam results weren't brilliant, but I didn't fail, and I didn't quit. Eventually, I ended up doing very well, but I never forgot the sense of intellectual isolation I experienced during my first few months.

Sam, once he got over the fear of student loans, was excited and proud about my whole law school thing, and helped me with enthusiasm and humor, playing the bailiff at my moot court arguments. When we needed someone to play a female witness for another assignment, he cheerfully stepped in. He gave me countless pep talks about famous athletes or business leaders, cut out newspaper articles for me with one-liners highlighted in yellow which were supposed to help me find my inner strength. I never understood what "inner strength" was, or where I was supposed to find it if I ever had it, but his positive energy touched me deeply and I couldn't help but feel lucky.

Sam and his very good-looking business partner, Lenny, used to go out a lot to meet with marketing people, vendors, potential clients. They met at restaurants, at bars, at people's offices, even at people's homes, and business mixed with pleasure. I always knew where Sam was, and even who he was with, but I began to resent his social lifestyle and my self-imposed lack of freedom with my law studies. I felt miserable and unfree. Why was he allowed to enjoy himself, while I did not allow myself to have any break? I was told that if I wanted to make it through the first year of law school, I had to suffer, so I was suffering. While I was sitting at home surrounded by books, trying to decipher my own illegible notes, Sam was enjoying himself building networks, giving pep talks, even flirting. I knew he was doing business, but the nature of his meetings was very social, so how "business" could it really be? Today all this looks funny, but back then, at twenty-three, I thought my life consisted of books, tests, and losing control of my boyfriend.

As if that was not enough, I began wondering about marriage. Everyone around me was either married or getting engaged with lightning speed. Some of Sam's friends were already having children. I knew that the second that tiny marriage worm got into my brain, it was there to stay permanently. The question of marriage wasn't just a curious thought—it turned into a poisonous obsession. Obviously, I wanted him to be the first one to think of marriage, because for me, it should be the man who asks the woman.

The demon of impatience had overtaken me, and I approached Sam with my serious question about whether he was thinking of.... of....of getting married? God! It was so embarrassing to be asking something like that, an offense to all my illusions about love and marriage. Later, his friends' wives, all those nice women with impressive diamonds on their manicured fingers, told me they, too, had to be the initiators of the marriage conversation. Sam seemed unshaken, and not displeased by my question. There was no sign of any awareness on his part that he should have been the one to bring it up. He told me we were moving in the right direction. Yes, after over a year together, sleeping together, going away together, being introduced to each other's parents and grandparents, siblings, uncles and aunts, and cousins, we were solidly moving in the right direction. Just that once, my sense of romanticism and pride were satisfied, but just that once. Innocently and cluelessly I thought I would never have to raise the subject again.

Just then, Sam's mom, Esther, got sick. It was stage four lymphoma, and the prognosis was not good. Sam was always very close to her. He was the middle child, five years older than his boisterous younger sister Debbie, and five years younger than his rascally older brother Jacob. In moments of family crisis, Esther relied on her diplomatic Sam. He never caused her much trouble, never got into drugs, or drinking, didn't even smoke, in contrast to his playboy troublemaking brother and his fun-loving sister. Sam was always much softer and much more tender with her.

It was a very rare type of lymphoma, and the situation looked desperate. Within a week, she began aggressive treatment at Memorial

Sloan Kettering. Until then, I never saw Sam get upset, but now he was distraught. I never had anybody so close to me suffer like that. Suddenly, I needed to put away my own convenience and my emotional concerns, and simply make myself useful. I wasn't really part of the family, and it was their private nightmare of disease, uncertainty, and numbing fear of imminent death. Who was I to intrude? Some girlfriend.

Esther's first chemo was scheduled. She was frightened but kept a courageous face. I wanted to be there for her, at least at the beginning, but I had no idea how the family was going to react to my presence. I thought about my father, and decided he would have done what he honestly felt in that situation. I liked Esther, I felt for her, and I thought she was going to be lonely and scared sitting there all by herself. I had no idea who else was going to be there, but I knew I wanted to be there, and nothing else mattered. I often ask myself whether my behavior back then was initiated by self-interest. Perhaps. But my self-interest arose from the need and deep desire to be loved and accepted by the family I adored. I found out the exact time and walked into the room when the nurses were getting her prepped for her first dose of chemo. The room was white, deprived of wellness but filled with fake neutrality. She looked like she was happy to see me, and that was enough for me. It took months of agonizingly painful chemo treatments and radiation therapy but against everyone's expectations, Esther not only got better, but reached remission. It has been over twenty years since her diagnosis, she has overcome many things, and life has been good to her.

My grandparents were getting older. The grandeur of their past was a memory, and now they were immigrants in America. As I see it now, their sense of self-worth remained in Russia. My grandfather Saul, already in his eighties when they arrived, never learned to speak English. True to his aristocratic self, he thought it was his duty to learn how to say "thank you" and "excuse me" but that was about as far as it went. My grandmother Marina, thirteen years younger, was much more willing than her beloved to learn English. She signed up for an intensive course of classes, which required her to complete homework, and soon became proficient enough for them both. They enjoyed themselves here, with old friends and relatives in New York, Boston, and Los Angeles who had immigrated years before them. My grandmother made new friends wherever she went. Their Russian fame traveled with them. People remembered them, and that made their lives in this country much more meaningful and entertaining. My grandparents' spirit never diminished with age. It was this very spirit that had carried them through the war, through the Leningrad siege, through the purges and through stagnation. Immigration did not crush them.

Torn from their magnificent Leningrad, from their privileged lifestyle, they accepted the new world with the most genuine happiness. Marina couldn't just be satisfied living a senior citizen's life the way her friends did. Her essence craved to be on stage. Whenever she could, she managed to perform at different Jewish Centers, synagogues, clubs, restaurants, and various events; she never turned down an offer. She just needed to hear the audience, she desired to hear that anticipated ovation, and most of all the sound of music as its unearthly electrons traveled through her thick fingers. No matter how snooty the restaurant, if there was a piano, she would march over to the tranquil looking pianist in his cute tuxedo and in her imposingly charming alien English would seat herself next to him and begin her show, upstaging him effectively and without remorse. People who didn't come to restaurants to listen to music were forced to stop eating and listen to an elderly lady in her bright, extravagant clothes with jet black hair and red lipstick. Her repertoire was vast, and she knew her audience; she played classics, jazz, blues, old standards from the forties and the fifties. What she didn't know, she could pick up from a couple of notes sung to her by the crowd. I witnessed fancy customers forgetting themselves and their manners; they couldn't get enough of my magnificent grandmother. During those moments, nobody adored and loved her more than her Saul. Like a king, he sat calmly in his chair, his back straight and his head held high, his index finger and his thumb supporting the noble bones of his face.

When my grandmother came to America, she found her friends living adapted versions of Russian lives. Her lifelong friends did not bother themselves with cooking and receiving guests as much anymore. They either bought prepared or half-prepared foods from grand Russian supermarkets, or they invited everybody to huge Soviet style banquets in some kitschy venue in Brooklyn or Queens. My grandmother still shopped, the way she did in Leningrad, and threw parties, cooking everything from scratch for twenty or more people, the way she did back home. She was scolded, criticized, and envied for staying true to her skills, for not giving in, for not adapting. She was also revered by the same people who criticized her.

She even made her own vodka. She would buy a bottle of regular Stolichnaya; to it she added her own concoction, the cranberry compote, which she cooked slowly, mixing in a certain amount of sugar. She never knew how much exactly—she measured by eye, based on instinct, useless to teach this to others. It ended up being sweet, but not too sweet, like some exotic elixir. What an illusion that was, and what a mistake to have one too many! It was a very strong drink, much stronger than regular vodka; it must have been a mixture of sugar and cranberries that turned that banal *stoli* into something much more sinful. My mother's Eddy used to order it from her for his restaurant from time to time, where it was billed as "Marina's Vodka."

Sam loved my grandparents. Despite their difference in age, language, history, experience, emotional intelligence, and everything that one calls culture, they were able to form a bond. Sam and Marina adored one another. They couldn't really speak to one another because of the language barrier, but my grandmother's limited English mixed in with bits of Yiddish and Russian expressed everything she needed to say to him. She called him her grandson. Sam loved it. He adored her food, of course (she always tried to feed him), but more than anything, he loved the genuine warmth and strength of her personality. She used to say to him: "Come to my houze, my grandson, I veel feed you!" which meant, "come see me, I will take care of you, love you... and feed you till you can't move because you are my family, and I know how to take care of family!" He recognized that she was like no one else.

Grandfather Saul didn't say much these days, even in Russian. Sam used to tell me how much he wished he could ask my grandfather about his life. My grandfather was already in his early nineties when Sam came into my life. He spoke little, unless he spoke Russian to his family and friends. He knew I would always translate for him, but I think he didn't want to impose on me. Once he asked to translate for Sam when we were visiting: "Tell him, Anichka, he has a nice punim (*punim* means *face* in Yiddish)". Timidly, I interpreted the phrase. In my grandfather's language it meant that Sam had a good, honest face.

He was ninety-four when he got sick with pneumonia. My mother was away in Russia; it was just Marina and me. My grandparents lived in Queens, in Forest Hills, all the way out at the end of the F train. The hospital was nearby, and I visited my grandfather practically every day. He had good care, a very good doctor, but he was getting weaker.

Every day was the same routine for me. Morning. Train to Westchester. Classes (I was in the middle of my first year of law school then). Back to the city. Sam's partner lent him his truck, so Sam could drive me to the hospital in Queens. He took me almost every day, came into my grandfather's room with me and sat there. Passover was approaching, and all my grandfather dreamt about was to savor his Marina's delectable Seder dishes.

Sam and I were sound asleep when the phone interrupted the night's clammy silence. Someone's indifferent voice on the other end of the line told me my grandfather was dead. I went to dial my grandmother, but she was already calling me. "*Anya, shto delat?*" What are we to do? Her voice was heartbroken, yet undefeated. She really didn't know what to do, and for the first time in my life I saw her not as my formidable Marina, but as an old woman who had just lost something big and important, something without which the rest of life would seem dimmer and more fragile. At that moment, every fiber of my body began to fill with pity, sorrow, regret, and physical pain for one life that was just extinguished and for another that was beginning to lose its luster. But there was no time to sit around. It was three a.m. Sam and I rushed to the hospital. There she was, my grandmother, *moya babushka*. Her's and Saul's sixty-seven-year journey together ended under the fluorescent lights of that Parkway Hospital in Queens.

Everything needed to be organized for a Jewish funeral, and Marina and I had no idea how to do that. We needed a rabbi, a Jewish cemetery, and it was the eve of Passover. We had no idea which way to turn. My grandparents were not observant. Saul grew up in a religious household, before the Revolution, but that was in a very different Russia. In America he loved attending services, but mostly on High Holidays. They were mostly cultural Jews. My grandmother's Jewish soul expressed itself best though music and through communication with people. She had discovered that American Jews understood her better if she threw some Yiddish words into the mix, and with time this helped her to create her own language. Everyone ended up understanding her, Jews and non-Jews. She talked using her hands and her eyes. Jews are good at languages. Sometimes, people understood her better than they understood themselves.

None of this was any use when it came to organizing funerals. Sam and his family came to our rescue; they took care of everything. We came back to my grandmother's sad apartment and Sam began his search. He spoke to his family's rabbi; he got his entire family involved. He contacted every funeral home for miles around and negotiated the price, which was the most uncomfortable, difficult thing to do. While he visited the funeral home to discuss the morbid details, Rabbi Fenster spent over an hour with my grandmother and me talking about my grandfather. My mother, my uncle, and my sister arrived the next day from Russia, and Rabbi Fenster called again and spoke to my mother and my uncle about their father. He wanted to make sure not a single important moment of his life was overlooked or forgotten. I had never before seen the observance of Jewish grief. Even though I wanted those days of sorrow to pass, be gone from my memory, my heart kept being grateful to Sam, to his family, to the Rabbi, and to my ancient faith for not letting my grandfather's death turn into a pathetic spectacle.

Everyone showed up to say goodbye: the relatives from America, their old friends from Russia, the new ones they made here, their neighbors, their doctors, the cleaning lady with her husband. Ex-husband Eddy came; he adored them both. Sam's entire family was there, and even my law school friends, who had never even met my grandfather. They were there for me, even though I didn't know who had told them. Somehow, they all knew. People would rather see one another for a good time, and yet very often they don't think twice about canceling. But people always show up for funerals, even if they are not invited; they honor the ritual of saying goodbye.

So ended my grandfather's long life, in his ninety-fifth year. When we came to the hospital the night my grandfather died, I saw Sam wipe away his tears. Perhaps I only saw him cry two more times after that. I shall always be grateful to him for that sadness, and for helping my grandfather Saul be buried with dignity as a Jew, far away from his home, but surrounded by those he loved most.

It brought Sam and me closer together in a way pain and loss always does. He was so kind to me and my family. Every other week-end, especially during the warmer months, we attended his friends' countless brises, baby-namings, and housewarming parties. There were no more engagement parties or weddings to attend because all of Sam's friends were already married. My law school friends were either married or engaged. People began to ask me questions. "What is Sam waiting for? What's his plan? Are you guys planning to get married?" Even my grandmother in her humorous way began to wonder. I didn't know either, and it infuriated me. I wanted to be married, I wanted a wedding, and I was petrified that if by the age of twenty-five I was not about to be married, I was never going to get married.

I never forgot those women who used to come and spend their afternoons at Eddy's restaurant: professional women, regular girls dressed in casual clothes. They seemed to be in their mid- to late thirties. They would perch themselves on those bar stools like spiders and patiently wait for their male prey as they sipped their drink. Some women were more successful than others, either because they looked less desperate or because they looked younger. Often enough, for the pleasure of spending an evening in the company of some mediocre male, this frantic female creature would end up paying for her date's drink.

It was pathetic, but I wasn't doing any better. I was getting bored. Sam still did not have a place in the city. He was still saving money. He came into the city to meet people for business, and we went to movies; had a bite to eat, visited his parents and their friends, got a hotel room. I asked again, and Sam, without losing his cool, repeated that we were moving in the right direction. Some months later, one of my best friends got engaged and again I approached Sam about his future plans. Again, I did not receive a satisfactory answer. Everything in my book was so simple: I knew who he was, and why I wanted to be with him. I was ready to start, and I wasn't afraid.

Sam was good, honest, noble, loving, loyal, open-minded, and the fact that he was not making money, the fact that he wasn't a connoisseur of intricate intellectual discussions, that he was not made of nerves and passion, did not bother me. I knew I had made my choice. He still didn't talk to me about marriage, but whenever I initiated those talks, I could tell we both wanted the same thing. But our inertia was giving our relationship acidic qualities that eroded the sweetness and warmth between us. I wanted to love Sam, he told me he loved me, but it wasn't enough. I wanted something real. Here they call it a commitment. I knew he was committed to me. I wanted more. I wanted a life together, and I wanted him to tell me that in plain English. It wasn't just about the wedding; it was about his inability to speak to me about anything relating to our future together. The fact that I had to initiate this conversation irritated my sensibilities; it turned poetry into prose.

One summer evening we were having dinner at some restaurant on the Upper East Side when he abruptly changed the subject and asked me: "What if I never become rich? What if I never end up making enough money?" It came out of nowhere, like a bomb, and it wasn't like him. He was always so positive he was going to end up making a lot of money, his energy was always so naïve and contagious, why did he suddenly ask me those questions?

I might have taken a moment to consider what this question really meant. Was he unsure of me, unsure of himself? Instead, in my desire to move forward at all costs I told him the things we both wanted to hear. Every entrepreneur goes through difficult times, the best thing about him was that he was his own master, one day soon I would become a lawyer, money comes and goes, it's such a relative thing anyway. I talked so much I never really answered his question. I didn't want to upset him, but more, I didn't want to admit to myself how alarming the question was. Had I been older, braver, or had I not wanted my white dress so passionately I might have insisted on an answer.

In late 2001, my mother and I were to receive our American citizenship. The date was December 21, 2001, and the venue was the federal courthouse on Centre Street, in downtown Manhattan. My sister was in Russia at the time, she had not yet satisfied the continuous residency requirement and it didn't look like she ever would. In that grand hallway, holding our voluminous paperwork, encircled by other immigrants whose dreams and experiences were unknown to us, we felt the realization of my father's dream. Most of the people were there with their families and friends. We didn't ask anyone to come. It was a busy time, right before the holidays. My grandmother would have been only too happy to take trains, buses, or even walk to come see us become American citizens, but we thought she would be better off at home. The courtroom was crowded and hot, no one was guaranteed a seat. The judge began his speech, and suddenly I saw Sam's father in the crowd, looking at my mother and me with modest happiness. I remember how desperately I wanted to leap over those weepy people and embrace his big body and thank him for his miraculous appearance, for his quiet pride, and for him smiling at us so generously.

When Sam didn't propose to me on New Year's Eve of 2002, I made the decision to break up with him. I didn't know when and how, but I had resolved to do it. I couldn't do it before January 3 because he told me he had an important party he was invited to, and he wanted me to come to it as well. He said it was good for business. I thought that one or two days were not going to make a difference. By that time, Sam already had a place in the city, a one-bedroom apartment in a walk up building on 47th Street between Ninth and Tenth Avenues, in the heart of Hell's Kitchen. With a heavy heart I traveled that evening to his apartment. I had a new outfit with me to change into, new shoes, makeup. What was it all for? Another useless party with a boyfriend who couldn't make up his mind. In any case, it was all going to be over soon; even my mother knew about it. I arrived in a bad mood, changed into my party dress and beautiful stiletto hills. Still, I hated the way I looked: everything seemed to look crooked on me that evening. Then, I applied some makeup and under the deceiving electric lights of his minuscule bathroom I thought I looked pretty. Sam told me I looked beautiful, but we didn't have a minute to waste. I looked outside the window: I could see nothing but flurries pushing each other in different directions. The dull light coming from the streetlights veiled everything on that street with silent drama. We rushed downstairs, stepped outside the building, and the freezing air immediately shocked every inch of my unhappy body. Within moments I observed how my delicate satin four-inch heels were converted into two whitish bumps, my torso robed in a flimsy party dress was shivering underneath my coat; the wind was playing with my hair twisting it into knots and my nose was getting larger and redder with every second. We were supposed to be picked up by Sam's friend. He was nowhere to be seen. I begged him to take a cab. My new semester was about to start, and I didn't want to get sick. The flurries stopped, but it was still very cold. I saw available cabs and signaled them to stop, but Sam said his friend was just around the corner. A lonely looking horse-drawn carriage drew up by our building, and I thought about the coachman losing his way in that wild weather. Sam told me to hop on, and not without hesitation I got on. I nervously began to laugh because I had finally guessed the entire thing and because I couldn't believe the moment had finally arrived with such simplicity and under such awkward circumstances. Sam was sitting just across from me. With his right hand he was reaching into the left inner pocket of his coat. In a matter of seconds, a velvety black box made its appearance. With the fingers of his left hand, he opened the box and in it was a beautiful diamond ring. With great nervousness and great happiness, he had asked me to marry him. All I could do was to shout out "Yes!" I looked around, and everyone on the street was watching us. Under Manhattan's frozen sky, in snowy streets with a rowdy audience screaming out countless congratulations and mazel tovs, I was beginning to imagine how great of a wife I was going to make, and how safe and secure my life was going to be from now on.

VII.

The Women: Young and Old

I WALKED AROUND THE CITY IN A FOG OF HAPPINESS, THINKING OF my blissful wedding and the joys of my future marriage. Sam and I agreed on a short engagement, a wedding at his synagogue in Long Island, and no kids right away. That night he called all his family and friends to let them know. We were so happy. Now that I was engaged, I felt different, new, like I could do anything. Life was now going to be easier, clearer.

The idea of belonging to someone other than my mother excited me wildly; I felt a primitive feeling of security. It occurred to me that since my father's death when I was thirteen, I had found myself in constant want of a male presence. The women in my family fed each other with falsities and memories about our past, our illusions sustained by my mother's forced, unnatural willpower. Now I was getting a new family, who loved me and wanted me.

Sam was the first among his siblings and his cousins to get married, so there was a big fuss about the wedding planning and many parties in anticipation of the blessed event. Gifts came pouring in, threatening to crowd us out of our tiny walk-up on 47th Street and Ninth Avenue. Sam was uncomfortable with the registry at Bloomingdales, as he was with anything having to do with money, but eventually he gave in and got used to being engaged. The law school semester had already begun, so I was relieved of all duties, except for my dress and our honeymoon. I was so happy I agreed with almost everything.

My dress came all the way from Russia, from Nadya, one of the dressmakers from the Bolshoi Theatre. My mother could achieve anything in Russia. We went to see her, a tiny, doughy woman of indeterminable age and few teeth, who knew every bit of gossip and dusty secret of the Theatre going back decades. She looked me up and down, measured my entire body with an old measuring tape that seemed about to crumble in her fingers, wrote down some numbers on the material we brought her. It took about fifteen minutes. The next time I saw my dress was in New York. It fitted perfectly.

I thought more about the dress than I did about the wedding, certainly more than I did about marriage. I can never define and explain my emotions; they are made up of colors, symbols, impressions, incomplete phrases. My wedding dress, on the other hand, was a tangible beautiful thing.

I wanted everyone to be as obliviously happy as I was, but in this my sister would not oblige me. She liked Sam very much, saw my girlish happiness, but her joy for me was somewhat restrained. The longer she lived in Russia, the more distant she was becoming. People don't change, my sister least of all. We may change our fashion sense, our taste in foods, our habits, but the core of us, our sense of morality always stays the same. Kind and compassionate people don't become unkind no matter what happens to them in their life, while liars and cheats will always carry seeds of dishonesty within them till the day they die. My sister had always been a quiet and private person. She never talked about boys, and we knew not to inquire too closely into her affairs. It was hard to tell if she was a late bloomer, or just cold, detached, possessed only by her art, an aloof nymph like she was on stage. This question was settled when she fell in love. As it turned out, she had a passionate soul that once awakened by love, burned brightly toward a human being who had a wild soul himself.

He was a talented young film student named Misha, well-known in Moscow artistic circles. He saw her crossing the street not far from the Academy, recognized she was a dancer by her posture and her stride, the bun in her hair. They got to talking. He revealed in her an ability to love with blinding intensity. Unfortunately for her, he was not a worthy subject of her unwavering loyalty and kindness. This wasn't just a bad boyfriend experience; this was a bad person who stole her innocence and damaged her life.

My sister was living in our old apartment, and she and Misha turned it into a bohemian hangout featuring loud and intense discussions about the special path of Russian cinematography, art, and literature, accompanied by heavy drinking, with a fog of cigarette smoke filling the apartment long into the night.

Reports began to filter in from neighbors and friends about this Misha. Apparently, there was this older socialite in Moscow with whom he had an unresolved amorous relationship. The lady was reportedly heartbroken over his infidelities and at how much money she had given him. The neighbors were concerned that people at my sister's gatherings were using drugs, omitting, perhaps out of pity, to mention that my sister was also one of those people. My mother might not even have believed them if they had told her; perhaps that is why she never asked.

My mother and I had a misplaced confidence in my sister's sense of responsibility and her ability to keep things under control. She had her diploma and soon she made the Bolshoi corps de ballet, the most respected in the world. In a year or two with hard work she could dance solos. But her boyfriend was telling her she shouldn't bother with her career. Ballet or no ballet, he told her, her beauty could open any door. He worked on her like that until she repeated his views to us over the phone, as if she were his client and he was her professional representative.

The more control he seemed to be asserting over her, the more aloof and distant she seemed with us. We found out later he was telling everyone about Liana's mother and older sister living without a care in New York City. Perhaps he wanted my sister to marry him so he could come to America. Meanwhile the money my mother was sending to Moscow was disappearing quickly.

Sometimes, our friends asked us with bewilderment what my sister was doing in Russia, all alone in those crazy times, with her strange hipster friends? This was an accurate appraisal and a fair question, but my sister would hear none of it, and certainly no criticism of Misha. With her wild eyes she declared that she loved her imperfect Russia and loathed perfect America where nothing appealed to her, including her family.

But as time went on, I sensed things were getting tougher for her. Her career was not going anywhere, her interest in it was not the same, and nothing else seemed to interest her either. Even her romantic fascination with Moscow was fading. Every time we saw her, she was more dissociated and careless in her relations with us. Still shy, still silent, still loyal to those she loved, yet there was a noticeable crack in her. She seemed to have lost sight of her main target in life: professional ballet, the toughest art form, the profession that forgives not a single misstep and gives no second chances. Because she was always able to withstand great difficulties for the sake of her profession, we thought she was the strongest of us all. Yet here, the instant she found herself under the spell of a force stronger than herself, she collapsed under its seductive pressure.

We were slow to realize what the problem was, but my shrewd grandmother was worried. It broke her heart to feel that somehow Liana had stopped being the child she loved in her. Also, Marina was all fire, and unless she received the same fire back with the same sincerity she turned into a cinder. She couldn't fully understand what was happening, but clearly something was terribly wrong, and she was offended, confused, and sad, because she couldn't do anything to help. She took to venting to me about my sister's spent past and her lost future, and in these discussions my mother came in for a great deal of blame.

Liana was to be maid of honor at my wedding, she was bringing my wedding dress and my veil from the Bolshoi, but the minute she stepped off the plane I noticed how absent her smile was. We hadn't seen each other in many months, but she was no more than simply glad to see me, in a nonchalant, rather removed way. She passed the dress over to me as soon as she saw me, as if it was too much of a burden for her.

Back at the apartment it always seemed like something else was on her mind. She kept herself busy all the time, yet her behavior was more chaotic than busy and productive. She would have a quick breakfast chattering about something irrelevant, never keeping to one subject; then she would ask me to connect her with someone on the Internet, which she never learned how to use herself. She'd make a plan, very politely ask me for a little bit of money, and then run off telling me she would meet me later. I never knew where she was off to, although a few times she mentioned it was Brighton Beach, the Russian neighborhood in Brooklyn.

Liana and I were on our own that hot hazy summer in New York. Our mother was in Russia. She had sold the big apartment in Moscow and was buying Liana a new, smaller one. It wasn't supposed to take longer than a month to get all the documents in order, but in Russia you never know. Liana attended my pre-wedding gatherings, but she had no interest in my silly pre-wedding jitters. Her mood changed all the time along with her plans, she missed our appointments, lost her keys, kept asking me for money. I couldn't wait for my mother to come back and straighten everything out the way she said she would.

On August 5, Liana told me she was going to see her friends in Brooklyn, perhaps stay with them overnight. She was wearing a beautiful black Chanel dress and black patent leather Ralph Lauren pumps, perhaps a tiny purse, her black hair pulled back in a ponytail. She didn't come back that night, nor did she appear the next morning, or that evening, when our mother came back from Russia. Out of town guests were arriving, the apartment was full of people, and it was impossible to conceal our panic from Marina, who felt it in her bones already.

We found a phone number in my sister's messy handwriting and called it. After a while a girl answered, and what a strange voice she had. She said she hadn't seen my sister since the party the day before yesterday. She took some amphetamines, they were smoking pot and drinking and then she left to walk on the beach, all on her own. The girl on the phone was not very coherent, and we were lucky to get as much out of her as we did.

The police were in the house by now, asking the same questions over and over. It was a missing person report on a young lady, maybe a homicide, they were taking it seriously. My mother and I were desperately afraid. Sam arrived instantly. I wasn't supposed to see him for seven days before the wedding, but now the majesty of tradition had given way to emergency measures. He called every hospital in Brooklyn, using every possible spelling combination of her last name and her first name. He was on the phone all night. Our guests had a close-up view of the crisis; it couldn't be helped.

I heard myself pleading with God inside my head: "I will do anything you ask of me and never complain again, just return my sister to me alive." How many times has God heard that one? I always knew I believed in God, in my subconscious, but I never knew how to pray to Him or what to say to Him on account of my lack of religious training. Despite his official rejection in Russia, people still believed in Him. "God sees everything," they would say. He seemed powerful, omnipresent, not always kind, but, perhaps, just. This last notion came into question when my father was murdered, but even then, I thanked Him for sparing my mother. As long as I believed in *Him*, I could question Him, interrogate Him and be angry with Him all I wanted. (God is always a "*He*", because in my view only masculine beings possess the right combination of strength and calm.)

The day before my wedding was my birthday, August 7, and the first words out of my mother's mouth before "happy birthday," were: "No matter what, you are getting married tomorrow." Sam still had the phone to his ear, he hadn't slept at all, but suddenly an answer came. It was the Coney Island Hospital. They had the correct last name, but not the first name, she had given them two upon admission. She was alive, but her condition was serious. They had found her on a boulder at Brighton Beach, alone, unconscious, and barely breathing, with algae or seaweed covering her body and her face. It was an overdose. The doctor told us she had a long and horrifying list of chemical compounds in her blood, of which I remember none. She was alive. Her being alive was my birthday gift that year, the only one I wanted.

We went to the hospital, and she was confused, unbathed, exhausted. She gave us a vaguely familiar smile. I wanted to kiss her, for her to embrace me, but she looked like she barely wanted anything to do with us. All the way back home, my mother was stroking her disheveled hair, her rough skin. I don't remember how we explained things to my grandmother, we couldn't comprehend the gravity of the situation ourselves. We thought things like that only happen in other families, with other types of people, not our kind, but of course everyone thinks this way.

Once we got her home, all she wanted to do was sleep, and when she woke up she wanted to go out and see her "friends." We understood what she wanted, but by now we understood that wasn't what she needed. She would not listen to us. She was despondent and threatened violence. The men in the blue suits came and called the men in the white suits who took her to the psychiatric ward in a straitjacket. She begged me to ask them not to do this to her. "Anichka, you are my *sestrichka (my sister)*, how can you do this to me? Please ask them not to take me, why are they tying me?" They had to take her through the lobby past our doormen who had known her since she was a timid, graceful teenager. She cried. Her mind was clearing up, and she understood she was not going to be able to make the wedding the next day. I went with her in the ambulance. The doctors allowed me to stay a bit, and watch her through the window, and she looked back at me with her eyes swollen from weeping.

The wedding was as beautiful as my new family could make it. All the traditions were observed, the bridal veil, the broken glass, ecstatic dancing with the bride and groom on chairs. My mother escorted me down the aisle. The last people in my family to be married in this way were my great-grandparents, in a small village near Vitebsk in Belarus. When the war came, they were exterminated by the Nazis. During the ceremony I thought of them, of my grandfathers, Saul and Misha, brought up as observant Jews in the most anti-Semitic country in the world. I tried not to think about Liana; I desperately tried to feel happiness, because it was *my* wedding day. After the ceremony, by tradition, there is the *Yihud*, or seclusion, where the bride and groom are allowed a few moments alone together, and I called the hospital. I couldn't talk to her, but they told me she was stable and peaceful. Thus relieved, I went back out and enjoyed my wedding.

Over two hundred people came to watch us get married. Many of them I did not know. Still, many of the guests were friends from my distant past, they knew me as a little girl, they remembered my father. My law school friends were there as well, all dressed up and not so miserable and flustered, but like respectable guests at some-one else's wedding. I danced with everybody, walked from table to table thanking everyone for coming, smiling all the time, receiving many envelopes full of cash and best wishes.

While Sam and I were off in Italy, not worrying about a thing, the way you are supposed to do on your honeymoon, my sister was discharged from the hospital. To my mother's relief, she was quiet and never left the apartment. Sad and detached was the way she described her. She had no desire to stay in America, and she refused to seek any further treatment or even undergo medical evaluation. She wanted to go back home, and so my mother let her go, saying it was useless to argue with her. A few days before we returned from Italy, she went back to Moscow and never came to America again.

How could we let her go after what she had been through? But how could we not let her go back to her Russia? Legally, we thought, we had no power over her. She was twenty-four years old, and no doctor had diagnosed her with any chronic mental disorder which prevented her from making seemingly rational decisions. At the hospital they got her back on her feet; she was physically in satisfactory shape. All my mother thought we could do was accept her decision and resolve to stand by her. Apparently, the Baker Act, of which we knew nothing at the time, allows families to request the intervention of the court and a three-day mental health evaluation in the case of family members who pose a danger to themselves or others. I don't know if this would have changed things, if that would have kept my sister from leaving the country. But I was not yet a lawyer and there were things I did not know. To me, my mother still painted rosy pictures about my sister's future, but deep in her heart she must have known that Liana's life could never be normal again and that she would have to dedicate her life to the well-being of her adult child.

I struggled with the reality that my sister had changed. I had seen it, and I knew the reason. It was so banal, so old, so well-studied, almost a cliché, yet no less real for all that. Many people use drugs and escape unharmed, others see their personality melt in the heat of their need. Many people are intrigued by addicts, like my mother with her drunk cokehead Eddy, but it didn't break her because, at bottom, her life was more important to her than her addictive love for him. Perhaps, in the same way, my love for Dan was infected with this aching sense of permanent agony and fear of betrayal. But in the end, I too had discovered that I loved myself more than my prodigal, passionate boyfriend. How was it, then, that my sister was unable to resist that force personified by her wicked Misha, which proved even stronger than her own stubborn personality? Many people fall in love for the first time with stupid or bad people, but then they eventually graduate to someone less disappointing who can soothe the wounds inflicted by predecessors. My sister did not move on. He was her first, her last, and her only. No matter how many times he abused her, no matter how many times he abandoned her and then returned to her, she always forgave. She never complained about him and never allowed anyone else to say anything bad about him.

Upon her return to Moscow after her near-death experience, she shut herself off from everyone and became a recluse. From what we knew, she not only stopped using drugs, but she also stopped seeing her Misha, as well as her other friends and acquaintances. She began watching her health and threw herself into her career, which she had neglected for some time. But this temporary reformation was no more but a brief interlude in the middle of a cheerless play. She had quit the Bolshoi, she told us she simply could not handle the pressure anymore, or maybe they knew about her drug issues, which would be hard for a dancer to conceal. She had a few ballet students of her own, but not enough to support her in what had become one of the most expensive cities in the world.

Helplessly, from afar, we watched her melt away, losing the ability to work with people or live with anyone. She had disconnected herself from the wicked influences of her past, but she didn't replace them with anything or anybody good. She stopped abusing her body with drugs, but it wasn't like she was healthy. She avoided doctors, even when she was sick, fearing interference with her natural state of being. Her mistrust of people deepened into a fear of interaction with others. She would not allow workers into her apartment, even when urgent repairs were necessary, and the neighbors were all complaining. Even my mother lost the privilege to enter her daughter's home. My sister didn't mean any insult to my mother, but she felt uneasy with anybody inside her home. I think she felt dirty and oppressed in anybody's presence, unless she was outside in the open space. In the open space she could run away from the unwanted environment and from those she feared. Was it something to do with her experience in the psychiatric ward in New York or did something happen in Russia? I don't know.

My mother visited her regularly in Moscow. She wanted Liana to change her life, she wanted her to get married, she wanted to figure it out for her, but she was bound to be disappointed. In Moscow my mother stayed at the historic National Hotel on Red Square. Upon arrival, she went to Liana's apartment and left handwritten notes underneath her door saying where she was staying, what room, for how long, asking her to call, telling her she loved her. She almost never called us, unless it was urgent. I think Liana hated to disturb my mother's peace, as much as her own, because our mother's worries must have made her anxious as well. Liana wanted to remain like a lake: utterly undisturbed. My mother never knew for sure whether Liana even knew she was in town. But sometimes she did call. There were magical moments when my mother thought she detected in my sister's voice notes of openness. Then she would hang on every word, deceiving herself that my sister was changing back to her old self, but she was getting worse. It was impossible for us to help her. We knew so little about her life in Russia. She loved her Russia, but the Russia she loved was not the Russia she lived in. She needed a good man who could love her and help her, but she was not the type to go for such men. Despite her innocence or because of it, her soul sought demons. She never talked about Misha; her feelings remained her own.

She became increasingly withdrawn, sometimes even refusing to see our mother when she came to Moscow. My mother would stay in Moscow for weeks at a time, keeping herself busy with friends and glamorous cultural engagements, to cover the emptiness of her visits, the constant worry. She called me regularly, and sometimes her voice sounded happy; that meant she had finally communicated with Liana and there was a plan to meet. Next, I would receive the news that Liana never made it to the rendezvous, that our mother waited for her for hours without knowing whether she was simply late or had changed her mind altogether. Then there were triumphant days, when they met, sat together for a long time, talked about everything, about the past and even about the future, which always gave my mother hope.

Sometimes my mother's trips to Russia ended without a sight of her daughter. She would leave yet another note in which she expressed her infinite love and worry for her, promise to be back in a couple of months, and carefully folded cash in the same envelope. We wondered whether Liana's strange behavior meant she was on drugs again, but we concluded that she was not. Drugs require money. My mother had access to her bank account, and my sister used money very modestly.

Liana never called me, rarely even asked about me. My normal life seemed to hold no interest for her, or perhaps she felt that because our lives were so different her interest in me would be unwelcome. I had so much to share with her, my marriage, my struggles, my failings, my dreams. I wanted her to sympathize with all that, be my sister the way she used to be, but her heart was hollow, and she had nothing to give me.

I last saw my sister about thirteen years ago, at a café in Moscow in the winter. She was already broken, sweetly strange, but still my

Liana. I could see what an effort it was for her to come out, and what a joy for her to be there with me. My mother and I were wearing our mink coats and warm boots; Liana had on a sad-looking denim jacket and a clean but battered polyester scarf, and she looked cold. We both felt shy and awkward, she stroked my back, and kept saying how thin I looked. It was time to go, it was late, and as we stood there, engulfed by our city's impermeable freeze, frivolous snow-flakes caressed our happy cheeks. She asked if I thought Moscow was beautiful, as if she were responsible for its beauty.

I always thought we were going to grow old together, my sister and me, walking through life hand in hand, shoulder to shoulder, in the comfortable wisdom of years gone by, unharmed by memories and protected by each other's growing families. Instead, my younger sister Liana died alone in her apartment in Moscow at the age of forty-two. My mother saw her last in February of 2020, right at the start of the COVID pandemic. She told her about the upcoming world crisis and shutdown, but my sister didn't seem to care about any of that. She didn't follow the news; her phone didn't even work properly. She refused entry to the world outside, but the virus got in there somehow. In the end she succumbed to COVID like so many millions of others. She was known to go silent for weeks despite all efforts to reach her, and then reappear. My mother would have gone to Russia, but travel was suspended. The only way we knew something was very wrong was when my mother saw no money was being taken out of the bank account she kept. That was sometime in May of 2020. When she was finally discovered in her apartment on the last day of August, we were told she had apparently been dead for many weeks.

I was the one who received the call from our childhood friend who was on the scene at the time. Heartbroken, he uttered the words that our Lianochka was no longer with us. Somewhere in the background, indifferent police voices were reciting the details of their macabre discovery. The medics suspected she had suffered a brain aneurism because of COVID. I couldn't get over how simple the information I had just received was, and yet how grotesque and how unfixable, how final it was. I had just received the information about the death of my little sister, but with what words was I to tell my mother? I was not just a messenger, but a bearer of my sister's death. I was the executioner. She had all the right to hate me for this, just like I hated her when she told me about my father. But when I told her of her Liana's death, she didn't think of me at all; her thoughts were only of Liana, she who constituted the purpose of my mother's entire existence, who grew up in Moscow like a little princess, only to die all alone without her mother by her side. I rarely talk about my sister, and almost never to my mother. Mercilessly, I leave her to deal with that dirty business of loss on her own. She lets me be because she loves me. She goes on with life and she smiles in the same way she has always done.

Somewhere there is a video of Liana in the role of the dying Swan, a dance originally choreographed for Anna Pavlova by Mikhail Fokin to the music of Camille Saint-Saëns. No more than twenty, she wears an old-style tutu of feathers hanging over her body, her head in a crown made of swan's feathers almost too heavy for her, with the light shining upon her long white arms and the red mark in the middle of her chest. Sometimes I ask myself whether I neglected or even unconsciously rejected my sister because of the way she lived; of the way she was? Had I become tone deaf to her seemingly comfortable life in Moscow, to her desperate loneliness, to her fears and her pains? I was my sister's hero, and yet, I neglected her, and I abandoned her. In the moments of loneliness when grief for my sister cloaks my mother's existence, she tends to question my love for my sister. She thinks that because I never talk about her, I might have forgotten her, removed her from my relatively pleasant reality. It is not so. I would like to think that because of what we shared together throughout our luminous childhood, my love for her always remained intact, undisturbed by the anguish of her adulthood. I was not as good to her as she was to me, and her death broke my heart.

𝕊

Sam and I came back from our honeymoon that summer of 2002 to begin a new life together as husband and wife. He went to work every day. I began my last year of law school.

All this third-year commotion of applying for jobs and going on interviews made me nervous. Pace was not a top-tier law school, so the top firms did not visit to recruit; students had to bring themselves to the attention of prospective employers. I was not looking for a job, partly because I couldn't articulate to myself what sort of law I was interested in practicing, and partly because I lacked confidence. Sam's entire family came to my graduation and even made a donation to the synagogue in honor of the first Meltzer to earn a law degree. They were all counting on me. They weren't flattering me with their questions about my imminent plans and their naive talk about me becoming a "big shot lawyer," they really believed in me, yet I felt overwhelmed by their expectations.

Before I could do anything, I needed to pass the bar exam and get a license to practice law, otherwise my fancy doctoral degree would be worthless. The New York bar exam, named for the bar that divides the lawyers from the spectators in every courtroom, is one of the most difficult in America: two grueling days of strictly timed testing on everything you should have learned in law school. A full 56 percent fail their first time.

I was overcome with dread of the test, sure all the other people in the review class I joined were cleverer than me. I could tell by the speed of their confident note taking. I heard people talk of being recruited by fancy firms or hired to clerk for formidable judges. I kept reminding myself to take it easy, but it was worse than my first year of law school. I was so miserable and full of helpless anger I decided to quit, and even my mother folded in the face of the tantrum I threw. It was only through the intervention of my brilliant friend Marina, who asked me if I had lost my mind to throw away three years of law school, that I was persuaded to continue.

On the last Tuesday of July 2003, I entered a vast hall of the Jacob Javits Center to sit with a couple of thousand others for the New York bar exam. I could smell disaster in the air on that hot and indifferent morning, and once the exam began, I saw how underprepared I was. Everything looked like a trick or an impenetrable riddle. I kept running out of time, even on the multiple choice. The essay questions were even harder, the fact patterns deliberately misleading. I kept jumping from one question to the next, hoping to see a glimmer of light. Then, at the break, talking with friends, I realized I had missed an entire essay. In my haste and nervousness, I forgot to turn the page and see if there was another question. Up until then I was discreetly harboring a dim hope of success, but clearly, I had blown it. I'd already handed in my booklet. Now there was the whole second day to sit through, to no apparent purpose. I lost heart, walking home in that heat under that impervious sun, feeling like too big of a failure to take a cab.

Stung and humiliated yet somehow undeterred, I resolved to try again. People taking the February bar exam differ from those who take the exam in the summer: many are re-takers, they are older, not as noisy, with jobs and families to support. I signed up for a different course that was not any cheaper and I felt like an impostor among all those busy, hardworking people. I took the exam, failed again, and overcome by sadness and disappointment with myself, apathy toward the future, and a sense of intellectual uselessness, I decided to give up and try to forget about it.

Eventually I found there were jobs for law school graduates without a ticket in the field of document review, where a law firm working on a major case will hire people like me to go through tens of thousands of documents in preparation for trial or an investigation on behalf of a client. The firm charges its client anywhere from $400 to $900 or more an hour while paying the document reviewers $27 to $40 an hour, and pockets the difference. The money was all right, nothing like I'd be making if I was a real lawyer, but the job was dull and oppressive as a sweatshop, in the basements of fancy law firms or at some grim "off-site" in one of Manhattan's forgotten neighborhoods. We worked ten- to fourteen-hour days and were watched, supervised, and micromanaged by trained staffers, who made sure we worked constantly and made our quotas. Often, we were forbidden to speak to one another. I waded through the dull contents of financial statements, personal emails, analyzing each with respect to its relevance, confidentiality, and its privilege status.

It was a hateful and oppressive employment, and I could feel it slowly eroding my intellectual capacity and self-respect. I had nobody to talk to, nothing to do worth doing. My law school friends were already practicing law. My transitory acquaintances in document review were passing the bar and getting better jobs. Only I was stuck. What had happened to the dreams I used to have, the poetry I used to write with breathless sincerity?

On the other hand, it was an easy, mindless way to make $27 an hour, and once you hit the forty-hour minimum you got time and a half. It made sense to grind away at it because you never knew when it would end, the case would settle, or the client would run out of money, and you'd be back out on the agency job market. You learned never to get cozy, and always to expect the worst.

It felt good and self-regulating making those meager $27 an hour, and certainly we needed it, because money was tight. I avoided asking Sam about his business because I sensed instinctively that there was no good news, none that I could see from the bank account. We couldn't go on vacations, we had to watch what we spent at the supermarket, we were almost always late with our rent. At times things seemed to get better, but this never lasted.

Sam was the same; happy-go-lucky and detached both at once. He was almost always in a good mood, positive about everything, happy about his friends' professional and personal successes. Nothing seemed like a big deal to Sam: the squalor of our living conditions, how he was almost always late and never reachable. Everybody loved him, he was such a nice Jewish boy. Yet the more generous and empathetic he was with everyone else, the less intimate he seemed with me. I don't think he set out to be like that on purpose, he was just built that way. He used to explain to me in his disarming way that there was nothing personal in what he did or didn't do, and therefore no reason for me to get upset. It was hard for me to accept that, because to me, everything seemed personal, especially when it came to gifts.

Shyness and pride prevented me from asking Sam to buy me pretty things, but that didn't mean I didn't want them or that my feelings weren't hurt when we stepped into a nice store, and he didn't offer to get me anything or did his best to avoid walking in at all. I could empathize with his inability to afford nice things, but I was hurt by his lack of understanding of who I was, of where I came from. Somehow, he missed seeing in me not only a girl who wanted pretty things, but also a beloved daughter of a doting Russian father who once upon a time used to give me beautiful things, not only on birthdays and holidays, but on the most unremarkable days of the year.

In the Soviet Union, women were deprived of luxury. After the revolution, they were not supposed to want nice things anymore. Pretty clothes, hairstyles, makeup, even flowers were vestiges of the tsarist past, or worse, artifacts of Western capitalism.

Lenin was not a romantic, but he could never eliminate in Russian women the instinctive desire to be women. When Perestroika came, the Dior lipstick my grandmother used to get on the black market and a hundred other sparkly things magically appeared on the barren shelves and racks of Moscow stores. Like wild she-beasts let out of their cages, the women attacked those goods, willing to trade all their rubles. Supply could barely keep up with demand, and women rejoiced that luxury had arrived to free them from their unglamorous and unfeminine past.

I was already in the West and was used to the sight of seductive merchandise, but I have a Russian girl's taste for splendor, for being and feeling feminine. Even if I couldn't live in luxury, I adored the idea of it. All these thoughts were in my head, but I knew I couldn't talk about them with Sam, because I sensed my thoughts did not belong in his world.

I was disappointed, but I did not want to admit it to myself, and I suddenly noticed it was time to have a baby. It would not only obliterate my insignificant past, but justify my future failures. My family would adore me more than ever, my status would be elevated, and above all, I would have something to do. Motherhood was something I could hide behind indefinitely. I was twenty-nine years old and all at once, it was unimaginable to live a life without children. I had always wanted to live to a very old age, surrounded by a rowdy family made up of dozens of grandchildren and great-grandchildren, whose names I would have difficulty remembering. I had no idea what to do with a baby, but I was sure it would come to me the moment I got it. Everyone around me was getting pregnant and giving birth, getting that special attention, just like it was when everyone around me was getting married.

My baby fever can only be called normal. Even busy successful career women, hitherto focused on their professional future, are subject to this partly hormonal, partly social frenzy. The biological clock is a cliché, but clichés are repeated because they contain a kernel of truth. I heard the alarm go off and it was time.

We had moved to the Upper West Side, a large two-bedroom apartment in a modest but solid elevator building on 92nd Street and Amsterdam Avenue. It was a much nicer neighborhood, a new horizon. We got to work in the baby laboratory, but after a few months there were no results to show. We went to the "top" doctor and got tested: Sam was perfect, but my hormones seemed a bit thin. Dr. Kohn didn't see a problem. I was young and healthy, a good candidate for the basic procedure of intrauterine insemination. I would take hormone pills and present myself at his office every day for a sonogram, and blood work (I can't recall now whether blood work was done every day). As soon as I was ready to ovulate, he was going to initiate the procedure.

I waited two weeks; first patiently, and then impatiently, and on the fourteenth day I bled. I tried again, and again, and again. I had side effects from the hormones he gave me. With every disappointment came a new wave of hope; the more I failed to get pregnant the more I wanted to have a baby.

Another month, another cycle, another round of treatments, another hopeful procedure. I waited some more, and on the fourteenth day of that new month I did not bleed. Impatient, I took the test in the bathroom at work. The mysterious stick with its miraculous lines said I was pregnant. I had tears in my eyes, although perhaps that was the hormones. I felt as if I had won something. Sam was ecstatic to see the flickering heartbeat on the doctor's fancy machine.

I couldn't wait to announce it to everyone, as if I was the only person in the entire world who had ever gotten pregnant. My wise grandmother wished I would not talk about it so much; in Russia it is not recommended to get too excited too soon, so as to avoid bad luck. But I was experiencing a happiness of a primordial nature on my way to the endocrinologist's that December morning. It was a crazy morning in the city because the transit workers had gone on strike and it was freezing cold, but I didn't care. I was pregnant, everything had a new purpose, even the transit strike. There he is, that clever doctor again. The top doctor. He is so busy, works so hard, when does he go home? This nice, cheery nurse, and the one who always looks like she is cross with me, but she is not cross at all, she is just tired. I have been her favorite patient all along. This doctor, he is the "top." He did it! I shall miss this room with its mollifying pictures by Rockwell, with its smooth equipment, subdued lighting, and soft sounds. I will send them a huge basket of flowers as a thank-you, but my flowers must be the most beautiful, to distinguish me from his other patients. It took him a few moments to get my attention: "I don't think it's going to happen this time. There is no heartbeat, honey. Not this time. We will try again."

I thought I had gone deaf for a moment, because there was a harsh ringing sound in my ears. I asked him to take another look, and he did, but the answer was the same. I was going to have a miscarriage, soon, in just a few days. He was disappointed, upset even, but he had dozens of other desperate women in his waiting room. He had to see them, now. He patted me on the shoulder, gave the kind nurses a few instructions and left the room. I was waiting for something else to happen, but nothing else was happening. I had to go now. They needed the room for other patients, less or more fortunate than me. Tears in the back of my throat were choking me. The nurses helped me out through the side door, so the other patients couldn't see me so upset.

Down in the lobby, I realized that I had no strength to get myself home. What a shame, what an embarrassment! What would I tell Sam? What would I tell him? How can I disappoint him when he was so happy? What would I tell my grandmother? She had been right to tell me to keep quiet. It was all because of my vanity. I couldn't go to work in that state. Let them fire me. But I couldn't go home and be on my own, either. I called my husband and told him how sorry I was about everything, especially for not listening to my grandmother. I had blabbed about something so fragile and private to the entire world like some common peasant, and now I was paying for it. I was inconsolable and outside it was cold. I walked a long time until I was able to find a taxi uptown to my mother's.

I fell into her arms and she at once got me on her sofa covered in her fragrant robes and her soft blankets. Almost immediately, my grandmother appeared, all the way from Roosevelt Island where she had moved after her Saul had died. She walked into the living room in her matching brown mink coat and hat, face flushed, eyes tearing from the wind, her lips brightly painted with love and courage. "*Anya, pervyi blin komom!*" ("The first pancake is always a messy one.") She made me laugh. I miscarried in a few days, in pain and heartbreak. Our family gynecologist, Dr. Tabakashvili, a Georgian Jew from the former Soviet Union, listened patiently to my story, the latest he had heard in his long career, and then told me in his shrewd, charming Georgian accent that this kind of thing happens all the time, a loss but not a tragedy, I was going to have more children, as many as I wanted. I believed him.

I went back to the specialist, who now made me give myself painful shots in my stomach, and about two months later I got pregnant and this time it took. Ariella Rene Meltzer, named after my father Arkady, as I had intended since the moment I learned of his death, was born on October 23, 2006. There she was, so little, such a person, all on her own and yet all dependent on me. I felt no motherly connection with her, no more than curiosity and a sense of amusement when the nurse put her minute body on top of me. I felt relief that the pain was gone, and I was very hungry. I loathe hospitals, their texture, their funky smell, their sterilized look, their policies and procedures. I wanted Sam to stay in the hospital with me that night, and I wanted to go home. I told the nurses I was leaving, but they said I couldn't go home because I'd just had the baby, and until the baby was safe to leave the hospital, I had to stay with her. The realization that I had no right to leave, no right to do what I wanted was suffocating. I understood for the first time that I was never going to be free again. I fell asleep sobbing into my hospital pillow.

A few hours later they woke me up in the middle of the night. To do what? To feed it? Her? With what? I had no milk. It was all so awkward, and strange, and nothing was happening; I asked them to take her away; the nurse insisted that I try harder. I refused, and she took the baby away, to feed her that cloudy liquid I had seen advertised on TV.

We hired a twenty-four-hour baby nurse for when I got home: Naeema, from Trinidad, who at once took charge of Ariella's feeble body with her infinite largeness and softness. I was tired and not thinking very clearly. Ariella was like a strange little animal I had to keep with me all the time. I loved dressing her and undressing her, touching her soft outfits gave me immense pleasure, caressing her supple skin, marveling at her meaninglessly adorable facial expressions, aimlessly combing her delicate hair. I didn't see her as a real human being, but only as an adorable toy. It was as if my body was a separate entity that had, through some strange process and without my permission, produced another body from which I now desperately wanted to be free. Staying home with the baby was either boring or upsetting; she was too young to interest me, but when she cried, I went to pieces.

Becoming a mother, having everyone call me "*Mama*," suddenly made me feel old. I was not a young, carefree girl anymore, but a matron with never-ending obligations, an agony I had imposed on myself. Again, not thinking clearly, I decided now that I had accomplished my biological quest, I could resume my old, normal life right away. Still sore, the day after I came home from the hospital, I confidently passed the baby to Naeema, got myself dressed up, put on my high heels, and went over to Sam's office to use the computer, apply for jobs, be useful, feel busy.

All was going well until I started to feel cool and unpleasantly wet underneath my blouse. I looked down, and I discovered embarrassing blotches all over my pretty top. I appeared to be secreting mother's milk from my breasts. I couldn't believe it. I thought I was done now that I had given birth, having considered myself under no obligation to breastfeed. Science had produced the formula, the rest was a matter of choice, my own personal convenience, but here it was, the maternal substance. I galloped home like some deranged animal to the baby. "Naeema, here I am!" I cried.

"No, Ms. Anya, we are all done here. Ariella is all fed and happy." Now I was disappointed. What a waste, what a farce. What a nuisance that little creature is. I had to run all the way through the city like some sweaty mad prehistoric thing just for her? She, of course, was gazing at me with a look of wonder and self-satisfaction. She could be fed and be happy with or without me, yet somehow through some biological action my body kept producing that strange liquid in response to her needs.

Now that I was utterly robbed of my personal freedom, I had time to focus on the culprit of my nonfreedom. Everything about her obsessively worried me, even though I consistently tried to appear serene: rashes, fevers, cries, colds, stomachaches. Little Ariella depended on me, but her dependence on me was purely physical. I, on the other hand, was addicted to her reliance on me, and that was the very essence of my prison; there was nowhere else to go. I had no maternal feeling for her, no warmth, no interest in her as an individual, no love which alone could make me stop feeling like a prisoner. I knew how to change diapers and wash bottles, I knew how to burp her, and even how to administer medicine to her through a tiny syringe, but I had no idea how to play with her because I could never form any eye contact with that little baby of mine.

I was not unlike other inexperienced mothers. Some people thought I had postpartum depression and perhaps they were right, but I didn't like them hanging that label on me, putting me in a box so they knew how to think about me. I was imprisoned by my hormones, exhausted, overwhelmed, and in a bad mood, but there was nothing so special about that. Millions of women have given birth over centuries through wars, poverty, and revolutions; I had food and clean sheets, although I would have liked some more sleep. As unbalanced as I felt, I refused to join the group self-diagnosis with this self-indulgent ailment of the twenty-first century.

Naeema took weekends off, leaving me to rely on sheer luck, fresh air, and Sam's tranquility. One Saturday evening I came home from my bar exam studies to find the apartment a mess of dirty diapers, milk-stained blankets and bibs and pastel onesies, with a layer of ripped up baby books and toys on top. The sink was full of unwashed dishes and the place smelled of milk vomit. Baby was making cooing noises in her new playpen as Sam watched sports on TV. I knew he had been watching the baby all day by himself. It would have been unfair of me to ask him to be a housekeeper in addition to burdening him with this unmanly task of changing his daughter's dirty diapers, no matter how cheerfully he did it, but none of my patriarchal upbringing could stop me from being mad upon seeing him in that state of detached peace with the mumbling baby in all that mess. On the way home I had seen people going out to places, looking effortless in their happiness, while I felt miserable and dull. I began by complaining about the messy apartment, then I moved on to how he was not paying enough attention to me, not listening to me, forgetting about romance, always reminding me how we had no money. I deserved to have some fun because in the end it was me who had just had the baby! I refused to stay home like some old matron. From time to time, he tried to interrupt me, to calm me down, but it was hard for him to get in a word. The baby was beginning to whimper in her crib, but I kept up my tirade. Her voice got louder, firmer, more acidic. She wasn't letting up, but neither was I. She wanted attention but so did I. I knew what she wanted, she wanted to be picked up, she wanted to be held. She was glaring at me, not Sam. I folded my arms and turned away, letting her know that I was ignoring her. She was the reason my life was in such a twisted place, it was never going to get untwisted again, she was my penal colony.

Sam picked her up, held her in his arms, and she went back to her cooing, her blue eyes helplessly smiling first at him, then at me, her tiny fingers playing with his nose and the sleeves of his T-shirt. I looked away. "Come on, Anya, just look at her. How can you be mad at something like this? Here, just take her." What could I do? She was the skin of my skin, the bone of my bone. I couldn't say sorry, it would have been too banal for my taste. Nevertheless, I was crushed by the moment's simplicity. It humbled me, and it saddened me. I picked her up and saw in her eyes for the first time a glimmer of acknowledgment. She smiled at me, not as a baby but as a human being. One more second and she was going to look away; her blue eyes would find some other object to gaze at. But I was wrong. This little fidgety thing did not look away but kept holding my gloomy face with her puffy wet hands and she smiled, and made me laugh. My Ariella!

We needed a full-time nanny and housekeeper, so we contacted one of those Russian agencies taking advantage of the phenomenon that a woman could make more money as a nanny in New York than as an astrophysicist in Russia. My mother conducted the interviews, she had a much more imposing personality, the look of a true employer that I lacked.

The one my mother liked best was Adinai, a Muslim from Kyrgyzstan with a medical degree. She liked her for her modesty, her quiet manner, and her conservative ways. Her good housekeeping and understanding in the ways of babies left nothing to be desired. When she first took Ariella into her arms, I could see her shielding her from the world.

Sam liked her, though she spoke no English, and he spoke neither Russian nor Kirgiz. She worried they wouldn't understand one another, and I practically had to beg her to take the job. She had just left another family where she was taking care of newborn twins, because they treated her unkindly. I promised her that our entire family was a bit loud, but kind; we had this little Ariella and we desperately needed someone who knew something about babies.

The very first night I met her, when I came home from my studies exhausted and anxious, she sat me down to tea and talked to me as if I were a child myself. Adinai slept with little Ariella every day for nearly seven years, from the time that she was three months old. She became part of the family. She taught little Ariella how to hold a cup, how to eat, how to dress, how to use a potty, nursed her through every sickness, calmed every tantrum. Maybe I could have done it all without her, but it wouldn't have been easy. I thought I needed her much more than she needed me, but this was not altogether true. When she moved in, I quickly realized she was completely without money, not even a dollar, and that the agency was exploiting her in an unconscionable way, taking advantage of her illegal immigrant status to deprive her of the larger portion of her wages. When we realized the scheme, we secretly upped her salary to compensate her for the money she was losing to the agency.

We paid her weekly, but on holidays and birthdays I bought her gifts and paid her double. It was partly the Russian way, and partly my way. Adinai hovered over our Ariella as if she were her own golden child, and I wanted to pay her back with the same generosity, as when she would shower her beloved Ariella with gifts, brought flowers and chocolates for everyone's birthday, jewelry, and silk scarfs from Kyrgyzstan. Where she came from, the value of a personal relationships was at least equal to the value of money. In Soviet times, money did not have much value, but loyalty and friendship saved lives. She had left her family and her sacred Muslim traditions to come and work in America where she knew very few people, without a word of English, and our family had become her world: she gave herself to us, became a part of us.

Sam could never understand my relationship with Adinai. He didn't mind us speaking Russian, but he was surprised at Adinai's lack of English, as if every immigrant should be fluent the instant they landed. He liked her and respected her for the job she did, but "thank you" was where it stopped for him. It was useless to explain to him how when people give gifts it's not just about the gift, it's about the gesture, the thought, the effort. Sam thought I was spoiling her, trying to buy her, he said it like it was a bad thing and told me I was on my own, which allowed me to ignore him where Adinai was concerned. I bought her loyalty, yes, and it was worth it, for the sake of my time and my freedom.

She said Ariella needed to eat, and the same went for me: I looked like a teenager, with my ripped jeans and ink stains all over my hands. Why, women my age in her country, a very poor country mind you, were well fed and looked much more like mothers than like adolescents. After a few months she gave up on the idea of fattening me up and took to feeding me her special brew of Kyrgyz tea, which came in the mail from friends and relatives in her remote land. Every time she saw me upset, on account of my studies, my work, my bickering with Sam, she sat me down, stroked my back, and gave me tea. She brewed it her own way, with loose tea leaves. Every night, in her heavy-handed Russian, she would carry me off into an unfamiliar world of her life in Kyrgyzstan filled with hardship, mystery, and infinite unfairness. As a young girl, she was kidnapped by her groom to be married, an ancient custom seldom practiced these days. She never loved her husband, a lazy violent drunk who ill-deserved this beautiful girl with a long, thick braid she could wrap twice around her slender waist. He beat her so badly she suffered a miscarriage, and could never have another baby after that, so she adopted her second child. Simultaneously, on a part-time basis, she attended a local medical school. Because her husband could never hold a job, she had to be mother, father, wife, breadwinner. Each of her stories invariably ended: "work hard, and you will get there, just keep working hard."

My squabbles with Sam were frequent by now, and any time she could not help but witness one, she would make an aloof gesture in the air with her plump hand and say: "Ahh, forget it, Anya; men, they are the way they are, they are men. What are you going to do? No use getting mad at them!" Her big, kind face smiled as she advised me to resign myself to my fate. She had no idea what we were arguing about, but it didn't really matter.

In her culture, as to a lesser but still significant degree in mine, religion and deeply rooted customs give men the leading role in society. A man, no matter how cowardly or insignificant, is always the central element of a family unit. Women like Adinai in traditional, patriarchal societies don't rate men highly, especially when it comes to their emotional abilities. Unlike American women, who fight their male partners over every spoken and unspoken word, women in Adinai culture don't fight their men, nor do they seek to change them. Either they submit or give an appearance of submission in order to outwit them, like the seductive Scheherazade in *Arabian Nights*, who uses her wit and the power of her sex to tame a powerful man. The genius of the role is that it is compatible with any male partner, be he a king or a pauper. American women take themselves far too seriously to play the role of a seductress who uses her wit and the power of her sex to tame a powerful man. She would rather lecture a lover on his damaged morals than use her feminine wisdom to persuade him to behave differently. The power of the feminine self in relation to the inherent weakness of the masculine is as immutable as human nature. A woman's ability to intuitively hear her man's needs, to restrain him without destroying him, is a timeless quality.

Kyrgyzstan is a former republic of the Soviet Union, southeast of Russia bordering on Afghanistan. It is a remote and poor country of mountains, woodlands, steppes, tundra, and deserts. The dominant ethnic group are the Kyrgyz, a Turkic people who follow Islam. During the Soviet era every person in the Republic was fluent in Russian because it was taught in schools.

Adinai's family had a farm with a couple of cows, some chickens, and a private house, and that gave them status in society. It took her many years to receive her medical degree, attending the local medical school on a part-time basis. Eventually she became a virologist, but even this was not enough, as she was the only moneymaker for the family. Adinai learned she could make more money as a nanny in America than as a doctor in Kyrgyzstan. The plan was to make as much money as humanly possible and return home within a year. In my thirty years in America, I haven't met a single immigrant who stuck to their original plan of returning to their desperate native land as soon as they accumulated enough cash. "Enough" is a relative term, especially in America, where there is no such thing as enough. Even the folks back home can never get enough.

She sent the money back to Kyrgyzstan to support her children, her relatives, and her husband Umar, but he really was no good. He squandered the money she sent him to finish the house and buy more cattle on drink and his mistress, selling his own cows, her cows, at a loss. Adinai was angry about the cows, but she was beside herself at the thought of losing her husband to another woman. He might be worthless, but he was the only husband she had, and she went so far as to borrow money from her friends to get him out of debt because indigency for the Kyrgyz is a shameful business, it will follow you even to America where the Kyrgyz community still lives by tribal rules of honor and dignity. Adinai had no choice but to keep working and borrowing money in America. It took her almost ten years to get her green card, and only then could she see her home again. She saw it, shed her tears of nostalgic joy, and came back to New York.

Umar was perfectly content to spend the rest of his life where he was, supported by Adinai, in peaceful cohabitation with his sympathetic female companion. He was not interested in making any changes to his life nor in helping Adinai in any way. Many of her friends, we included, advised her to forget him, to divorce him, to find herself another man. This was America, where a woman could start anew, be absolved of old sins and welcome new adventures. Adinai wasn't buying it. She had a husband, and he might be an idiot, but he belonged to her and not to this other woman she was now supporting, and in the end she won. Her son and his young family won a green card and came to live in America. Her daughter got married, and even though she cared for her aging father, she was planning to have children of her own. With his family gone, he was turning into an old, depressive drunk. Even his carefree mistress left him. Adinai somehow knew at once and chose this moment to tell him she wouldn't send him any more money. She wanted him back, and she got him back, her broken, treacherous, useless, but one and only husband. I never saw her so happy as when that tiny, feeble man stood next to her in our apartment. This was not the wife-beater I expected. He spoke almost no Russian; his only tool was his smile which was timid but full of quiet joy. He was wearing a sweater Adinai had carefully selected for him for the occasion, a little man, neat and peaceful and so happy.

Adinai took him in hand at once, and within a few days he had a job at some shoe repair shop and had made a pledge to stop drinking, strictly enforced by her. It wasn't about love; it was about duty. She never thought of men badly. Those who were good, kind, and successful she put on a pedestal, but those who were less than great and less than good she treated as a mother would treat her disobedient child: scolded, given a lesson, but later fed well and perhaps given a delicious dessert. With men, the situation was a bit more hopeless, because children grow up, while men do not. Still, no matter what she felt inside, on the outside, Adinai and women like her would teach her daughter, Ariella, and even me: "He [whoever that "he" is] is a man, he is the nucleus of a family, he is the protector and defender, he must be given respect, and therefore always fed and cared for before anyone else." With those words her index finger invariably would go up pointing to the sky, in a way that defied argument.

As I watched Adinai cook her delicious meals for Sam, I couldn't help but admire the dedication with which she went about her task, the act of cooking and feeding the man of the house. According to Adinai's cultural norms, the man of the house needed to be fed first. He always got the hottest bowl of soup, the largest portion, the most succulent piece of meat. That was how she expressed her womanhood, her femininity. I saw Sam's eyes, and he looked satisfied, pleased, at peace, and it gave me peace and a sense of self-worth as well. I absorbed her lesson so well that even when I was mad at Sam, I thought he deserved that best piece of meat, because he was the man of our household. We feed and serve our men, keep them warm, well fed, pleased, possibly happy. In return we expect security, strength, and protection.

My husband was older than me. I wanted to look up to him, learn from him, and seek his protection. In exchange I was willing to give myself to him, my loyalty to him. But I couldn't look up to a child, even if he was six feet four inches tall, even if Adinai insisted he was the king of the family. I liked the idea of him being a king; being a king is sexy, but kings have duties, responsibilities. Also, they are supposed to be in love with their queens and princesses. Adinai's wisdom was silent on this point.

It was February and I was taking the bar again, hoping to escape the intolerable world of document review. Sam's business was shakier by the day. He was making some money, but I never inquired how much because I knew it wasn't enough, even if he was doing his best. Without the money I was making, we could not afford our nanny, without whom we could not function, so I couldn't quit my job. I felt like I was in a constant race in which I was the only contestant.

Everything depended on the bar exam, and I failed it again. It had been four years since my graduation, and still I was not a lawyer. I was crushed, again. There was no point thinking what to do next, I had to review documents and keep making money while I could, because the job could end any day. Ariella was playing with her funny toys, gazing at me from time to time, trying to play with me, while I felt I had no right to enjoy her. I was not worthy.

In the autumn of 2007, the world economy fell into a recession. I was working downtown by the stock exchange, and the people on the street seemed to lack the usual arrogance and vigor in their stride.

There were fewer of them, too—the competition for my favorite bran muffin at the neighborhood delicatessen fell off to nothing. Sam's business did moderately well during good times, but when the recession hit, mugs and bag packs and T-shirts with logos and happy tag lines were the last thing big corporations facing bankruptcies and government inquiries needed. Sam dissolved his business with his longtime partner, closing his showroom, selling his inventory, and planning to begin a new if ill-defined phase of his business working from home. Perhaps he would even start a new venture. We tried to stay optimistic, but we had no savings, and the future did not look bright.

Fortunately, there was a rise of class action lawsuits against major banks because of the subprime mortgage crisis, so there was plenty of document review work. I had to take a pay cut since our wealthy clients were no longer quite as wealthy, but I worked extra hours to make up the difference. Sometimes I was hired to do jobs that required Russian-speaking attorneys, which paid at least double in comparison to English language reviews, and offered flexible hours, unlimited overtime, minimal supervision, even working from home. I stacked up the hours, knowing it couldn't last.

It was a stressful time. Sam kept telling me I needed to learn how to save money, but I didn't know how, since the money I made we spent on the life we lived. You have to have money to save it, and we couldn't do without rent, food, or Adinai. I wasn't ready to accept the notion that enjoying life was a luxury I couldn't afford. My luxurious childhood and comfortable adolescence were nothing but a distant memory now, but I refused to let it go. I didn't want furs or diamonds, I just liked going to restaurants, museums, and movies, and I didn't want to worry about the price of milk. I had a law degree, but without a license it was like a misplaced prop from some forgotten play. I would have to take the bar exam for the fourth time. It meant more expenses and lost wages, and lost weekends, it meant more uncertainty. One thing I did not think of was the possibility of failing again. I studied all day at my mother's place and attended classes at night. I spent the same number of hours studying as I did before, but this time the quality of my studying was different. For the first time I understood what it was I was learning and the method behind it. Once I had learned it, it seemed so ingenious and so simple. Everything turned into a game of spot the issues; the players had become friendly with me, and I smiled each time I recognized their faces. I found myself obsessed with the law, not with the test.

There was a moment of panic when two weeks prior to the exam I still hadn't received my ticket. It was a credit card snafu, and the Board of Law Examiners said it was my mistake, which, narrowly construed was true, but I had to sit for the bar and this awful bureaucrat in Albany could not seem to understand the gravity of the situation. It was outside of his control, he said. I called Sam in tears. He asked for the phone number of the man in Albany. Twenty minutes later he called me back and told me where to express the money order. "Get back to your books; you are taking the bar," he said. How had he managed to convince that obstinate, narrow-minded man? He must have said it differently, in man-talk, that's all I can think.

The next crisis arrived five days before the bar exam when Sam fell ill with a dangerous form of appendicitis. He'd walked into the emergency room by himself not feeling well and they forgot about him on the gurney for twelve hours with abdominal pains and a 102-degree fever. I got there after work and started making a lot of noise and then both our mothers showed up and made even more noise. It was a famous Upper East Side hospital, so when he finally met the surgeon, he *did* save his life. The young doctor came out of the operating room in his smock and told me my husband was a very lucky man. His eye fell on the books and my notes spread on the coffee table. "What's all this?" he said, and I told him about the bar. He looked me in the eyes and said very quietly, "Do me a favor, I know it's hard to do, but leave your husband to me. He is my responsibility now. I will take care of him, and you take care of what you have on this table."

A few days later, I went back to the Javits Center and took the exam. The voice over the loudspeaker announced time, and I felt an unpleasant chill penetrating my spine. I could barely read the first question I was so nervous, while everyone else was filling in those pink bubbles. It was all so familiar, and suddenly, I got angry, and with that anger came the focus. There wasn't a question, essay or multiple choice, I was unfamiliar with. I spotted issues, I applied them to the presented fact patterns, and I could see how everything had its logical resolution. When the loudspeaker ordered us to put our pencils down, I felt almost indifferent to my fate. Thousands of people were exiting in silence, and on that day, I stood in silent solidarity with them all, tired from the test, but not tired from my emotional reaction to it.

The next day it was back to the whirlwind of money-making activity. The winter passed, and spring arrived to remind me of my triumphs and my failures. My nervous heart and that May wind were making me breathless as I was rushing to get to the office that morning. The bar exam results were about to reveal themselves on my computer screen in a matter of minutes. What if I had failed again? I felt sorry for myself, for trying hard and yet for getting nowhere, for absence of hope, for my weakness, for the futility of my efforts, and for realizing that hard work and honest effort, two things I had relied on the most, were about to mock me. It was early, not even eight in the morning. I turned on the computer, punched in my username and my password, got online, made sure no stranger was looking over my shoulder, and logged onto the New York State Board of Law Examiners website. There were more numbers and more passwords to punch in; my fingers were cold. I minimized the window to make my failure look less prominent. I closed my eyes, sure I had failed, and then slowly opening them, I read the word "Congratulations." I enlarged the window, double checked the name and the relevant numbers, and then silently admitted to myself that the word belonged to me. I had passed the bar! I took myself out for a fifteen-dollar cup of coffee at the fancy hotel around the corner, with the cherished secret safely tucked into my heart—a real lawyer: powerful, independent, cool, brave, and rich, drinking extravagant coffee like this all the time.

At day's end, I flew home like some fairy tale fire bird, with flowers for everyone in the family. The keys rattled in my hands as I tried to open the door, falling on the prickly mat at least twice before I got a hold of them. Our apartment door, painted in cheap dirty green, looked so dear that evening. The door opened, I inhaled the sweet odor of home and all those who filled it with their presence, and through my tears I cried: "I am a lawyer! I am a lawyer! I am a lawyer!" I showered them with my messy flowers and wet kisses, desperately trying to seize that precious moment. Little Ariella began to cry. I was trying to explain to my two-year-old that this was not time for tears, but for happiness, at last.

Shortly after, I was admitted to the New York State Bar in solemn ceremony at the Appellate court downtown. Those who loved me were there, including my Ariella. But that was my father's day; it belonged to him more than it did to me, and my entire being demanded his presence. I knew how much he loved me, and I wanted to make sure that he didn't love a nobody. Even before he died, I looked at life through his eyes, and made it my goal to do everything as he would have wanted me to. I didn't become a doctor like my father, but I thought he would have loved seeing me become an American lawyer. He who had spent his entire life challenging the Soviet anti-freedom machine and its crooked codes of morality, adored America and its rule of law. Knowing this inspired me and gave meaning to all those years of failure that had finally culminated in a win.

❦

I'd like to say that my life changed once I became a lawyer, but it didn't. Sam's bad luck in business, our constant lack of money to support our standard of living, such as it was, made it impossible to think of starting a law practice. Even getting a job with a firm meant investing time and money that I didn't have. I stayed with document review; they were paying me more now that I was admitted to the bar, and there were opportunities to employ my language skills. The money was good, even if the job didn't require an attorney so much as an obedient clerk. Maximizing my hours was the only thing that mattered, I tried to work eighty hours a week, but the most I could ever manage was seventy. This way I could eat out, take little Ariella to museums or strolling along Madison Avenue. I loved grocery shopping, because it distracted me from the monotony of my job and my squabbles with Sam. The markets were colorful, fun, full of joyous foods and eccentric people. I walked out feeling like a successful person, with all this lovely food in a bag for my family.

Then I would get home, and Sam would inspect the groceries, criticizing me for spending an extra dollar on milk or some other item which could be more cheaply obtained at some other location further away. In Sam's view, everything was always overpriced, everything needed to be bargained for, bought for less money. To him the value of a thing was not in the way it looked, felt, tasted, or made you feel, but only in its price. These conversations humiliated me, hurt my pride in my status as his wife. I wanted our life to be beautiful, graceful, elegant, the way it was in my Russia, where my existence was lubricated by my parents' love and by my childhood's exclusivity. I guess it was an unfair request, an impossible task, and yet I still wanted it.

Sometimes, we socialized with Sam's friends, who lived in big American houses in lush neighborhoods of Long Island and New Jersey. Suburbia was never anything I wanted to try, but I respected his friends for the way they made a good life for themselves. They were his childhood buddies, and they genuinely loved him, but they also saw no competition in him, and therefore it was easy for them and their bossy wives to treat him with genuine kindness. I was always bored in this company. Some of them were doctors and lawyers, but every conversation revolved around sports, with perhaps a little business and a bit of the stock market. Perhaps it was my fault as well; it was not like I had much to say about my work.

I knew I had no career, only a succession of money jobs, like a car stuck in the mud. I was in my mid-thirties now and as much as I loved life, I found it to be dull. I had nobody to keep me interested. At work I was surrounded by smart sardonic lawyers who were stuck doing the dullest work imaginable, overworked, self-effacing men and women diligently reviewing thousands of pages of documents without omitting a single detail, observing every rule and procedure of the office, keeping their heads down and saving every dollar they made. There was this one little man, he must have been in his fifties, and he came to work early and stayed late, always carrying with him a large bulky rucksack. No one knew anything about him, no one ever spoke to him, and he never spoke to anybody. He reminded me of some inanimate object, or a character from Gogol's world. One morning we received the news that the night before he had collapsed and died in the middle of Grand Central Station with nothing but his work ID to show who he was. I pictured his small, anonymous figure lying still on the marble floor, overpowered by life. We all felt sad, less for his death but for his life. We had trouble remembering his face.

I had a collection of poems, all in Russian, I'd been writing since I was eighteen. Around this time, I got this urgent need to publish them in a book. I found a Russian publisher who offered to do it for $500. His house had a very good reputation in the industry, and he liked my poems and I liked him and we shook hands on a deal. I told Sam about my project, how it would cost money, and he nodded silently, which always meant I was free to spend my own money. After a few days deliberating whether to splurge on proving to myself that I was not a nobody or a nothing, since probably the book wouldn't earn me back $500, I told the publisher "no" after I had already said "yes." What humiliation! I had allowed myself to be weak and pushed away my chance to be inspired. My grandmother would never have done that, she would have given him her last $500, saying "Take this money, because publishing my poetry will inspire my interest in living." But I was not my grandmother, and my grandmother wasn't around to make me do what I really wanted to do.

We had celebrated her ninetieth birthday at her favorite restaurant, the Russian Samovar on Broadway, and everyone had a wonderful time, as we always did. A few weeks later, I called her, the way I always did, to see if she needed anything, but she didn't pick up or return my message. After a while, I began to worry and then I decided to go to her place on Roosevelt Island. When I buzzed her doorbell, she opened the door, but she didn't look right, and she said she had a terrible headache. That was the first time I ever heard her complain. She had heart problems and high blood pressure, but she was bored by medicine and doctors always telling her what to do. She loved good food, had no interest in exercise, and treated matters of her own health with an airy carelessness, like it was an inconvenience. At ninety, she was as sharp as she had ever been, but now she was half-dressed and terribly red in the face. "My head," she said, "my head!" On the wall I saw tiny traces of blood. The stove was lit but there was nothing on it. Some Russian program was on TV, with the volume turned up. I saw that her left arm had turned black, a humongous hematoma. She held her head in both hands. "Babushka, ty upala?" I asked. (Grandma, did you take a fall?)

She denied it. She had always been clumsy, always in a rush, and her tripping and falling used to be a family joke, and even she would laugh as she lay on the ground: "Saul, come help me up!" Now it was just me with her. She wanted me to go home to my husband and my Ariella, she didn't want the ambulance, but when she sat down on the couch and grabbed her head, crying "My head!" I dialed 911. What to say to those operators? Panicked, I realized my phone battery was dying. Her landline phone was either dead or broken; when she took a fall she must have been holding the receiver and dropped it on the floor. When I walked inside the apartment I saw it on the floor, shoved to the corner. I looked for the cord, still mumbling directions, when I heard Marina's voice. Not the voice I had known my whole life, loud, interfering, full of zest and courage, but quiet and full of agony and fear she asked: "Anya, are you there?" I was busy charging the phone, so without looking around I assured her I was right there, that I wasn't going anywhere, that she had nothing to worry about, that help was on the way, but when I turned around and looked at her face, I saw that she couldn't see me anymore. Her green eyes without any expression, every trace of Marina had vanished from that beautiful face.

Was that it? The end of that whirlwind, fiery, magnificent life, my grandmother's life? So, that's how it is, I thought. She had had a massive stroke, and this is the end. Once she was taken to the hospital and evaluated, the test showed a severe head injury. The doctors tried to be kind but there was no hope. She was on blood thinners for her heart condition. She must have been taking a nap, the phone rang, she got up too quickly, got dizzy and fainted. Why did the phone ring? Was it me calling? I was in agony.

She spent three weeks in intensive care, helpless, covered in bandages, in a coma. I sat by her bed every day, but I could barely bring myself to touch her. This wasn't my dazzling Marina. I lost heart; all I could do was stare at her. My mother, though, caressed her, talked to her, covered her with blankets, the way Marina herself had done for my Dedushka Misha in his dying hour. He was ninety-two, blind and in and out of the hospital with his stomach ulcer. His devoted housekeeper Gla was by his side, but she was in her eighties now and none too steady herself. This was in 1993, and Marina and Grandpa Saul were getting ready for their big move to New York, but she would spend weeks at a time in Moscow taking care of Dedushka, then rush back to Leningrad to manage all the logistics of immigration.

They were an odd couple: she the performer, dramatic and emotional, sensitive and shrewd. Dedushka had none of her sensitivity; he'd seen too many people die on his table to be sentimental. In the family, they were like two fireballs, constantly colliding in what sometimes appeared to be conflict, creating more energy, making life happen. They were two great tireless fighters, tough, selfish and selfless at the same time, both in love with life. They understood one another, and they loved their children. Dedushka was glad to have his devoted Marina next to his bed in the hospital, embracing his weakening body with her strength. Unable to move or to see anything but visions from his past, he could still feel my grandmother's presence. At one point one of the doctors said something about his kidneys failing. He looked up into the white ceiling, patted her hand and said: "Agh, Marinochka, I am done for."

My grandmother lasted three weeks in the ICU, but never recovered consciousness.

Still, my grandmother's life, I felt, was stronger than her death. Her humor, her star power, her passion for life, her feminine glamour, her love affairs, her true heart had found a home in every fiber in my inexperienced body long before I could realize what sort of person I had for my Babushka. I had none of her willpower. I was too shy, too soft spoken, too polite, too moody. She was too wise to give advice, but she was full of comical stories and comments, which gave hints about what she really thought.

Little Ariella was never quite comfortable in my clumsy, bony arms, on my hard chest, but whenever Marina would pick up her tiny body and press it against her soft, confident chest, Ariella would stop fidgeting, yawn, and fall asleep. My grandmother was too busy being a star, it took most of her time. Even as a grandmother she was not particularly grandmotherly, as strict with my sister and me as she was with her own children. All that changed when Ariella was born. She became tender, she became gentle. She hated the fact that I was never home, that I worked all the time, was always exhausted from drudgery. In moments of frustration, she would shout: "This is not a family!"

She came from Roosevelt Island on the bus a few times a week, with homemade pies and other foods. She took Ariella for strolls in the fancy pram, in her dark mink coat and her matching mink hat, her head held high, occasionally peeking inside the pram just to make sure whether her *Ptiza Moya Yasnay*, her Shining Bird, was doing all right.

When she died, I lost all joy in my life. It worried me, frightened me. My mother this time had no strength for me, no answers, no support. She felt the way I had at thirteen, an orphan, helpless, and exposed. Who was going to help me get rid of *my* suffocating sadness this time? Time? But time takes time. My grandmother was my only source of wisdom, humor, my link between the old and the new, the nuclear reactor who had been the source of my inspiration throughout my whole life.

Now she had vanished and, in the vacuum where she had been, there was only the memory of her voice, the things she said. Her attitude, her mannerisms, her edgy jokes, her tough criticisms, how I missed them, how I wished I could turn into her and be as strong, as honest, as resilient, as uncompromising, and yet as charming as she was. She always used to say that without inspiration life was not worth living. For every birthday or big celebration, she wished me inspiration. I used to wonder when I was small, but when she died, I realized it was her. She was my inspiration. After my grandmother's death, something shifted in me. I became obsessed with life, and now that nobody else was around to provide me with inspiration, I was going to make my own.

VIII.

Rupturing

S AM AND I HAD NOT BEEN ON A REAL VACATION FOR MANY YEARS. There was never any time or money. A year after my grandmother's death, with our ten-year wedding anniversary approaching, I wanted to do something marvelous for us both. Our life in America was so stale, so mediocre, so utilitarian. In my view, this could only be fixed if we were to go away to Europe. We could pretend that we were still carefree, still loved one another, and all our problems were imaginary.

I wanted to go for the whole month and take Ariella with us. My plan was to spend a day or two in Paris, then go to the French Rivera for two weeks, then to Bordeaux, where my mother's friend had a home. Sam said he was not opposed to the idea in theory, but on a practical level it was way too extravagant and there was no way we could afford it. Rather than argue, I decided to organize the whole thing as a surprise and to tell him it was my anniversary gift to us both.

I booked the flights, and announced we would stay at the Ritz in Paris. Sam seemed pleasantly surprised, but soon he began to say he couldn't go, couldn't afford it, had to work. Things with him and the landlord had gotten ugly, and now we had to move very soon. Take Ariella, he said, your mother can help you. I was furious, how could he ditch me at the last minute? We compromised: he would come for the week of our anniversary and my birthday.

Each of us saw that trip all wrong. For me it was an absolute solution to all our problems. For him, it was a path toward disaster. The luxurious Ritz hotel, the cobblestoned alleys of St. Tropez failed to distract him from his troubles, he couldn't get his mind off what it was all costing, and his feeling that he didn't deserve any of life's pleasures. I couldn't afford it either, but I always thought that money was made to enjoy life. Sam thought it was made to be saved. This was a fundamental disagreement we had.

On our wedding anniversary, we spent over an hour in search of a restaurant that would fit Sam budget. I knew each group of chatty waiters could tell he was reading the prices, not the description of the dishes. I was almost ready to spare us the embarrassment and pay for my own wedding anniversary dinner, but I decided to uphold a tenet I considered essential to my femininity: that the wedding anniversary dinner check was for the man, not the woman. Somehow, we found a suitable place and even managed to maintain a celebratory mood. Sam seemed cheerful, sitting there under that navy sky with its yellow stars like in one of Van Gogh's paintings. In a day or so he went back to New York.

I didn't want to enjoy my holiday without my husband, but I still managed to have fun without him. Ariella still talks about our extravagant French holiday, the wonderful ice cream, the cafés, the colors, pushing through the crowds of tourists at the Louvre to see the *Mona Lisa*, how they treated her like a fairy princess at the Ritz. It convinced her that life outside her tiny banal world was magnificent.

Until now I had never traveled anywhere without my husband, because I never wanted to be looked at as a lonely, single woman without a man to watch over her. With all my love of freedom, I had never been able to free myself from people's opinion of me. What will people think? A single woman in her thirties with a child on her hands is utterly deprived of romantic mystery, she is nothing but one confused clumsy object called *mother*. Gone are her effortlessness, her lightness, her charm, her careless gaze. Motherhood limits a woman's interests, narrows her viewpoint, makes her nervous and anxious. There were all these young, free, breathless, light girls twirling around me. I needed my husband; his presence next to me would have made me feel better. Even if only temporarily, together we would have played correct roles: I, a desirable wife who needs the company of her man; he, my husband, who makes me feel wanted and secure. Still, he was right to go back, he knew he couldn't afford to live the life I wanted him to live, and he didn't want to appear like he was taking advantage of me. I was happy not to meet his disapproving gaze whenever I wanted to buy a couple of souvenirs or an extra portion of ice cream. I spent freely and by the end of the holiday, I didn't have much money left. I took a deep breath, and told myself that no matter what, my job was still waiting for me back in New York.

§

When Sam picked us up at the airport, we were barely on speaking terms. I didn't sleep that night, and early the next morning I was already back at work. Sam and I never talked about France. I knew he was angry with me for spending the money, even though I was the one who had earned it. He thought I was selfish and irresponsible and not a good "team player," a phrase I despise because it smells of socialism. In Soviet Russia, everybody was expected to be a team player. I only wanted to be his wife, with my own strengths, desires, weaknesses, vulnerabilities, questions, and only occasional answers. But I couldn't explain these things to him, how I was convinced that taking myself and my family away to Europe had inspired me to go on and to feel life again.

I worked myself to the bone for the next week or so, but suddenly the client settled the case, the job was over, and I had to find another. This kind of thing happened all the time. I had no outline for the future. I only knew that I wasn't happy in the present. My month in France had showed me I was trapped and I didn't know how to pull myself out.

I found a new job and set about turning time into money, to make up the ground I had lost. For the next few months, I barely noticed how mornings turned into nights. I felt tired, dull. I had no time for books, newspapers, theatres, concerts, museums. Even when I found time to read, I had no one to talk to about it. I read and watched the wrong things, I met and talked to the wrong people. I was becoming the wrong person.

On rare occasions, I would go to a ballet, with Ariella or Mother, no matter what the tickets cost. I needed to have the best seats and it was my money. Those magnificent evenings reminded me of Russia. I could see there was a whole realm out there that existed in parallel to my office full of disgruntled document-review lawyers and my squalid apartment, where I bickered with my husband. It was now a one-bedroom on 72nd Street and York Avenue. Adinai and six-year-old Ariella slept in the living room. It didn't bother me so much: I had given up on the idea of living space. I woke up at 5:30 in the morning and worked all day, and came home late in the evening. Whenever I craved to be on my own, I went to my mother's. So much of my stuff was still there. I never really moved out, never separated myself from her, from my childhood. Her place was my harbor, my oasis. I worked late hours, and sometimes I even went out with my friends.

I craved to be on my own a lot. At home I always felt I was missing out on something, that the world was happening without me, while I sat in the airless cell of whatever office I was assigned, I let myself miss the world's momentum. I was not in a rush to go see Ariella. After a day at my stultifying job with its enforced silence, I couldn't face her childish chatter, even if she was showing me how she was learning her ABCs. Even if it was my own beautiful child.

Sam usually wasn't home to greet me, although I always knew where he was, and what he was up to. We had no secrets from one another, at least as far as I knew. We stopped having time to make love, but we always had time to quarrel. This we saved for weekends, when I had time to notice how much worse things were getting. I was always the one who started it. Sam never got irritated with anything. For him it seemed it was all the same.

After his business failed, he found a job at an online travel agency company. It was a job without any career prospects and with very limited financial compensation, so Sam did not stay there for long. Soon he found a job working for a former competitor, bringing in deals on a commission basis. For this, he made even less money than the little he made before. To take his mind off his troubles, he focused on turning his body and his mind into a temple of physical and spiritual health. His entire life he had suffered from psoriatic arthritis, a painful condition where the skin breaks out in red patches and silvery scales above the affected joints. It was a bad case and he'd been prescribed strong, effective injectables, but because of the side effects he resorted to them only when the pain became unbearable. One day he came home with two huge black binders with hundreds of pages of nutrition advice and announced his decision to stop using medications altogether and rely only on alternative medicine and nutrition. He arrived in the apartment with bags filled with plants, all in different shades of green, and told me to ask Adinai to boil them without salt. He had fallen under the influence of a nutritionist who told him that this diet was going to end his arthritis, and he was convinced our entire family should follow this regimen, eating only green plants. He even suggested little Ariella should give up ice cream; you can imagine what she thought of that.

Adinai, in particular was unable to comprehend this metamorphosis in Sam's thinking. Everything she cooked had salt, meat, and dough in it. In her view, strongly influenced by her culture, human survival depended on getting enough meat to eat. Life without meat meant bad times. The rest of us agreed: this was not a diet; it was a starvation kit.

She shrugged and cooked up the vegetables the way he said. They were unappealing. He ate this way for many weeks, like a monk, and to me he didn't look healthy, but his condition improved until winter came and his arthritis got worse, as it always did with cold weather. Still, he felt his food regimen was important and life changing. He never ceased to lecture us about it.

I was prepared to live with this neurotic dietary routine, but then he joined a men's group. He was always part of some self-improvement group, like Toastmasters, but this was something different, a male support group. It was weird. They met every week, they would form a circle, chant, walk around, talk about their life, their frustrations, make promises, set goals, see how they could help each other and others. On Sunday evenings the men had to meet via conference call, which usually lasted over an hour, sometimes two. Sam took these calls outside or locked himself in the bathroom. I couldn't help eavesdropping. They were giving each other an account of the week gone by, this or that one had sent out job résumés, made up with a wife or girlfriend, quit smoking, taken out the trash. Everyone had to attend, everyone had to be in it together. He came back from the first meeting with these men and his eyes were shining; I could see he was inspired by something. He told me it was the most important thing he had done in his life; it was going to help him be a better man, a better father, a better husband.

Occasionally they went on weekend retreats, to some rustic place in the woods where the real bonding took place. I was never supposed to know exactly where. Sam has never been very outdoorsy, but on these occasions, he bravely ventured into the wild, spending nights at the campfire with his new male friends and exposing his not so young bones to nature.

They called each other "man," and they called the group "Wolfpack." One evening, after a meeting, he came home with a huge wooden stick, six feet in length, and about two and a half inches in diameter. Every week it was someone else's honor to keep the pole stick at his home until the next meeting. He looked like Moses carrying it around Manhattan. "I take it you are the wolfpack's fearless leader?" I inquired sardonically, and with eyes expressing pure faith in the cause he told me there was nothing funny about it. Those men understood him, he said.

I bit my tongue. It would have been unfair and cruel of me to mock him the way I felt like doing. He had lost his business. He was not a success, but neither was I for that matter, so who was I to criticize him? More importantly, what I observed was more alarming. My husband was no longer the master of his own fortune, unable to control the course of his family's life. Some of these guys had it even worse, and that gave him comfort, made him feel less insecure and less exposed. They sympathized with one another, and their troubles led them to believe they understood one another as well. He was a mentor to an inner-city kid, from a broken home, a good kid, but already scarred by the worst of what the city had to offer. Sam played basketball with him, he spent time with him, and involved him with his wolfpack group. I don't know what happened to the kid in the end, but I know Sam needed that boy more than the boy needed him.

I decided not to interfere. Sam was good, kind, honest, loyal, always wanting to help. That was the guy I married. Now, his altruistic interests had become an obsession, to the exclusion of his real responsibilities in life: making sure we didn't get evicted again or giving me a chance to work less than sixty hours a week. They called it a men's group, but these were not masculine qualities, or at least they did not seem masculine to me.

He was on the phone with the wolfpack men all the time, and sometimes I came home to find one of them at our apartment for an overnight stay. Sam knew I would never refuse a guest. In Russia, hospitality is a sacred obligation, guests must be fed, smiled at, conversed with, given a bed. I did all that, but I was not happy.

The less time we spent together, the less of it both of us needed and desired. Intimacy? I had to remind him. He never refused me, was always kind, loyal, and agreeable, but it was always me who had to initiate our doomed bedroom game. Sex did not seem as important to him as it was to me, the miraculous thread strong enough to hold us together. Without it, I thought our marriage was in name only. I could either encircle him with gentle foreplay or simply announce to him that it was time, but I was getting tired.

I knew Sam wanted another child, and I knew it had to be done, because, as my grandmother used to say, "one child is not a child," and it had to be with my husband Sam and nobody else. In those days, despite everything, I felt I owed him a duty as his wife to keep him happy, even though I was full of fury with him and at my life. Having a baby with him was one of the ways of keeping him happy. In a fight, I would sometimes threaten that I would never consider having another baby.

In his novella *Kreutzer Sonata*, Tolstoy says that a woman has only two choices: either to kill the woman within herself by never becoming a mother, thus allowing a man to enjoy her sexually, or become a mother, a nurse, and a mistress. According to Tolstoy, no woman has the strength to be all three, and therein lies the cause of much hysteria. "If they would only reflect what a grand work for the wife is the period of gestation! In her is forming the being who continues us, and this holy work is thwarted and rendered painful . . . by what? It is frightful to think of it! And after that they talk of the liberties and the rights of woman! It is like the cannibals fattening their prisoners in order to devour them, and assuring these unfortunates at the same time that their rights and their liberties are guarded!"

There was also my vanity to consider. Because I needed to work, it gave me a perfect excuse to not be at home; it was a perfect escape into the world. I had to admit that the work I so despised gave me the freedom to spend my own money and enjoy life's little pleasures. I had friends I enjoyed, and it didn't escape me that I was still young and pretty, I could make men smile that special smile which made me feel effortlessly beautiful and free. Even if my husband had grown tired or fallen out of love, there was still much in life to entertain me. But once I had another baby and become the mama of a newborn again, that would all go away. The very thought of myself all caged up again, voluntarily, made my throat feel dry with anger. I wanted to play on my own terms, and I didn't want anybody to ask me any questions, least of all my own husband. Was I becoming a real American woman for whom femininity has become a dirty word? Where was my uniquely Russian desire to belong to a man?

A worm deep inside me was poisoning my mind with the notion that perhaps Sam was just not in love with me anymore. For his birthday that year I got us a room at the Carlyle Hotel on Madison Avenue. Perhaps it was more a gift for me, who adored luxury, comfort, loveliness, and illusion, but I could count on him not to refuse a good meal at the best vegan restaurant in town, a few blocks away from the hotel, where I planned to order almost everything on the menu and not think about the price at all, followed by a luxurious bed with me in it.

We agreed to meet at the hotel at noon on a Saturday, and I checked in right on time to inspect the marvelous, pristine, fragrant rented heaven where everything seemed to have a seal of wealth and security. It was a bright crisp February morning, and the sunlight was illuminating every corner of Madison Avenue; I could see it from my glowing window, but where was Sam to make the picture complete? He was always late, and that day he made me wait over an hour. So typical, and it made me mad and sad, but I decided to ignore it. He showed up in the end, and he was happy, and so was I, and we spent that day as if that *other* life, a few blocks away, did not exist. Nothing was troubling us in that warm room, on that lush, soft bed. I forced myself to feel carefree, loving, sensual, and by the end of the evening when I looked at myself in the mirror, I saw a different person: newer, younger, happier.

We went to dinner at the trendy new restaurant. Since everything was vegan and organic, Sam felt it was safe to consume food there, and we spotted a few famous people whose names I cannot recall participating in what was then the latest trend. I tried to pretend that we lived like this not only on his birthday but on all days of the year. The afternoon in the hotel room was still fresh in my mind, I felt we still had so much to look forward to. We discussed our plans for the future; about Sam's business plans and about the endlessness of opportunities.

More than anything, I was just enjoying the thought of waking up in our rented splendor. We got back to the Carlyle, weakened by the evening's tenderness, softened by our own optimism, and slept a sleep that was restful, healthy, and deep. We woke up, had a lovely breakfast, and checked out. Sam wanted to walk back home, but I insisted on a taxi, my treat.

Life went on. Things were actually looking up for me at work, I was at a good firm, they needed someone who spoke Russian, and the pay was pretty good with overtime. There was still reason to believe that one day my life was going to be wonderful. I was already planning our next summer getaway, imagining myself in the latest summer fashions somewhere on the Italian Riviera.

In the middle of all this, my breasts began to hurt. I went to see my Georgian doctor, who had helped me so much the last time. He looked me over, took my blood, and called me a few days later at work to say he had diagnosed me with a very early pregnancy. "What?" I said. "How? When? Where?" He gave a witty smile I could feel over the telephone line and replied it was for sure what, but it was up to me to remember how, when, and where. He'd see me soon, he said, and passed the phone back to his assistant. I was all dressed up for work. I had to go to a meeting. I looked down at my waistline and detected no difference, the bathroom mirror could not confirm anything either. I went back to work thinking it was cool I could get pregnant just like that, on my own, without a doctor's help. It must have been the beautiful Carlyle Hotel, that evening, right before dinner.

I called Sam and told him. He was surprised and very happy, like a child. I walked home that night, forty blocks, thinking about the beauty of life. A very small, very insignificant part of me felt victorious. My body was capable of doing something like that on its own, voluntarily, without any plan, without my permission, surprising me at the age of thirty-five. It was truly a miraculous occurrence. At the same time, this had happened *without* my permission. I was not sure I was in agreement, had no time to consider. Yes, I wanted another baby, but right this minute, in seven months' time? What was going to happen to my body, my sundresses in the summer, my vacation in Italy? How were we going to afford two children when we could scarcely afford one? That was our reality, banal and simple. I was thinking these thoughts in the middle of York Avenue when a car zoomed by me, missing me by inches.

At home, Ariella was exhilarated at the news, convinced it was her own doing. She felt triumphant. Later I told Sam all that I had on my mind. I told him that I had a change of heart, and I gave solid reasons which included my vanity, as well as realistic worries about our financial survival. I knew he understood that having another child, in our case, meant financial sacrifice and a lesser quality of life. He listened, he was patient, he was kind, he said nothing. On the one hand, he knew he was powerless to fight me when I got into one of my moods. But in no way did his silent response mean that he agreed with me. With his silence he rebelled against my hysteria. I wanted him to fight me on everything I said to him, I wanted him to reassure me that everything was going to be beautiful, but instead he kept to himself. He simply let me vent.

A few days later, still full of anger, on a bright, careless April day, I called my doctor. In a quivering voice I told him I didn't want it. It was not for me. He listened to me. He told me that he would always be on my side, work with me, and help me. He told me not to get upset like that. My appointment wasn't until the next day, but he said I could come see him right away. I had a choice. I could do anything I wanted. I thought of Sam who would be devastated, and yet he wouldn't have been able to either influence or contradict my decision. I thought of Ariella, who would be so disappointed, of my mother and her abortions before she had me, of my grandmother.

I had a lot of freedom, but as it turned out, not enough free will. I was limited by self-imposed checks and balances. I was conflicted, constrained by fears and undeniable realities, by rules and laws and the physical limitations of my body. What if this was my last chance to have a baby? I wasn't exactly a fertility goddess, and my getting pregnant like that, for the first time in six years, was a bit on the miraculous side. I thought a lot about my grandmother, by now a permanent absence from my life, and of her contagious love for life itself. My grandmother had been such a free person; she never seemed to be chained to anything or by anyone, but that didn't mean she deprived herself of things or of people. Her children and her family were her fortress, but they did not define her because she was not restrained by them, because she was not attached to that fortress. "One child is not a child"—those were my grandmother's words, and I heard them with clarity. My grandmother was gone, and for whatever reason I found myself pregnant again. On that day I decided not to get an abortion.

All throughout my pregnancy I tried to pretend I wasn't pregnant. I couldn't smoke or drink wine, but I dressed glamorously and continued to live my life. At one point I worked three jobs, I walked everywhere, and I made sure I never refused an invitation. Since we first began dating, during good times and bad times, Friday night was always a sushi date night for Sam and me. We continued with this tradition even during my pregnancy. I spent every day planning out my return to normal life the instant I delivered my second baby. I planned to go straight back to work. I could eat and drink what I wanted, I could go back to smoking, I could wear my beautiful dresses, I could feel weightless and be slender again.

Marina Goldie Meltzer, named for her two great-grandmothers, was born on October 29, 2012, early and without advance notice, the same way she was conceived. The obnoxious gusts of Hurricane Sandy must have pushed her out of me as they pushed the tide over lower Manhattan and Brooklyn. We were lucky to be on high ground at Lenox Hill Hospital on the Upper East Side. Marina was a quiet little baby, with a formidable forehead, and large ears. I felt curiosity and pity at her small, helpless body, her facial features, those soft, floppy ears. While Ariella's eyes were crystal blue, Marinas were dark blue, like two deep sapphires. Sandy shut down the city for days, and we were all stuck at home in our one-bedroom apartment, Adinai, Ariella, our tiny Marinochka, Sam. Everyone was happy but me. I felt like I was back in captivity.

Marinochka was small and not a good eater. I was not the greatest breast feeder. I had plenty of milk, but again I found the entire thing to be a nuisance for which I had no patience. As a result, the baby became fussy. We had stacks of baby formula prepared for her, but she wouldn't drink it, she had stomachaches. She didn't seem to like my own milk any better. She cried, she screamed, because she was hungry. Her little routine of eating and sleeping was not tranquil, but whenever she was at rest, or simply stared at us with her clever gaze, even my disagreeable mind was at peace.

A week after I got home from the hospital, I went to work. My doctor wasn't too happy about it, but I had worn him down. It wasn't the work I wanted, of course, it was an excuse for being away from home. Nobody could blame me for working many hours, especially now that I had two children to support. I pretended that nothing had changed in my life. As usual, work was an excuse for not being at home. Sam's situation was no better, still working on commission, busy in the evenings with his men's group meetings, talking to them on the phone. I didn't feel bad about having to stay at work late. Sometimes we'd get a drink together after work, but he didn't want to meet any of my new friends. On weekends, if I had no work to protect me from home, on the nanny's day off, with no one and nothing to distract us from each other, we pretended to want to do something nice together, but really, we didn't. Sam would go off alone to work out or do something for one of his "wolfpack" members and he'd make sure it took half the day. If he had to meet me somewhere, he was never on time. I could never get him on his cell phone. Sometimes he'd disappear for hours, and I would be stuck waiting with the kids until he returned. He might have struck up a conversation with someone on the street; he still thought it might be good for his business. On some weekends he spent much time with the men doing altruistic work. After Hurricane Sandy hit, their wolfpack group spent days on Staten Island helping with cleanup and building temporary homes, which was admirable, and I dared not criticize him for that.

Sometimes I reflected that nothing tragic was happening. There was no infidelity, no abuse, but clearly, I had become secondary. He was not in love with me, or even interested in me anymore. That was infuriating. I picked fights. I told him his group reminded me of a sect, a cult. His devotion to those strangers, to the exclusion of his family, seemed fanatical to me. He got offended, he insisted his wolfpack was making him a better husband and a better father, and all the work he was doing was for me, for our family. But how could he be a better husband or a father by not spending time with his family? He could not see my point.

I met some of those men and heard about others from Sam, and as far as I could tell they all shared one common bond: failure. There might have been a point in their life when they might have had success, but now was not that time. The reason for their assembly was to justify their failure to each other and to themselves. In addition to professional lack of success, they all seemed to have problems with girlfriends, wives, and children. Sam was hiding from me as much as I was from him, and the group was his refuge for his wounded self-esteem.

I understood. I always felt more comfortable with people who had failed the bar exam at least once, had boyfriend problems or trouble getting pregnant. Misery, as the proverb has it in many languages, loves company. I don't blame Sam for seeking out people who could understand him, but he couldn't convince me that this self-absorbed activity, which further estranged him from me, was for my benefit. I saw Sam grapple with those men's emotional problems, their anger, their sense of victimhood, with *their* complaints, showing them far more attention and care than he ever showed me.

I knew I wasn't in love with Sam when I met him. I knew it later when we began to date, and then when we got engaged. I knew it because I had been in love once, and I could still remember how it felt. With Sam it was something dear, something wonderful, light-hearted, warm, but it wasn't being in love. *In love* meant being helplessly jealous and unreasonably beautiful. I waited for all these sensations to come back and visit me again, but they didn't. We got along just fine. Compatibility is important for a loving marriage, but not for passion and for falling in love. I saw how smitten with me he was, but I also saw that his passion had limitations. Still, I closed my eyes to that. I also saw that he was not an eagle, as we say in Russia. In other words, he was not a risk taker, a daring player, a fighter. That night at the restaurant, a long time ago, when he carefully asked me: "What if I don't end up making money, or be successful?" he wanted to see my reaction, or, perhaps, he sought my permission to not be successful. Back then, I brushed it off as something minor. I knew he was neutral toward art, music, and literature, preferring sports and current events. I knew he was careful with money, that he valued education and loved Manhattan as long as it didn't cost too much. I knew all that, and yet none of it seemed to matter, because I didn't want it to matter. I chose Sam for his goodness, his honesty, his loyalty to me and to my family, because he was Jewish and wanted to have a home, with children in it. Because all I wanted was to get married, I deceived myself, and I deceived him. I told myself I was marrying a good man, and even if I was settling for less, I could worry about that later.

Once Sam and I had satisfied the minimum requirement by actually getting married and procreating, I began to suspect that we might have reached the minimum and the maximum of our marital bliss. I began to suspect the vacuum. Looking back, I understand that I mistook Sam's virtues for qualities that would substitute for intimacy, passionate love, marital love, and most importantly, his ability to play the role of my king, who would protect me and support me and not give me away.

Baby Marina had terrible stomach issues. Her crying was so severe it caused her to vomit. I tried my best to be calm on the outside but seeing her like that tore me to pieces. Even though it was Adinai who took care of her day and night, I couldn't handle watching Marina's body shake from colic each time she had a bit of food or got a bit upset. Our pediatrician told us it was going to get better as she began to move more and that it would be fine once she began to walk. Taking care of her on Adinai day off was almost always a frightening experience. I would get home relatively early, before Marina's bedtime, and calm myself down with a cigarette before entering the apartment. Admittedly, it was not entirely unpleasant to find myself at home surrounded by those creatures who, with their helpless little bodies and funny voices and soft faces, would run toward me just to be kissed and cuddled, but after twenty minutes of sweetness I had no idea what to do.

We lived in a small apartment, the front door opened on the living room, where the children slept, first with Adinai, and then with a new nanny who came to replace Adinai shortly after Marina was born. I didn't want Adinai to go. I begged her to stay, I offered money. But she was done. She was tired. Ariella was beside herself, she followed her outside, crying at the top of her lungs, grabbing on to Adinai's clothes, biting her, trying to prevent her from going. Another lovely Kyrgyz woman came to replace her, and then another, Gulzat, who has now been living with us eight years. Marina refused to sleep in her fancy crib, so Gulzat and the baby shared the same bed. My father's antique desk from Moscow, with all those intricate drawers, now served as a changing table for our babies. I had to be practical, the desk had no other use.

The living room was the only one you could breathe in. The bedroom was cluttered, with room only for the bed and walls that pressed in on you when you closed the door, but this was the only place to be once the children went to sleep. We had to be very quiet if we wanted to use the kitchen. When I got home early enough, I cooked for Sam one of his healthy meals, helped Ariella with her homework, played with baby Marina until she reached her threshold of cheerfulness, and tried to envision the future.

One such evening Sam suggested moving out of the city. Roosevelt Island had a great view of Manhattan, there were nice areas of Brooklyn or Queens. This was a red line. I had told him long ago that Manhattan was the only place I considered worth living in. The city was exciting and fun, he said, but the suburbs were better suited for bringing up the family. At that point the conversation was over, and maybe the date and the relationship, too. I didn't speak to him for an hour, because to me those were irreconcilable differences.

All Sam's childhood friends eventually bought big cars and houses with backyards, modeled on their own childhoods. For them, Manhattan was a temporary playground. To me, someone born and raised in the gluttonous metropolis of Moscow, Manhattan was my whole idea of America. Immigration made no sense to me without Manhattan, the glittering island of the pursuit of happiness. It was true that I couldn't breathe in our apartment and avoided it when-ever I could, but I had never considered sacrificing my Manhattan address for a larger space away from the city. Sam knew it, and yet he kept bringing it up. So, we bickered, and when we didn't bicker, he was on the phone with the wolfpack. I began to avoid him, leaving home early, coming home as late as I could, to avoid bickering or really any sort of communication that would inevitably lead to a squabble.

One time I came home with a few new things for the apartment, perhaps some pretty new pillows, new sheets, or a duvet cover. I also bought new feeding equipment for baby Marina that the doctors said should help her digestion. I remember trying to be money smart about the whole thing so Sam would be impressed, but he surveyed the receipts, shrugged, and gave his usual speech against spending money. I helplessly mumbled that those were the things life con-sisted of; we needed those things, I worked, and I made money so we could have the things we needed, and I reminded him about his job. Rather than fight me, he simply nodded, fell silent, and went on working on his laptop. I knew that with him silence always meant disagreement and resentment.

I sat at the table, taking in my surroundings: the kids playing, our exhausted nanny, Sam's oblivious typing, and then a call came in, one of his wolfpack and he took it. Was this going to be my life? My whole being rebelled against the idea. I didn't know what I was going to do about it, but I knew I didn't want what I had. I despised it, and it embarrassed me, and I was ashamed of myself for being embarrassed by it. I felt neither loved, nor admired, nor needed, and as a result, any remaining love and loyalty that I once felt toward my husband began to slip away. It was a strange and dangerous feeling, a lonely feeling. But at the same time, something within me began to sense freedom, the kind that allows you to break away and run toward unbroken dreams and new hopes.

IX.

My King

I<small>T WOULD BE JUST THE TWO OF US IN BEAUTIFUL</small> C<small>ARNEGIE</small> H<small>ALL</small>, and no one to disturb our pleasure. Valery Gergiev, my mother's old friend from the Leningrad Conservatoire, was conducting an all-Russian program at Carnegie Hall. Many years ago, in the Soviet Union, my grandfather Saul put Valery Gergiev's name on the musical map of the country. As years passed and his fame grew, he never ceased to feel a special connection to my family. After the concert, my mother and were going to dinner with the double bass player in the orchestra, one of my mother's oldest friends.

It was October 11, 2013. I wore a flare skirt of black tulle which hugged my slim waist and a thin black sequined top, along with my favorite stiletto heels. My hair I wore in the French style: short, but not too short. Our seats were in the orchestra, where we met many of our friends in the classical music world, some of whom we had known since our days in Russia. It felt so pleasant to be talked to and to feel at ease with people. Even the vibrations of the orchestra, and most importantly, the Russian music itself penetrated me completely that night. I felt alive and young, like I had come back home.

When the concert ended it was time to go backstage, which I never much liked. There was always pushing and shoving, everyone thinking he was more important than the person next to him, so that the artist was going to notice or remember him. Meanwhile, all an artist really wants after a performance is to be left alone. My mother is a professional backstage person. She loves to mix and mingle with powerful people, make new connections and friendships, and she is good at it. I like to make a five-minute grand entrance, but I have no patience for making conversation about nothing.

I told my mother I'd wait for her outside, but she would hear none of it. I was going to mingle whether I liked it or not. I had to admit my spirits were lifted by how pretty I looked that night. I saw men glancing and smiling at me. In the elevator two unsuspecting young Russian orchestra players discussed my looks right in front of me. As the door opened, I turned to them and thanked them, in flawless Russian, for their performance, watching their jaws drop before I walked away.

The big reception room backstage was filled to capacity, with friends of the maestro, music critics, public relations people, businessmen, agents, musicians, protégés, people of unknown professions, fake and real celebrities, and most importantly, donors with bottomless pockets and passionate love not only for music but also for Valery himself, who is a charming fellow. My mother was effortlessly chatting with someone of visible importance who turned out to be Alexi Kudrin, the former finance minister of Russia. I had told my mother I was starving and given her fifteen minutes, but the maestro had not yet made his appearance. After a few polite words with the minister, I apologized and positioned myself in the corner where I could sulk privately. I was standing with my arms folded across my chest, thinking of the sushi dinner I was probably missing, when a man with a tray offered me champagne. I politely declined. He walked away, only to return a few minutes later. In my best impression of Greta Garbo, I told him I did not drink champagne. Thus rebuffed, he withdrew.

I felt my mother tapping my shoulder, inquiring why I was being so unsocial. She said that she had recognized the man. I told her that he was a waiter, and that I was not interested in waiters, and even less so in champagne. Irritated, she told me in Russian that I was never going to get anywhere in life with my defeatist, inert, timid, and unsocial disposition. Here were a lot of interesting people with whom I should try and make a connection. I was supposed to be building a law practice, and these types of evenings should be seen as an opportunity. I saw them as a waste of time. I gave her a dirty look and she went back to her brilliant social rounds.

I could see that my waiter friend had taken a liking to me. He kept staring at me from the opposite side of the room. He was wearing a natty suit, and he looked quite a bit older than the other waiters. Perhaps he was the head of the catering team. Why does everyone have to love champagne? This time without a tray in his hands, he confidently walked straight across the room and, ignoring my bad mood, and pointing to the Star of David teasingly hanging around my neck, he commented that it was "quite a bold statement." I remember being amused by the comment. He then asked me if I was Israeli. "No," I said with a slight indignation, "I am a Russian Jew." "So am I," he said. By the way he sounded out his vowels and consonants, I could tell he was an Englishman, but even this could not charm me. I was tired and hungry and irritated and not about to be chatted up by some waiter. Sometimes it seems like every other person in New York City is descended from someone who ran away from some pogrom in Russia. "I don't think with that accent you can pass for a Russian Jew," I said, this time flirtatiously, and with much less irritation. One might wonder, what does a Russian Jew of the twenty-first century look like? Without writing a treatise on it, I will just say that a Russian Jew of the twenty-first century sounds and looks (even if he wears a $3,000 suit) like his ancestors from one hundred, fifty, or thirty years ago. A Russian Jew always speaks with a mysterious accent, he is forever haunted by antisemitism, and in his eyes, you will always see hope fighting with despair. Westernized Jews, such as my new friend, did not possess these qualities. He gently protested, ignoring my scorn, and told me about how his grandparents on his mother's side came from a place called Ekaterinoslav in Ukraine. They fled the pogroms at the end of the nineteenth century and settled in Switzerland. His father's side of the family were also refugees from Russia, but ended up in Ireland and then England. He asked me again if I would not care for some champagne, at which point I confessed as charmingly as I could how much I detested champagne.

He was extremely charming, this Russian Jewish caterer, and evidently a person of importance because every thirty seconds he was interrupted by some important-looking person who appeared to know him and ignored me. I didn't mind a bit of flirtation, but I was already anticipating the predictable list of questions about Russia, immigration, and did I like it in America? Just another tiresome businessman. Can he help me with anything? A job? My business? I had no idea how to network. Even if I were in good spirits, this social small talk never led anywhere. On the other hand, I did notice the man had a playful look in his eyes, which I rather liked. When we got around to "What do you do?" I said I was a lawyer, and he looked a bit surprised. People usually don't expect to see a lawyer in me, but I am one when I need to be, and my British friend had ruffled my feathers when he questioned me about my trade as if I were I schoolgirl, so I asked "What about you? What do you do?"

"I run Carnegie Hall," he said.

The room was noisy, I thought I must have misheard him. "I am sorry, what?"

"I run Carnegie Hall. I am so sorry, but I have to go and make a speech for Valery. It's his birthday today." And he was off, to make a toast in honor of Valery's sixtieth birthday, and another to congratulate him on his triumphant concert. Everyone in the room was looking at him, especially me. Afterward, he was busy talking to people. I stood by my mother's side and shot discreet glances his way; delighted to see my Russian Jewish Englishman gazing directly back at me. I turned away. In two minutes or so I looked back; he wasn't there anymore.

I surveyed the room once more, and there he was again, staring at me, like I thought no man had ever done before. His stare was intense, attentive, and serious. It excited me because it made me feel as if I had been picked out from the rest. For the first time in years, my heart began to beat faster.

My mother said it was time to go, but now I didn't want to. How could I leave now when I had this feeling? He was still in the room, still busy talking to people. He had told me his name, but I wasn't paying attention. I have always been hopelessly timid with men, never knowing how to make the first move without feeling foolish, but that night I felt inspired. I couldn't let this sweet flirtatious meeting end right there and then. On my way out I made a gentle U-turn to where he was standing. I saw him watching, and I smiled at him. He asked for my card and gave me his, then boldly inquired if I would be interested in having lunch with him.

At dinner, I forgot about how hungry I was, ignored the guests I was supposed to be nice to, and buried my nose in my phone, googling Clive Gillinson, the executive and artistic director of Carnegie Hall. There was a lot about him: a talented mathematician, a prodigy on the cello, playing in the London Symphony Orchestra at twenty. He became orchestra manager there in his thirties and saved it from bankruptcy. In his second career as an impresario, he was a founding partner in the Pacific Music Festival in Sapporo, Japan, with Leonard Bernstein and Michael Tilson Thomas, established music education programs under the aegis of the LSO, and started a record label. There was more: he held a vast array of honors from all over the world and had been knighted by the Queen. His name was Sir Clive Gillinson, and, indeed, he was the executive and artistic director of Carnegie Hall.

I checked out his birthday, and he was a solid thirty years older than me. I smiled. I had always liked older men. Their ways with women are more tender. With women of their own age, perhaps, they are different, but with younger women, they are less judgmental, they are patient, they know how to adore and cherish all that is still young. A few paragraphs down, where it talked about his personal life, it said he was married and the father of three children. That last bit of information only whetted my appetite.

I had to chew my food and to swallow, and during those moments I thought about him, my new acquaintance, the knight. I recollected every moment of the evening: his gaze, his voice, what he said. Would he invite me to lunch? Who knows? People say things they don't mean, or, even if they mean the things they say, they forget about them. Feelings and words are fleeting, especially when uttered to strangers by strangers, but in the middle of the day, I received an email from Clive Gillinson's assistant inquiring whether I was free to have lunch with Mr. Gillinson.

I ran to my mother, excited and out of breath, even though she was only in the next room, and asked her what I should do. "He invited you to lunch? You go to lunch!"

Our date was at the famous Petrossian restaurant, now sadly closed, near Carnegie Hall. Ostensibly it was a business lunch, but I knew I was flirting and dressed accordingly in a Calvin Klein silk pencil skirt and a cropped cashmere V-neck navy cardigan with high heels.

I was older now and aware of it. Females either spend fortunes on aging gracefully, or they simply spend the rest of their days in denial about this cruel inconvenience called the process of getting older. The truth is, and all women know it, there is no such thing as aging "gracefully" for women. They just age. A woman's age is reflected in the way she looks, she walks, in the texture of her skin, as well as in the way she thinks. Even if her thoughts become wiser, they lack freshness. A young girl's silliness can be forgiven because of her youth; an older woman not so much. This is not so for men.

I never eat lunch. It's a day destroyer, messes up one's thoughts as well as one's digestion. I despise it as much as I despise champagne, and as much as eating dinner before eight or bed before one in the morning, but here I was making an exception for Sir Clive. I was so nervous I ordered the wrong thing: a salad covered with bacon bits, not even kosher style, and had to spend the entire hour and a quarter pretending to be interested in it. No doubt this did not escape the attention of Mr. Gillinson, but he did not mention it. He was wearing a dark suit and a white shirt and tie, very correct. His face was serious and attentive, his eyes animated, his voice full of life. I was intimidated yet attracted. Our conversation was flowing, effortless, easy.

He told me all about his job, and then all about his children. At first, I thought they were small, but it turned out they were all nearly my age, with lives of their own. There were three of them and he seemed to love them very much. They all lived in England.

There are two types of men who won't stop talking about their children: first-time fathers of babies and unhappy husbands. My new friend was in the latter category. Tellingly, he never once mentioned the mother of these children of his. For my part, I said nothing about my personal life, never hinted I was carrying any baggage. I had both my diamond engagement and my wedding band on my left finger, so it was up to him to ask questions, but he wasn't asking any. Our lunch ended, and he asked if I would be interested in coming to a concert at Carnegie Hall someday. "Yes, but only to the very best one," I replied. He smiled. "All right, I'll make sure I only invite you to the best one, then."

I began to receive invitations a few times a week; the concerts were all the best, and any time he invited me to sit in the director's box #43, I came. I never declined a single invitation. Perhaps it would have been wiser to say "no, I have other plans" at least once. I never did learn how to play hard to get.

Suddenly, I was engulfed by the arts again. This was my new hobby, and it was exhilarating. A glittering world had opened itself to me, and I wasn't going to allow anybody to take it away. At home I told Sam almost everything about my new acquaintance. Sam never objected to my regular concert attendance; he knew he had no right to deny me something that he had neither the desire to participate in nor the means to support.

There was no physical impropriety in going to Carnegie Hall and sitting in the director's box. My Englishman occasionally invited me for a bite to eat or a drink after a concert, but none of these outings ever culminated in anything more than a friendly hug; he never tried to kiss me or touch me. Three months had passed since our first acquaintance, and I was getting more and more intrigued by the status of our relationship. Sometimes I thought he was not interested in me at all and just liked me for a friend. His British politeness was impeccable, inscrutable. His self-control was immaculate, and while there was always a hint of flirtation in his sharp sense of humor, he never allowed himself the slightest impropriety of speech. The subject of whether I was married or had children never came up. Did he not care, in the way I did not care? I couldn't tell. I had become ill with the sickening feeling of wanting to be wanted. I had neither time nor patience to decide whether it was physical or emotional. It was all merged into one sensation, accumulating in my stomach, and I knew I had got it from him. My heart was open, he had me from the first moment I saw him watching me that night. After three months of sitting in the director's box #43, of being wined and dined, I had had enough of polite hugs. I wanted to know if he really liked me the way I liked him, and if he wanted to kiss me on the mouth instead of just giving me a sweet embrace.

The holidays came, he was leaving for two weeks to see his children and his wife in England. We had our goodbye dinner, an intimate affair at a place way across town. I brought him a book on Pushkin, the poet who, to almost every Russian, including myself, meant everything. Another major Russian poet said exactly that of my beloved poet and writer, that "Pushkin was our everything." So, it meant something for me to give Clive that book that evening. That night I revealed to him that I was married and had two daughters. My younger daughter, Marina, had barely turned one at the time. He was touched by my gift, knowing the importance to Russians of our greatest poet, and he wasn't surprised that I was married, but small children were news to him. He said he didn't think I was a mother because I seemed to have so much freedom. I laughed and told him I believed in paid help. He walked me all the way home. We walked, we laughed, we barely touched. Upon reaching my street, I only got a sweet cuddle and a kiss on the cheek.

Then he went away and I didn't hear from him. I began to wonder what my odd friendship with him really meant, whether my desire-inflated ego simply imagined his infatuation with me. To review: he was thirty years older, a busy and important man who moved in the highest circles, where rules of relationship might vary dramatically from the ones I knew. After ten days, I was in despair, sure it was a lie that distance makes the heart grow fonder; distance makes people forget people.

Determined to celebrate New Year's Eve in style, I twisted Sam's arm to come with me to the Russian Samovar with some friends. My grandmother loved it there, she knew the owner and I used to go with her and watch her do her thing with the Russian musicians who all loved her. The music was the best part of the Russian Samovar. It was opened by Mikhail Baryshnikov and the poet Joseph Brodsky and the walls were adorned with pictures of Russian intelligentsia, refuseniks, and some of the world's greatest artists, writers, and musicians of the era, who were regulars. The décor, with red tablecloths and green lampshades, gave one a mixed taste of pre-Revolutionary Russia and stale Soviet Empire. The quality of the food has varied over the years, but I always loved the black bread, *seledka* (herring), and pickled vegetables. One never went there for the food, but for the state of *Russkaya Nostalgia* that could only be achieved at the Russian Samovar. The restaurant had lost some of its charm when the city's health-obsessed Mayor Bloomberg had outlawed smoking. My heart full of anticipation for the New Year, I got all dressed up and we all had a good time.

After midnight, I sent a clandestine email to my English friend, wishing him a happy New Year. I was sure he had forgotten me, but suddenly I saw his name staring at me on the screen of my phone. He said he was looking forward to seeing me, and I took that as a hint that he missed me the way I wanted him to. I didn't care if I was wrong about it because I desperately wanted it to be true. Replying, I told him I had just the place to take him.

I had the perfect occasion in mind for our welcome back date. On the eve of January 13, Russians celebrate Stary Novy God: Old New Year, which marks the changing of the year according to the old Julian calendar, used in Russia until the Bolshevik revolution in 1918. Old New Year is an informal, and very nostalgic holiday that marks the official end of the lengthy holiday season, a night of eating, drinking, singing, and lamenting the past.

We met at the very cosmopolitan hour of 10:30 in the evening at the Russian Samovar. It was already noisy and crowded with Russians from all walks of life. I had made a reservation weeks before and asked for a good cozy table in the back, but instead got a very seedy table near the exit by the bar. I complained indignantly in Russian, and they agreed to move us to a better one as soon as something freed up. I knew they were lying. I had wanted to impress my date with my connections, show him I had pull at the Russian Samovar, but it didn't look like I did.

He arrived punctually at 10:30 with a gravely serious expression on his face that gave me pause, but as soon as he saw me waving at him, the muscles on his face relaxed, and my courage came back to me. We talked about everything that evening, and we laughed much more than we ever did before. He was light, mischievous, charming, utterly captivating. We talked about Russia, about Mstislav Rostropovich, the greatest cellist of all time and his particular friend. My family and I knew Slava, as the whole world called him, as well. We talked about how he and his wife, Galina Vishnevskaya, the great opera voice, were exiled from the Soviet Union in 1974 for sheltering the writer Aleksander Solzhenitsyn in their home. We talked about Israel and about being Jewish in a non-Jewish world. He had been in Israel many times, and even volunteered for the 1967 war, but it ended in six days. His views by now were complex: he was a Jew and a passionate Zionist but also an atheist. I told him about my obsession with Israel, how my Grandfather Misha wanted me to go for him. He said he was planning to travel there in a couple of months for work. I had been waiting for someone to say something like that for a very long time. Even if he was lying, I was fine with it from his lips. Sometimes when a man lies to a woman he does so because he desires to be loved by her.

The restaurant was getting noisier and more boisterous, the spirit of the Old New Year filling every corner of the place. I took him upstairs to show him the room where we celebrated my grandmother's last birthday. We stood there in darkness, with sounds of Russian music, and party noises coming from downstairs to make the moment tender. I was nervous, but I was still expecting him to do the usual thing men do when they are left alone in the dark with a woman. Yet my English gentleman did not respond to the darkness in the usual way. He let the darkness hang in its lonely vacuum. Even though I was somewhat shy about being kissed, I wanted to be kissed, nonetheless. My disappointment was great. We went back down and on the stairs he held me firmly by my waist. I held my breath for the kiss I was expecting, but there was nothing more.

In the big room the celebration was in full swing. Almost everyone seemed to know one another and those who didn't pretended they did. I waved to some of my grandmother's old friends, and they waved back, I beamed with pride to be known and recognized. It was almost five minutes to midnight and the room was crowded, everyone breathing into each other, inhaling each other's body odor intricately mixed with perfume, stepping on each other's feet. Waiters began to fill our glasses with obligatory champagne, and everyone drank farewell to the old year, according to the old Russian custom. Within a minute or so with trembling hearts the crowd raised glasses to greet the new Old New Year. It was such an easy thing to do. Everyone was doing it. We were no different than other neutral people who were slowly merging into one nebulous, bright pile of something big and round. My face collided with Clive's and we kissed on the mouth. At first it was a kiss like all others, a New Year's kiss, but seamlessly it morphed into a kiss that broke the rules of propriety, the kiss I was waiting for. When it was over and before he gave me another, he said: "You are going to be my disaster." Those were the best words I had ever heard a man say to me, and they changed my life forever. We kissed all the way home.

Now I understood the meaning of the expression: "to be swept off one's feet." He did that to me with the very first kiss. It was the power of him. We stole moments not just from ourselves to be with each other but from time itself. Everything we did was immoral, and bad, and even illegal in some jurisdictions, but we had fallen in love and therefore morality had carved out an exception for us. I didn't care to know then, nor do I care to ponder it now, because it is useless to pretend that romantic love has anything to do with morality.

His work schedule was meetings all day and concerts at night, seeing people all day long: donors, trustees, government officials, artists. Sometimes he had to travel for business. To find time for me, he had to be inventive. He met me between meetings, during intermissions, after the show, unless his wife was in town.

In due time, he told me about her. They had been together for almost thirty-seven years, married for thirty-four, but he told me it was pretty much over soon after the birth of their first child. He stayed in his marriage for his children, but his safe harbor was always his work. I heard that Mrs. Gillinson didn't take to New York and took little interest in becoming part of New York society, which is an essential element of being the wife of the director of Carnegie Hall. She preferred England to America, and a country life to the big city. I also heard that she loved to garden. From time to time, she dutifully visited Clive in their magnificent Upper East Side apartment that Carnegie Hall had bought for him to use. He then told me he hadn't been in love with his wife for a very long time.

I told Clive where my marriage stood as well, how there was nothing but habit and fear of being left alone that held it together. Perhaps I kept quiet about the fear part.

Meeting Clive for breakfast, lunch, and even drinks was easy because I did it during work hours. Getting together later on was more complicated, but I did it. I made up stories about friends, business meetings, my mother. I lied a lot, but since I had a lover's exemption, I felt no guilt at all. Sam seemed to suspect nothing. Maybe he was afraid of what I would tell him, which I had decided would be "you have no right to question me." I never had to test this bomb: he never said "no" to me, and so my freedom was limitless. I felt that since he had stopped loving me, I had the freedom to do anything I wanted. I was falling in love, and hurting those you leave behind is easy when you are in love.

Once Clive whisked me away to Milan for a one-day business trip to the opera at La Scala. He had to talk to an important conductor. Afterward we had a 2 a.m. dinner in the middle of the Piazza del Duomo and then back to our exquisite hotel room for a few hours of sleep before our flight back to New York. When I came back, my mother asked me what I wanted out of all *that*. With my back

255

facing her as she was making coffee in the kitchen, I said: "I want him to leave his wife and marry me." I couldn't see my mother's face when I said that, but I could sense both her shock, as well as silent approval, because she always approved of everything I did, especially when I did things with such an absolute resolve. My mother was a strong human being in her own right, but whenever she saw me do something that was risky, unpredictable, and exciting, I reminded her of her Arkady.

Clive had arranged for me to come with him on his trip to Israel. Obviously, nothing was going to stop me from going. At home, I made up a lie about how my new friends at Carnegie Hall were organizing a trip and invited me to come with them. I was surprised at how easy it was to lie; how innocent I felt. Only my mother knew the truth. I packed my suitcase.

It felt like I was thrown onto the pages of a beautiful book I had never read. We went first class, with drivers and cars waiting for us everywhere, concierges to solve any small problem we might have. I never had to worry about what to do next. I had never been treated this way, and I immediately found that I liked it. Clive was working, there were meetings, meals for business, but one or two days were to be devoted to excursions.

Israel was strange and fascinating, but I felt very much at ease. I loved the fact that so many in Israel spoke Russian, and almost everyone there was Jewish, like me. People there are straightforward, crass, and brave, and interacting with them I felt an absolute sense of legitimacy. At home with my own identity, I didn't have to explain or justify myself to anybody. I'd never felt this way before, never felt like I belonged somewhere just by virtue of standing on that land and recognizing myself as Jewish in the eyes of other Jews.

In Israel I was Clive's open secret. We walked under a different sky there, me seeing it for the first time and him seeing it through my eyes. We felt free to be in love there. I attended every meeting with him, and not a single person made me feel uncomfortable. Clive was still a stranger, a beautiful stranger, but a stranger nevertheless, and spending ten days in a strange country with a strange man was something I'd never done. I was studying him, his body, his mannerisms, his habits, his work ethic. He came to give lectures, advice on music education and arts management, and maybe recruit a generous new board member; it all goes with the job.

The Wailing Wall made me think of my grandfather Misha. It even looked like him: very old yet relentless, unsentimental yet full of hope. After my father's funeral he had moved in with us for a while, sleeping in my father's study. He spent most of his time on the couch lying there, not talking, just staring at the pictures of his son. My mother came frequently to check on him. When she told him about her plan to move to New York and about Marik who had been so kind, he had one question: "Is he Jewish?" Reassured, he kissed her face with his parched, pale lips. I wished there was a way to let him know that I had seen the promised land, and it was beautiful.

After ten days it was time to go back to real life. We flew together through London, but he had to stop there for two days to see his family before he came back to New York, while I went back and pretended to be married to Sam. The thought of separating after the intensity of those ten days appalled me, but this was all part of having an affair.

I was coming home now, to my old life, where it had to be admitted that I was running around on my husband, always waiting for Clive to ask me out for a twenty-nine-and-a-half-minute lunch. I knew Clive was in love with me. He said things to me no man had ever said before, he looked at me in a way no man had, and he treated me with a knightly tenderness I found irresistible. At the same time, I instinctively felt I was also giving him something he was missing. He found me interesting, unusual, exotic, fun. I was enjoying my affair, and was desperately in love with its object, with Clive. But I saw it had to end. Because I was in love with him, I didn't want to be his mistress, no matter how wonderfully he treated me. A mistress, especially if she happens to be much younger than her lover, is always an added problem for him in a life that is already complex. Perhaps I would have been luckier than most, and he would have stayed in love with me for a long time, but one thing I knew I didn't want was to share him with someone else and be at the mercy of the phony loyalty he owed to his real family.

Sitting in the departure lounge at Heathrow with Clive, I wrestled with myself in a panic about how much to say to him of all that was in my heart, which was that I wanted to give him *all* of me. Nabokov says when you reveal yourself you run the risk of disappointing the other party. I didn't want him to think I was worried about his love for me, or that I was an unhappy and ungrateful neurotic, but I couldn't change who I was, and I didn't want to pretend either. I was insecure, I was impatient, I was weak. I was not ungrateful, but I was unhappy because I was in love and my state of being had been altered and there was nothing I could do about it, and where was it all going from here?

Tears began to pour down my face where words had failed me, while he watched. Finally, I said: "What now?" He went silent for what seemed a very long time, holding my hands, looking back at me with his clever black eyes. And then the verdict fell upon me. "Just tell me something," he said. "If I were to change my life, will you be ready for the consequences that might follow?" The only consequence I could think of was us being together. My Clive was changing his life for me in exchange for our uncompromising unity. I boarded the plane alone, but my heart was full.

Clive had promised to change his life for me, but he wanted to do it properly, without smashing into people and shattering the lives of those affected. Clive always has a plan for everything. He is neat and careful. He likes a challenge; he creates them and then he skillfully untangles them with an elegant solution, but this was the biggest one he had ever created, spanning his private and his public life. He was a public figure, with a spotless reputation. He was responsible to a board of trustees, solid and respectable citizens generously giving of their time and money to one of America's greatest cultural institutions. While there was nothing illegal about having an affair or leaving one's wife of thirty-four years for a much younger woman, it nevertheless unsettled the upper reaches of society in this city that likes to think of itself as liberal. I always thought good old jealousy played a big part in how people felt. One of his society friends raised the delicate subject over lunch, inquiring as to whether I was the *real deal*, or only what I appeared to be: a younger Russian woman taking advantage of an older distinguished Westerner. Another important lady had advised Clive to refrain from calling me his *girlfriend*, saying it was unbecoming of his dignity. I didn't like it either. As far as I was concerned, I could only be either his lover or his wife, because only in these two roles a woman can be true to herself. They are honest roles. The role of a girlfriend, especially in her late thirties, is a compromised, phony role. She is neither a girl, nor a friend.

I had no public image to be concerned about. I was a private person, with private needs and private desires, and I considered that I was the sole judge of my behavior. On the other hand, my private life, obscure as it was, was on fire. Clive lived like a bachelor, but I lived with Sam. I had to see him every day. I had to go to bed with him. It became unbearable to pretend I was still living a normal life with him, while in my head and in my heart, I was carving out a new model of life with Clive.

I didn't want to continue lying to Sam. A week before I left for Israel, he sent me an email asking if "something non-kosher was going on with my trip to Israel." Cornered, guilty, but above all afraid the trip could fall through, I lashed out: "You know I don't observe kosher. If there are people who are willing to take me on a trip to Israel, I am certainly going to go, and not spent the rest of my life regretting the missed opportunity."

Whether he believed me or not was of little significance in the end, because in a few weeks I confessed to Sam that I, Anya, a nice Jewish girl from Moscow, had violated the seventh commandment. I felt no remorse, no fear, no pain, and no pity for him. After the initial shock and anger, he was ready to forgive me and take me back, for the sake of the children and our future happiness. With a gesture to our beautiful Ketubah, the marriage contract every Jewish couple signs, looking helplessly at us from the wall over our bed, he told me I was breaking up the family. I didn't think the Ketubah was going to help his argument, seeing as it stipulates a husband's obligation to make sure his wife is fed, clothed, and otherwise supported, even if I was in technical violation of its terms as well.

He was trying too hard to save the marriage for the sake of the children; he never mentioned us, so I asked him whether he was still in love with me and he couldn't give me a straight answer. He avoided answering the question, again saying we should stay together for the sake of the children, but I told him the children were never going to thank us for staying together in misery, never going to thank me for sacrificing my own happiness and pretending to like it for their sake. I married him because I wanted to be loved and love in return, but my wants had not been realized and I had made my decision.

Even the nice rabbi, who we went to see at the behest of Sam's mother, couldn't talk me out of it. He put on his sympathetic poker face and listened to our story without interrupting, but I think he was taken aback by how made up my mind was. I wasn't trying to conceal anything or make any excuses. He also seemed astounded by Sam's gallant attitude, by his willingness to forgive and move on, but I said I wasn't looking for forgiveness because I was in love with another man who was in love with me, and I wanted a new life. There wasn't much the rabbi could say.

Then I found out I was pregnant, obviously by Clive. His aplomb almost deserted him for a moment, as it will any man who receives this news, but he gallantly and unselfishly offered to stand by me no matter what I decided. I didn't want to become imprisoned by yet another pregnancy, and I didn't want Clive to feel like he was the victim of some banal entrapment. I wanted him to be in love with me only for me, and he showed me that he was.

Both of us were still married and we were still a big secret, but he stayed with me all through my predicament. He took care of me; he was good and kind to me. He went with me to the doctor, he stayed with me for hours both at the clinic, and then later at my mother's. He made it easy for me to trust him. We think that just because we love we trust, but I had always feared to be a fool, the way I was with Dan, my first love. Now I was in love with Clive, who was older and smarter than me; his gentle voice knew secrets which allowed my fears to subside, at least for the time being. I relaxed and let him love me, and it felt good. I was ready to leave my husband for another man. Was this really me doing these things? Nobody (that I know of) in my family had ever done anything like it.

I moved in with my mother, leaving the apartment to Sam. Even if the lease was in my name, I couldn't bear spending another night there. My room in my mother's apartment was just the way I left it the day I got married. I never really left home, never packed my old life into boxes the way I had seen other girls do. I just left it where it was, and whenever I wanted to come back and visit it, I would open the door and the familiar air of security would engulf me completely. The desk, the bed, the mirror, and my friendly bookcases greeted me silently like devoted servants, trying to hide their happiness from seeing me. I stayed with Clive whenever his wife was not in town.

I couldn't alter my daughters' lives until our marital situation was settled, so I pretended everything was the same except I didn't sleep in the same house with them. After school the nanny brought them over to my mother's and took them back home at bedtime. I wanted nothing from Sam, only my freedom. Despite my lawyer's advice to seek sole custody of the children, I asked only for fifty percent. I knew he loved our children, and I didn't want to fight. When his lawyer did try and seek sole custody on Sam's behalf, because that is how divorce lawyers behave, the judge slapped him right down.

I didn't like the feeling of being on my own. Even being married to Sam and being broke most of the time made me feel safer than I did now. Divorce was expensive. I had to sell my diamond engagement ring to finance my lawyer's retainer. I was unable to work as many hours as I wanted because the divorce took a lot of time, I wanted to see my children, and time with Clive was most precious.

Clive could have resolved many of my problems, but I was ashamed to talk to him about money. Our love was unlike all others, our passion was ingenuous and pure, but it seemed to me like it was fragile. I was afraid the minute I mentioned money, it would crack. I always thought people with money have a much easier time asking for money than those who don't. It probably has something to do with confidence. And so it took me weeks to gather up the courage to ask Clive, who, true to form, did not hesitate to write a check.

That summer of 2014, Clive went on a long trip to England to tell his wife their marriage was over, and to have a long talk with his children. There were days when I didn't hear from him, and I fell prey to worrying whether he would change his mind, realize the madness behind the beauty of our affair and gently give up on me. Days went by with no news, and then I found out I was pregnant again. Frantically I called my doctor, telling him the news. He asked no questions, just told me to come see him. But before he passed on the phone to his assistant, I heard him blurt out in his wise Georgian accent: "Not to worry, Anya. I will take care of you." Clive wasn't shocked any less at the news this time around than the first time. Of course, the choice was all mine.

On the phone Clive told me he was waiting for the right moment to tell Mrs. G and the children. Alone with my various predicaments in New York City and feeling not a little sorry for myself, I felt impatient and perhaps jealous, and he must have sensed it. "Don't worry," he told me. "I will do right by you."

He kept his promise to me, but on the other side of the ocean it didn't work out the way he had hoped. His wife was shattered, and his children were angry and he wound up paying his own lawyer a lot more than he ever paid mine, as the thing dragged on for nearly five years. He came back to New York, to me, and I moved in with him that summer. He had stood by me, so I stood by him, as he remade his life to have me in it, so in turn was my life transformed.

He likes to say he was *smitten* by me, but it happened only because I resolved to smite him that night. I saw him, and I decided I was going to desire him with my whole being. Bursting into Clive's life and making him mine was easy. Had I not invited him into my heart that evening in October he would not have fallen in love with me, and we would not have ended up together. He was alone, unattended, there was no woman next to him. Even when I learned he had a wife in some village in England, I was neither disturbed nor deterred. A wife's place is next to her husband if she does not want to lose him. To leave him unattended is negligent, perhaps even reckless, especially if her husband is a star like Clive.

Had she been there on that fateful night chaperoning her inattentive husband and guarding his male virtue, he would never have approached me with his tray of champagne and if he had I would have never showed any interest in him, no matter how charming his accent. A pretty woman across the room is not enough of a reason for a man to unglue himself from his position guarded by his devoted wife. Some women say, "I trust my husband," but much depends on the strength of another woman's desire. A man needs to feel the warmth of a woman's body, he needs to feel seduced by her, he needs to be taken care by her, he wants to be watched by his woman without feeling oppressed and controlled. During various stages of marriages, this has always been a wife's job. When this disappears, another woman senses the void and steps in. Few things in a relationship depend on a man. A man will only scream "Help, get me out of here" when he is drowning, and only when there is another woman standing there to catch him. In all other instances men are either too lazy or too busy to act.

I saw an empty space next to him, and I stepped into it, but that was the easy part. I knew what I was to him at home; no one had ever paid as much attention to me as he did, no one had ever been as tender, as understanding, as pure, as passionate, generous, and loving. With him I became younger, more alert, with his every touch my heart trembled. I felt like I was a higher species, someone who had come from a different planet to make his life beautiful. My insatiable ego wanted me to become his everything. I wanted him to need me and adore me in private and in public.

In public, though, we were surrounded by people who either didn't understand or didn't want to understand who or what I was to him. The uncharitable view had me as some modern version of a Russian Cinderella. At first, Clive's sophisticated, wealthy friends looked at me with suspicion, but with time they got used to my face and my voice. I wasn't just any Russian girl. I was Anya, by now a well-adjusted New Yorker. I fascinated them with stories of my unusual Soviet upbringing, my grandparents' legacy, my father's brilliant but risky career, his murder in his beloved New York, and how we came to live here.

Every night there wasn't a concert at the Hall, we had dinners, parties, galas, and receptions to go to. This was high society, the crème de la crème sent each other printed invitations, and initially I went as his "plus one," a title I found insulting. In time I became his official girlfriend, so that they put my name on my dinner card: "Anya Meltzer." That was better, but what my heart really desired was more than a minor upgrade. I wanted to be Mrs. Gillinson.

We went everywhere together, and pretty soon I began to slip into my official duties. I'd get home from work in time for a quick shower, put on my best outfit, and be off to the Hall, where it was understood I was Clive's woman. He never mentioned it, but I instinctively understood that he relied on me to help him with guests he invited to our box. Soon enough I became acquainted with politicians, business tycoons, renowned authors, various celebrities from music, fashion, and film, and other dignitaries. My job was simple but subtle. I needed to talk to them as needed. I made sure they felt welcomed, yet not overwhelmed with attention. After the concert Clive and I would go backstage where he thanked the artists, and unless there was an official post-concert reception or a dinner he had to attend, we elegantly disappeared for a bite to eat by ourselves. It felt natural to me. I grew up around the theatre in Russia, but there was also something new about it. It was Clive himself.

It was impossible for my heart not to be smitten with him, and for my mind not to fall in love with him. He brought the world of art and music back into my life, he made me feel like a girl again. He brought my youth back to me, this noble knight who fell in love with me. I could have never loved a lesser man. He was the right man, the sort of man my father would have wanted for me.

Naturally I wanted the world of art and music I loved so much to like me, too, but here there were impediments to true love. The city's fashionable ladies couldn't get enough of Clive's wit and charm. He was *their* Clive Gillinson, a delicious, respected foreigner who had come to New York and infused Carnegie Hall with new life. Suddenly, I, a nobody, had interfered with this idyllic flow of things. I was not famous, nor was I rich; anyone could tell simply by looking that I was a divorced woman with two small kids to care for, trying to fit myself into his world.

Some mediocre cynics, thinking of embarrassing me, have asked me if I would have fallen in love with Clive had he not been Sir Clive, the Executive and Artistic Director of Carnegie Hall. It's a silly hypothetical question, and the answer is no. I fell in love with all of Clive, as he appeared to me when we met. If I had met him when he was a musician in the orchestra, I might have found him charming but no more than that. Few pay attention to a greenish bud; they wait for it to bloom into a succulent rose.

For Clive's seventieth birthday I arranged two surprise parties, a small one at work for his staff, and a big one at our home for a select group of about a hundred very important people. It was a fine big apartment, but I had a little panic attack when they all began to pile in at the same time. I was terribly nervous because at that time I didn't know how to arrange an event like that and couldn't have afforded it if I did. Without benefit of a caterer, I cooked most of the food, and what I didn't cook I bought at the Russian supermarket in Brooklyn, caviar and other Russian delicacies. Our nanny, Gulzat, was my main and only assistant. Most people had no idea who I was to be sending out invitations to Clive's house, and on the night of the party some guests thought I was a new personal assistant. I smiled magnanimously and gently set them straight. It was a fantastic success. Every single trustee showed up, perhaps curious to see who it was who had so unceremoniously replaced the seldom-seen Mrs. G.

I smiled a lot and people smiled back at me, and I was ready to trust their smiles. The surprise was successful, and Clive was amused to be fooled not once but twice. He was truly happy to see so many people come and wish him well on his birthday. Everything he does is for the benefit of others and the honor of music through the vehicle of the giant known as Carnegie Hall; it's never about him. This birthday party was an opportunity for others to praise him.

That night he was also proud of me. I was looking for that acknowledgment, and when he raised his glass for the toast, it was me he toasted, telling everyone about the happiness I had brought into his life. I hung breathlessly on every word. It was a big night, an important night, an exciting night, and it could have gone either way because I didn't even know whether Clive liked surprises. After that, everyone remembered my name and no one ever mistook me for an assistant again.

During the first few months, my daughters didn't stay with us too often because I was busy being in love with Clive, always afraid to disturb the balance of the relationship. I was busy working, attending concerts, trying to make an impression on society. I didn't want to overwhelm Clive with my "personal baggage." They would come by the humongous apartment to visit, and then back home to Sam or my mother's.

I have always been self-centered, and I rarely dwelled on my young daughters' inner world. As long as I was able to provide for their physical and educational needs I felt at peace. At the same time, because my children have always been a part of me, I never thought it was necessary to think of their needs apart from my own. I didn't think of them when I fell in love with Clive, when I first kissed him, when we first made love, or whenever he held my face in his hands as if I were a child myself.

One evening, in the early days of our relationship, about fifteen minutes before some banal Broadway show was about to start, I casually but lovingly asked Clive whether he loved my children. If I had been thinking clearly, I would never have asked an important question like that without knowing the answer in advance. It is like asking a man "Do you love me?" or "Am I fat?" Women are not asking these questions to know the truth. They know the truth. They want flattery; the sound of sweet words addressed to them. With a smile I was waiting for his reply but instead of a charming lie, he told me the truth.

"I think your kids are perfectly fine," he said. "They are wonderful. Of course, I enjoy them. But I have already been there. You know I adore *my* children. I've had three, and I've done my part."

I felt like he had hit me with a brick. My throat filled up with hundreds of cotton balls. The lights went out, the show was about to begin. Suddenly it felt lonely. For a few moments I felt like I was sitting with a stranger, not with my love for whom I had left my family. Could it be that no one but me was going to love my children, that even the love of a knight had its limits? Was I making a mistake? If he cannot love my children the way I love them, do I have the moral right to be with him, to desire him? Can I love that man? Can I even like him? I was so far ahead of myself I had no idea what was happening on stage. I couldn't wait for the intermission so I could run to my mother to embrace my children because I missed them, because I felt I was betraying them by loving this brilliant person who decided he wasn't planning to love my daughters.

Clive was watching the play. Clearly, he was unaware of the agony his words had created in me. But by the time the lights came back up, I had decided to act against my impulse. Instead of creating a scene and storming out of the theatre, instead of drowning myself in self-pity and blowing my chance at happiness, I decided to be wise, for a change.

People don't change, but circumstances change around us, and we adjust to them. Perhaps if I left this alone, I thought, something may happen to make him change his mind without even noticing it. I was surprised at myself for thinking in such a calm and rational manner, and indeed, the crisis, if there ever was one outside of my own thoughts, passed without incident. Without any interference on my part, Ariella and Marina have become Clive's children. Everything happened seamlessly and naturally. He was too honest and too busy to play the father figure with them, he was simply Clive: witty, funny, smart, playful, resourceful, generous, tender. He loves to spoil them like two princesses, he teaches them, he advises them when needed, he helps them with their schoolwork. Without any fuss, he made them part of his unusual life and everything we did.

For my part, I told my daughters everyone has only one father and one mother. Clive was there for me to make my life better, to keep me young and beautiful. I told them if they were both smart, they could make a great friend; if not, it would be their great loss. Whenever my daughters and I have disagreements, as happens between fiery Russian personalities, he is the one they go to seek peace and justice. Because my older daughter, Ariella, and I are so much alike, Clive is a helpful confidant for her. Marina, full of fire, mischief, and adventure, is his co-conspirator and playmate. She doesn't speak of love, but she cuddles up to him whenever she is tired, hurt, or happy. When I had nothing to give them except for my love, he gave them a home and security. Since that murky day on Broadway, he has told me many times he loves my children, and each time I hear it my heart beats stronger.

In this period between the scandal and the divorce, everywhere I went with him, at home and abroad, I was treated with respect, and even love by his associates and friends. In Europe, as well as in Israel and Russia, it was normal for me to accompany Clive to meetings, but not in Japan. Because Japan is the most rigidly patriarchal culture in the world, resisting all efforts at reform, a Japanese tea ceremony was arranged for me while the men talked business. Three exquisite elderly Japanese ladies who spoke no English dressed me like a queen in a bright green kimono with exquisite red flowers, like an exotic butterfly, and arranged my hair in the Japanese style, whereupon we engaged in the highly ritualized traditional tea making and drinking ceremony, and I was taken to the most beautiful garden where they took pictures of me amidst magnificent Japanese flowers.

We went to Buckingham Palace for the Anniversary Gala of the Welsh National Opera, with King Charles III (then Prince Charles) as the host. Clive had met the Queen and the other royals before, but for me it felt like a fairy tale. I got dressed up in tulle, lace, and velvet for the pinnacle of my social life at that point. The best part was when we stepped into the cab all dressed up and the cabby said, "Where to, my dear Sir?" and when Clive said "Buckingham Palace, please," his expression never changed. We walked calmly up to the golden gate and we were admitted; I could hear the whispers and feel the stares behind me.

Her Majesty was not in attendance, but the place was swarming with dames, knights, earls, lords, and other distinguished persons all perfectly dressed, with beautiful manners and wearing a little pin or ribbon indicating their title. Clive had either forgotten, or simply decided not to take his decorations from home, but everyone in the receiving line where we shook the royal hand called him Sir Clive. The reception was followed by a small concert and a dignified and hearty dinner which I could not fully appreciate due to its meatiness. One elderly couple who looked especially aristocratic wanted to know every detail of our improbable romance; their faces smiled kindly as I let them in on the fun. I've been to dinner at some of the fanciest homes in the world, and these people are all generous and gracious with perfect manners, but sometimes it can all seem a bit pompous. Buckingham Palace was not so gaudy as I had pictured it, but with a quiet dignity that was very regal because it was real. Eventually Prince Charles got up and bid everyone a good night and that was it.

Next time I'd come to Buckingham Palace, I decided I wanted to come not as Clive's girlfriend but his wife. His divorce, involving more ill will and money than mine, dragged on forever without resolution, complicated by the necessity of making it legal in both countries. We lived as husband and wife in all respects but the legal one, and I, never known for my patience, felt it was draining our romance of its poetry. Clive said it couldn't last forever, and when he got it done, we were going to get married and I would be his Lady Gillinson, just like he treated me everywhere we went.

Clive is on the cello jury section at the International Tchaikovsky Competition in Russia, so we went to the Moscow Conservatory. Our seats were in the second row. I looked around and saw many familiar faces I had known since my childhood. I greeted them politely and proudly introduced them to my Clive. Everyone knew who Clive was, and it was not without pleasure that I'd noticed their prying eyes as we walked in holding hands. In Russia, things were different: I couldn't introduce him as my boyfriend, because that would indicate I was his mistress, and I couldn't use the word fiancée, either, since it was a fact that he was already married even if I, by then, was finally divorced. A tricky situation, and best not to identify him as anything at all, and simply tell people that we were together if they were rude enough to ask, which fortunately no one was.

The elite of the Russian oligarchy was there, and the atmosphere was electric, all lights, TV cameras, diamonds on naked shoulders, and a lot of men from the Russian secret service because everyone was expecting the arrival of the tsar, Vladimir Putin.

Clive was a star and free to behave as he pleased, and he exercised that freedom while proving to me how much I mattered to him about ten minutes before the concert began when two men in immaculate dark suits and morbidly serious faces approached him and in painfully heavy Russian accented English conveyed the invitation to come and join President Putin for the duration of the concert. Clive smiled a brilliant diplomatic British smile and innocently inquired whether the invitation also included his lovely companion. The answer was an unequivocal "nyet." Clive did not flinch. "Please thank Mr. President from me, but I cannot abandon my girlfriend." Everyone around us saw and understood what was happening; I heard the whispers behind me and could not help beaming with pride. I felt like I had just grown a second heart either from vanity or from happiness.

Back in New York, I was working extremely hard to support myself and the kids and not very much enjoying being divorced from Sam, since the court had decided because I made more money than he did, most of our expenses were on me. My role as Clive's companion demanded that I appear elegant and glamorous at all times, so I never wore the same outfit twice. Clive had no idea how dire my finances were, he was so generous, but I didn't want to ask him for anything after the way he helped me with my legal bills. It would have been too humiliating, too trivial, too ordinary.

Once he surprised me by telling me he did not care much for poetry. I laughed and told him the sad story of my book and how I almost published it. It upset him, so he gave me the money on the spot. My long-lost publisher had not raised his price, and the book came out. A large group of my Russian speaking friends came to my book launch where I read from my book, and we all ate, drank, and carried on in Russian.

In the summer of 2018, Clive's divorce finally came through. We were in Taiwan, and the hotel phone rang at five in the morning with the news that now he too was an unmarried man. The fact that my Clive did not legally belong to another woman anymore meant freedom. Now we almost completely belonged to each other. Almost.

On my birthday, August 7, at our favorite French restaurant, Vaucluse, he proposed to me in front of my children. He'd cleared the whole thing with my mother ahead of time, asking her permission to marry me. I had insisted, for I adore tradition, and he had happily complied and she was delighted.

I had been waiting for it every day since the divorce came through, but when the ring appeared it was the most delightful, most perfect surprise. Underneath my other gifts for the day was a bride, the doll had a pink dress and a pink veil and tiny pink shoes. Underneath, I found a white box, which was hiding another smaller white box, and this one said in silver letters the word De Beers. Inside this box was another, in black velvet. I opened it and saw the symbol of this world's materialism, vanity, and euphoric happiness. Did we kiss? On the mouth, sinfully, disastrously, just like that first time at the Russian restaurant. It was a very posh restaurant, and everyone was looking at us, they were happy for us in a New York sort of way and broke into cheerful human applause, although those who took themselves too seriously did not clap.

I knew Clive was in love with me; his face had an expression of most genuine happiness that night. I also knew that he was not gaining as much by marrying me as I was by marrying him. He had my love, as I had his, but he was still going to remain the same Clive Gillinson while I felt like a whole new person in my new status as his wife, not only the feeling of security but his name, his protection. I was gaining the old-fashioned respect of New York society, which is only liberal when it comes to fashionable political and social issues, not human vulnerabilities. I knew that marriage offers no guarantee against falling out of love, but I had fought for this one so hard and for so long, I was sure our love was not going to be extinguished with marriage.

The girls were very excited and immediately began to plan the wedding. I wanted a traditional Jewish wedding, with a huppa and the seven circles. Clive is an atheist, which is fine with me, but he told me he was not going to be able to say anything that implied he believed in God. I, on the other hand, needed my God to hear me. We went to our friend Rabbi Shmuley Boteach to help us; his wife Debbie and I are friends. Shmuley, an orthodox rabbi and occasional figure of controversy who calls himself "America's Rabbi," is a scholar of great depth. He told Clive he did not need to believe in God in order to be Jewish. Clive was taken aback, as this seemed to contradict everything he had so far been taught to believe, but Shmuley's explanation was persuasive. It was simple: as long as Clive was born to a Jewish mother whose mother was also Jewish, as was the case, he was Jewish, and his faith or lack thereof had nothing to do with it.

Shmuley wasn't going to preside at any wedding where anyone didn't know what they were doing, so to help Clive reconcile his Judaism and his atheism, we went to his home on the Upper West Side for serious discussion six times before the wedding. Shmuley is the author of *Kosher Sex*—not to mention over thirty other books on theology, relationships, grief, Judaism, social issues, and politics—so there was nothing dull about these evenings, filled with discourse on history, philosophy, and religion. Shmuley and Clive, who have almost nothing in common except for their devotion to Zionism, Jewish values, and the ability to think freely and deeply, became great friends.

According to Orthodox practice, I had to procure a Get, a ritual Jewish divorce, from Sam, who good-naturedly agreed to appear before the rabbinical court in an office space in the garment district. The other people in the waiting room looked grim and uncomfortable, some of them were there with their parents. Then Sam appeared in his shorts with his large sneakers and a big orange basketball in his hands. When we got in the room, we had to separate and sit on opposite sides of the room. We read some scripture and repeated some prayers. As with everything in Judaism, we were surrounded by symbols, mysticism, solemnity, and common sense. The rabbi gave us a piece of white cloth to hold, and then, with the words: "I divorce thee! I divorce thee! I divorce thee!" It was all over.

Three days before the wedding, my friend Debbie took me to a Mikveh, a ritual bath. I grew up in such isolation from Jewish laws and customs that when I encountered them, they felt new and exciting. They took me to a specially prepared bridal suite where I showered and removed all traces of cosmetics. I had to look, feel and be utterly pristine, almost uncomfortably clean. The silent attendant lady came back and made sure I was ready, then escorted me to the Mikveh through a private entrance. The Mikveh bath used to be rainwater; now it is meticulously cleaned through a special natural oxidation process. I felt like the water was washing my old life off me, purifying me for the new life I had chosen and done so much to make mine.

So many important people were coming to see us get married, everything had to be perfect. The venue was the great hall of the Cunard Building at 25 Broadway, a huge room with five vaults in the ceiling and maritime themed decorations, big enough to hold the whole of New York society. We hired a professional who made everything come out perfectly and the only decisions I had to make concerned the music for the ceremony and the all-important first dance. Music has always been the barometer of my state of being. Without it I cannot feel poetry. I picked Shostakovich's Waltz #2 from his Jazz Suite for the first dance, and for my daughters' processional I picked a song by one of Russian bards from the Soviet Thaw period, Bulat Okudzhava, one of my father's favorites. I knew there would be Russians who would recognize and love that music. During the ceremony, I would make seven circles around Clive, symbolizing holiness and completion, as with a wall of a house. These rituals express laws governing the foundation of human relationships, without which the Jewish nation would have never survived, and as we repeat them, we think of those no longer with us. I walked down the aisle to the theme from *Schindler's List* written by John Williams. Jewish happiness always has a shadow of sorrow, and I felt it as the music started to play. I had my mother holding me by my right elbow, our dearest friend Sereja holding my left, and I began to walk very slowly so as not to waste a single note. As I was walking down that aisle, I kept wondering about the guests and why they were not standing up like I had seen it done at other weddings. I was blinded by the lights and by the vision of Clive standing near the rabbi. He looked small, and I wanted to make sure that he was smiling, but I couldn't see clearly. I remembered then that my veil was keeping things away from me. I kept walking, sinking deeper into my music, feeling shamelessly triumphant, defeated by happiness. When I approached Clive, I looked at him, seeing his approval of my dress and the music I chose in the look in his eyes and the way he smiled at me. I picked up my heavy dress, took a deep breath, and began to make circles around him, seven times. I looked up and saw everyone standing, and I was surprised to think they were standing up for me. It was so silly at a moment like that to think of myself, but I couldn't help it. I was so happy. It was a beautiful wedding, a victorious wedding, a courageous wedding. Again, I thought of my father and his dreams for me, how he kept me warm and well-fed, made sure I was clever, interesting, and well educated, taught me about beauty and kindness. My mother told me he saw his girls as two jewels entrusted to him, and his main purpose in life was to protect us and make sure we were happy women. With his death I lost that sense of security and with it my sense of self-confidence that had taken me so long to recapture. The image of my father as my only king had never left my mind, but now I had a husband. The day I married Clive was the day that feeling came back to me, for the first time since my father's death. Standing in front of my rabbi and half facing that dazzling crowd of guests, my broken adolescence and my wandering woman-hood finally took refuge in the embrace of my new king.